TARGET RICH ENVIRONMENT

VOLUME
1

Baen Books by Larry Correia

Saga of The Forgotten Warrior
Son of the Black Sword
House of Assassins (forthcoming)

The Grimnoir Chronicles
Hard Magic
Spellbound
Warbound

Monster Hunter International
Monster Hunter International
Monster Hunter Vendetta
Monster Hunter Alpha
Monster Hunter Legion
Monster Hunter Nemesis
Monster Hunter Siege

with John Ringo
Monster Hunter Memoirs: Grunge
Monster Hunter Memoirs: Sinners
Monster Hunter Memoirs: Saints

with Mike Kupari
Dead Six
Swords of Exodus
Alliance of Shadows

To purchase these and all Baen Book titles in e-book format,
please go to www.baenebooks.com

TARGET RICH ENVIRONMENT

VOLUME 1

A Collection by

LARRY CORREIA

BAEN

Copyright © 2018 by Larry Correia

A Baen Books Original

Baen Publishing Enterprises
P.O. Box 1403
Riverdale, NY 10471
www.baen.com

ISBN 13: 978-1-4814-8344-5

Cover art by Kurt Miller

First printing, September 2018

Distributed by Simon & Schuster
1230 Avenue of the Americas
New York, NY 10020

Printed in the United States of America

10 9 8 7 6 5 4 3 2 1

CONTENTS

Tanya: Princess of the Elves ❖ 1

Dead Waits Dreaming ❖ 29

Sweothi City ❖ 49

The Bridge ❖ 75

The Grimnoir Chronicles: Detroit Christmas ❖ 91

The Grimnoir Chronicles:
Murder on the *Orient Elite* ❖ 123

Father's Day ❖ 155

Destiny of a Bullet ❖ 165

Bubba Shackleford's
Professional Monster Killers ❖ 179

Blood on the Water
By Hinkley Correia and Larry Correia ❖ 203

The Losing Side ❖ 223

The Great Sea Beast ❖ 235

Force Multiplier ❖ 253

The Adventures of Tom Stranger,
Interdimensional Insurance Agent ❖ 273

ACKKNOWLEGEMENTS

We had a contest on my blog, Monster Hunter Nation, to come up with a name for this collection. I want to thank Logan Guthmiller for suggesting *Target Rich Environment*. It was a great idea, and it hearkened back to the opening quote used in my first novel.

I also want to acknowledge all of the editors from the various anthologies these stories were originally published in. Gathering a bunch of authors together for an anthology is like herding cats, and editors often have a thankless job.

TARGET RICH ENVIRONMENT

VOLUME
1

TANYA: PRINCESS OF ELVES

I posted this intro on my blog on April, 2010.

> This is just a rough little snippet that I wrote set in the
> Monster Hunter universe that doesn't actually fit into any
> of my current projects. Tanya was originally going to be a
> background character in Monster Hunter Alpha, but
> didn't quite fit. So think of it as a deleted scene on a DVD.
> Maybe I will revisit Tanya's story in a future MH novel. I
> know that it would be a lot of fun. Enjoy.
>
> —Larry

*Then I posted the rough draft of what would later become the opening
scene for* Tanya, Princess of the Elves. *Originally I planned for Earl
Harbinger to have a sidekick in* Monster Hunter Alpha, *but that didn't
work out because Alpha needed to be a darker book, and Tanya was just
too funny and upbeat for what was basically a horror story.*

*Little did I realize that the fans were going to fall in love with the
princess. Shortly after posting the snippet, Toni Weisskopf, publisher at
Baen and all around genius super editor, asked me to write the rest of the
story so she could buy it. At that point I decided to have a bit of fun by
adding one of my other favorite characters, and beginning MHI's answer
to Romeo and Juliet. Tanya's unconventional romance and quest to
redeem the elves has been showing up in MHI novels ever since.*

ONCE UPON A TIME, in the state of Mississippi, there dwelt an elf
princess. The princess lived in the Enchanted Forest with her mother,

the queen of the elves, in a ninety-foot-long aluminum double-wide trailer.

"I'm bored, Momma," the princess of the elves whined. She was sitting on the couch and painting her toenails. The princess had been complaining a lot lately. "This is stupid, stupid and boring."

Queen Ilrondelia grunted and used the remote to turn up the volume on the TV so she wouldn't have to listen to her youngest and only daughter. It was an infomercial about some blanket thing with sleeve holes for your hands so you could sit all warm on the couch and still work the remote. The queen decided she needed one of those and wondered if they made it in her size.

"Tanya! Write down that number," the queen ordered. "I need one of them snuggly blankets for keeping warm."

"You ain't listening. How come you won't let me do nothing?" Tanya said.

"You wanna do something? Get that skinny ass offa' the couch and get a ink pen like I said!" the queen bellowed.

"Yes, your majesty," Tanya answered sullenly, got up, and went to the kitchen.

"And fetch me some Ho Hos while you's at it . . ." the queen said, then thought about it. "And some ranch dressin' for dippin' sauce." She returned her attention to the TV. Tanya came back, but as usual, took her sweet time, so the phone number was gone, and the queen would be forced to wait on getting her snuggly blanket with sleeves, but she did bring the box of Ho-Hos and the bottle of ranch dressing like she'd been told. The queen took the snack and glared disapprovingly at Tanya's too-small shirt. "Your belly's stickin' out."

"It's fashion," Tanya said. "You're just jealous."

The queen snorted. *Fashion.* The girl had no sense. Tanya went back to the couch, but one of the cats had taken her spot. Tanya tossed it on the floor and went back to painting her toes.

The queen forgot about the TV for a minute and concentrated on her kid. She didn't do that very often. "So . . . You wanna do somethin'?" the queen asked.

Tanya sighed. "Yeah, I do."

"So the Enchanted Forest ain't good 'nuff no mo'?"

"That ain't what I meant," Tanya said. "But elves used to do stuff. You know. *Outside.*"

The queen of the elves pondered on that while she unwrapped a Ho-Ho and squirted ranch dressing on it. Her people had a sweet deal. The government paid them good money to stay right here in the Enchanted Forest, but some of the younger elves were getting uppity, talking about *adventure*. They'd been watching too many movies with fancy movie elves in them. They didn't realize how good they had it here in the Enchanted Forest.

The world had moved on. It wasn't a magic world no more. It was a world of techno-thingies and computing boxes and inter-webs. It wasn't a world fit for her kind.

The queen knew her youngest was going to be a problem child since she'd gotten that butterfly tramp-stamp tattooed on her back. Somehow she'd gotten it in her head that she wanted to "see the world" and such nonsense. She even talked to those damn pixies. Hell, the girl probably didn't have the smarts not to consort with a filthy orc if left on her own. But since Tanya was the prettiest girl in the trailer park she had all the boys wrapped around her finger. Her crazy talk could cause trouble. Trouble could make it so that the government checks quit coming.

The government didn't want people knowing about monsters or magic or the things that lived on the outskirts. Other than shopping at the Walmart, the elves kept to themselves. All it would take was one dumb youngster to go and pull something stupid in town, and their sweet gig would be up. And with Tanya flouncing around like a cheap pixie, talking to humans, and sneaking out, it was only a matter of time. The princess was a pain in her ass.

"Tanya, Tanya, Tanya," the queen said around a mouth full of Ho-Ho, "what am I gonna do wit' you?"

Tanya looked up from her toes. "Let me travel. You let other elves go out. You let Elmo and the trackers get work."

That much was true. She wasn't above farming out her people for odd jobs, under the table of course, to supplement the government checks. In fact, Harbinger from MHI had called earlier, saying he needed a diviner, and he was willing to pay big bucks for only a few days' labor. "So that's what you's all spun up on? 'Cause I'm sendin' Elmo with that boss Hunter? That's 'cause there're some elves smart enough to do some job, get paid, and get back! You'd just screw it up. You ain't wise like them yet."

"I can do magic, too! And I'm educated!" Tanya shouted loud enough to make two cats retreat under the couch. "I got my GED."

The queen frowned while she chewed, chins bouncing. She never should have let the girl take that correspondence course. It had made her even more uppity. It was time to put the royal foot down. "I forbids it. You'll be queen someday, so you need to learn 'bout how to be a proper type ruler, meanin' you ain't goin' nowhere."

Tanya screeched in frustration and stomped off. She slammed the door to her room hard enough to shake the whole trailer.

It had taken another hour for her momma to fall asleep on her recliner. Tanya waited until the snores were nice, even, and loud before sliding out the window. She'd snuck out many nights before. She knew every bar from here to Tupelo, and had danced on most of them.

But this time was different. Tanya wasn't coming back. It was time to make it big. She was sick of the Enchanted Forest, sick of her Queenliness always bossing her around, and bored out of her mind. She was too big for the trailer park, and she was going to show them. She had a backpack full of clothes, spell fixings, a pocket full of money (mostly stolen), an iPod with every single Eminem song on it, and her dreams.

She'd heard the legends. Elves used to be beautiful, immortal and magical. The elder Vartinian used to tell the youngsters the stories. Their people had been brave, and had fought mighty wars against the fearsome orcs and the evil fey. It was impossible to imagine her mighty ancestors living in the Enchanted Forest and being happy. She'd heard about other elves across the sea. They had to be cooler than her stupid relatives. She watched a lot of TV. She knew what was out there.

It had been on one of her weekend *scouting* trips that she'd finally come to the realization that her destiny lay outside the Enchanted Forest. After hitchhiking to Tupelo, because she'd heard about an awesome kegger, Tanya had come across a magical shrine where a mystical hero had been born. She still wore one of the great one's holy symbols on a chain around her neck, a solemn reminder that a legend could come from humble beginnings, plus she thought her Elvis Presley medallion looked wicked cool in her cleavage when she wore one of her low-cut tops.

If a human could go on to become a god, what amazing things

could an elf of the royal line accomplish? All sorts of badass stuff, that's what. But first she needed a ticket out of the Enchanted Forest, and by royal decree, elves were not allowed out without leave. Sure, the queen looked the other way for Tanya's sneaking out, as she knew that youngsters needed to blow off steam, but leaving for good would be different. Momma would be sure to send the trackers after her. So she needed to hatch a scheme that would let her go in a way that the queen wouldn't dare drag her back.

The getaway plan had been in her head for quite some time. The idea had started a couple years back when she'd watched some Hunters come to bug Momma for information. Tanya had always found humans interesting, especially the cute boys, but most elves hated their cousins because they were squishy, mean-tempered, and short-lived. But they respected the Hunters. The Monster Hunters put boot to ass on a regular basis, and even the snootiest elf in the Enchanted Forest had to admit that they were the real deal, so fearsome that they even owned a tribe of vicious orc barbarians, let free only to eat the babies of their enemies.

There had been a funny-looking red-bearded one, a big ugly with a scar face, a black guy with badass dreadlocks, and a blonde girl with attitude, so pretty that she had left Tanya jealous enough to start bleaching her own hair. All of them except for the ugly one had come back the next year, and Tanya had eavesdropped again. These people had adventures *and* they made serious bank. They were feared and respected, riding to battle on a flying death-machine driven by their insane orc slaves, and living in a mysterious palace known only as the Compound. Now that was living large.

Summoning up all her courage, Tanya had confronted the Hunters as they were leaving and had asked what it took to become one of them. They didn't laugh at her at all. The one with the red beard had seemed a little confused, but had started to give her a serious answer, until Momma had hit her with a well-aimed bunny slipper and ordered her back into the trailer. The slipper had nearly put out her eye, but it was worth it. Just the fact that they hadn't laughed at her told her that there was no reason an elf couldn't join up.

When she'd overheard Momma saying that she was going to assign that idiot Elmo to do a little job for the king of the Hunters, she knew that she'd have to move quick. She was a much better diviner than

Elmo was, probably twice as good when he was liquored up, which was most of the time.

After sneaking out the window, Tanya had hunkered down behind the back of the trailer and waited. Most elves slept in pretty late, so if the Hunters were coming in the morning, then she'd have a good chance of reaching them first. Momma wouldn't dare send the trackers after her if she was working for the Hunters. Tanya congratulated herself on the brilliance of her plan.

It was getting cold, early winter, but she'd worn a nice coat. It was a letterman's jacket from the Boonville Blue Devils, lifted off a stupid human. Human boys were even dumber than their elven counterparts, but she did appreciate the muscles on the ones that played football. Luckily it didn't take too long for her ride to show up. Even with her earpieces in, she still heard the truck arrive. It was a huge, black pickup truck with a winch on the front and a shell over the back. It had to be the Hunters. This was perfect. Everyone else was asleep. She turned off the *8 Mile* soundtrack, grabbed her backpack, and ran over to rap her knuckles against the window.

It took a second but the window rolled down and the human behind the wheel gave her a funny look. If she were hitchhiking, this was normally when she would have leaned forward so the driver could see down her shirt, but that didn't seem like the *professional* thing to do. She had an act to keep up. "Heya," Tanya said, standing perfectly straight. "You the Hunter?"

"I am," he said politely, tipping the brim of his ball cap. It had a green happy face on it. If he was an elf he'd have been in his mid-hundreds, but Tanya figured that made him about forty in human years. Wearing a really old leather jacket, he seemed bulky by elf standards, but probably lean compared to most of the humans she knew. He wasn't handsome at all, kind of plain with a hard face, like someone who spent a lot of time outdoors, and eyes that seemed to look right through her. Elves had blue eyes too, but his were the color of ice and just as cold. This was the kind of man who made his living face-punching monsters to death. "I'm here to see the queen."

"She's probably gonna sleep until about noon," Tanya answered, thinking quickly. "She went on a real bender last night. I'm talking like a gallon of Thunderbird! She didn't want to be disturbed. So she sent me to meet you. I'm your diviner."

The Hunter seemed a little surprised. "You're Elmovarian? The master tracker?"

"Of course," she answered proudly, the human hadn't been expecting a *babe*. Tanya prided herself on being the hottest of all the elves in the trailer park. "That's my full elf name. Whenever I work with humans I let them call me Tanya."

"I'm Earl Harbinger," the Hunter said. "Ain't you a little young?"

"I'm an elf. I'm older than I look." Which was true; Tanya had been able to successfully buy beer when she was only fourteen with her fake ID. Momma had always said she was an early bloomer. She was twenty-two now, which was positively *ancient* by human female standards. "Besides, I'm the best tracker in the Enchanted Forest." Tanya didn't hesitate. She went for the gold. This was her ticket out of this dump. "All righty then, we better get going, I'm guessing you've got lots of things to murder." Not wanting to give him time to think about it, she immediately walked around the front of the truck to the passenger side. She held her breath until he unlocked the door. She threw her pack in the back seat and climbed in the front. "Okay, let's go."

The Hunter shrugged and started the engine. "Seat belt," he suggested. She complied. Tanya was terribly nervous, but Momma didn't come lumbering out of the trailer. Nobody raised the alarm. The trackers didn't come out with their sawed off shotguns and compound bows to massacre the Hunter for kidnapping the royal heir. They crossed the threshold of the Enchanted Forest and then they were free.

"Where're we headed?" Tanya asked, eager for adventure.

"Indiana," Harbinger answered.

The princess of the elves was intrigued. "Ooohh. That sounds exciting."

The Monster Hunter just watched the road. "Uh-huh."

Exszrsd Hgth Frhnzld Wrst was Uzbek Orcish for *Stab-Fighting Warrior of Righteous Vindication*, but he was just Edward to his friends. And today, Edward had been asked to stay in the van. So he sat in the van, listening to AM talk radio and sharpening his swords.

Outside the van, the Hunters were preparing for battle. They would call when he was needed. Then Edward would kill things, and all would be well.

His older brother and clan leader, Skippy, had asked him to come along to support their adopted clan on this mission. Clan mother and holy woman, Gretchen, had dreamed a dream that had told her that Edward's life skill would be needed today to save their friends. All *urks* were born with a life skill. Edward's skill consisted of stabbing things, so any day that required Edward's skill was truly a good day to be an *urk*.

Skippy, or *Skull Crushing Battle Hand of Fury* as Mom had called him (strange humans, with their insistence on short names), was still busy fixing the MHI helicopter from when the giant tree beast had knocked it out of the New Zealand sky. So the Hunters were going to drive in cars, which were slow, lumbering contraptions compared to his brother's helicopter. So when the Hunters had assembled to leave on their latest quest, Edward had just shown up with a bag full of stabbing and slashing implements and tossed it into the back of the van, which had created an awkward situation. The Hunters had gently tried to turn him away.

That had never happened before and their actions had confused Edward. The Hunters always seemed to love when Edward stabbed things for them. Oh no, they assured him. They loved Edward, but they had warned him, this mission required the presence of an *elf*.

So that's why the Hunters didn't want him. Elves were disgusting, foul, loathsome creatures. As tuskless as a human, but way more uppity about it. Elves and orcs had been at war since the beginning of the world. Edward would rather eat his own sword than have to put up with an elf, but Gretchen had been adamant that Edward needed to be present today or the Hunters would get in trouble. So when he'd still insisted on going, they'd made him promise to stay in the van out of sight. Harb Anger was sleeping in from being a werewolf, so they'd have him pick up the elf.

So Edward kept out of sight, carefully running a whetstone down his sword while listening to Rush Limbaugh on the radio. Edward did not understand human ways, but he loved their talk radio and news programs almost as much as he loved their heavy metal. When he was not practicing his stab-killing, Edward watched the news. Owen Zastava Pitt, Brother of the Great War Chief, had laughed and proclaimed that Edward was a "Fox news junkie". Edward was pleased with this title, for he did love the human news channel, and not just because foxes were the most delicious of all mammals, which was the whole reason he'd started watching that particular channel in the first place. Anything named after the favorite animal to hunt with his bare hands was okay by him.

Tanya managed to fall asleep on the drive. At first she had only been pretending, snoring theatrically because the less she talked to Harbinger, the longer it would take for him to figure out that he'd picked up the wrong elf. Sure, she figured she was an amazingly good diviner, being of the royal line and all, but she'd never actually done anything with magic outside of the Enchanted Forest. She wasn't worried though. How hard could it be?

She woke up when Harbinger pulled into a gas station. The sun was high and annoyingly bright. She'd been out for hours. Blinking, she stumbled out of the truck and headed for the convenience store. Before leaving the bathroom, she reapplied her makeup and fixed her hair in front of the mirror, because she wanted to make a good impression on her new co-workers. Then she flirted with the cashier, shoplifted a couple bags of Corn Nuts, and left. When she got back, Harbinger was waiting.

"You forgot to pay for those."

"Oh, my bad!" Tanya exclaimed. "I must've been sleep walking still." She hurried back in and paid for breakfast with actual money. The boss Hunter sure didn't miss much. She was going to have to play her cards real careful with him.

Harbinger started talking as soon as they got back on the highway. "We got the tip yesterday. Some locals were tearing down an old factory and must have uncovered it inside. Some of the workers got killed. Local sheriff investigated, and he had some dealings with MHI a long time ago, so when they found the anomaly, they knew who to call."

Anomaly? That sure did sound all sorts of *sciencey*. Tanya figured that a real smart professional-type elf would ask all the right questions, but not the stupid questions that would make them sound like they really didn't know what they were doing. "What're we dealing with?" That seemed like a happy medium.

"The creatures haven't been identified yet, but it sounds like they're coming out of a pocket dimension. That's why I called your queen and asked for a diviner."

"Pocket dimension . . ." She racked her brain and drew a blank. "Yeah, I get those *all* the time."

Harbinger scowled. He seemed to make that face a *lot*. "I've only come across four in my entire life and I've been doing this for a long time."

Tanya felt a momentary stab of panic. "Well, all the time, relatively speaking." Good. That sounded vague. She tried to change the subject. "What kind of monsters do you think they are?"

"The closest teams were already booked, so my guys didn't get there until earlier today, but now that I've got Hunters on site, hopefully by the time we get there they'll have figured it out. We'll play it by ear. If the monsters are a pain to deal with, that's where you come in. You can find the anchor and just break the tether."

That was a whole bunch of words that apparently didn't mean what she thought they meant. "No problemo," Tanya answered, not really sure what he expected her to do.

Harbinger didn't seem too talkative after that. Tanya still couldn't remember anything about pocket dimensions, anchors, or tethers, so she pulled out her cell phone. It was a desperate gamble, but Tanya was an elf of decisive action. "Gotta check in . . . Queen's orders."

Ilrondelia, Queen of the Elves, stabbed listlessly at her bowl of cornflakes and bacon. Tanya had been nowhere to be found. Fool girl had probably run off, screwin' around again, so she'd been forced to call for one of her other subjects to make breakfast. Elmo was the elves' best tracker, and he had just been waiting around for the Hunters to give him a ride anyways, so she'd drafted him to cook her bacon. It was all soggy. Proper bacon stayed crispy in milk.

Elmo was a mighty fine tracker, but terrible cook. It wasn't like Harbinger to be late, so she'd ordered Elmo to vacuum the royal trailer instead of just standing around. The cat hair kept plugging up the vacuum, so it was taking him awhile and the noise was making it hard to watch TV.

Suddenly, the vacuum stopped. The queen looked up from her soaps to see what the matter was. "You ain't done. That carpet don't look clean to me!"

"Sorry, majesty," he answered blearily as he fumbled around in his pockets. As usual, Elmo was hung over. "It's my phone."

The queen didn't like those fancy cellular phones, too much communicating wasn't good for an elf, but she'd bought a few of the prepaid ones at the 7-Eleven for the elves that had to take care of important outside business. The royal family had all got some too, because royalty always got the good stuff. "Well, answer it!" It might be Harbinger, and she didn't want to miss out on any of that nice, under-the-table, MHI cash.

"Oh . . . it's a text." Elmo squinted his little beady eyes. The queen was actually surprised that Elmo could read. She hadn't known that about him. Literacy made her suspicious. Elmo started typing with his thumbs, all slow and fumbly, especially when the texter had the shakes. The queen thought that texting was a particularly stupid way to talk. "Well, ain't that funny?" he said.

"What's funny?"

"Tanya's gettin' serious about studyin' our ways." Elmo wiped his nose on the back of his hand and dropped his phone back in his coveralls. "Usually that girl's got her head in the clouds."

"Studyin'? She shoulda been cookin' my bacon," the queen said. She went back to her soaps. She'd punish the heir when she got back from . . . wherever she was. "Hey, where's Tanya at anyways?"

Elmo shrugged. "She didn't say. She wanted to know what a human would call a pocket dee-mention. I told her it's just human talk for an *eskarthi-dor*."

That was the old Elvish word for a portal world. Why in the world would Tanya care about one of those? "Gimmie that thingy," the queen growled. Elmo handed the phone over. Grumbling, she tried to dial the number, but her fingers were too chubby. "Damn it! Call that fool girl back."

Once she knew that what the Hunters were interested in was an *eskarthi-dor*, her confidence had grown. She'd never actually seen one, but Varty the Elder had taught the young elves about such things before he'd gone on to the Great Trailer Park in the Sky. This was going to be a piece of cake.

Tanya jumped when her phone rang, but it was only Elmo calling her back. She'd downloaded the ringtone of pigs squealing for Elmo, but right then she was wishing she'd downloaded something more professional sounding. She looked over at Harbinger. "Gotta take this. Important elf business."

He didn't so much as take his eyes off the road. "Obviously."

"Hel—"

"*Tanya*! You fool girl! I'm gonna wring your scrawny ne—" Tanya had to hold the phone away from her pointy ear. *Mom?* The Queen had a set of lungs, and when she got to yelling, you could hear her clear over in Corinth. Tanya covered the phone and looked over at Harbinger, but he seemed oblivious to the monarch's fury. "—idiot had to cook my bacon!"

She had to think fast. There was no way she was going back to the Enchanted Forest. If she didn't become an official Monster Hunter on this trip, she was screwed. "Why, yes. Everything is just great here."

"Huh? Get your fool ass back here befo—"

"Yes. Right away."

"Why you talkin' all funny?"

"Everything is fine here," Tanya said. Harbinger had no idea; he was just smoking and flicking the ashes out the window. Her plan was working perfectly; she might as well use the opportunity to build her street cred. She raised her voice so Harbinger could hear her over the wind. "Don't worry. I'll handle that huge infestation of horrible monsters as soon as I get back. Yes. I will be sure to tell them that I am the greatest tracker the Enchanted Forest has ever seen. Thank you."

"Tanya? You been huffin' paint?"

"Thank you. Bye-bye." Tanya closed the phone and checked Harbinger's reaction. The Hunter was clueless. *Yes!* She shut her phone off to avoid getting anymore unwanted calls. "Sorry about that, Mr. Harbinger."

"More important elf business?"

"Of course. I'm *super* important."

The queen stared at the phone in her hand. Something was wrong. Tanya had been talking all sorts of weird, and she hadn't even sounded drunk. She mashed redial.

"Hi, this is Tanya!"

"Girl, you better—"

"Ha! Gotcha! Leave a message!" *BEEP.*

Something was terribly wrong.

"Your majesty?" Elmo asked.

"The heir . . . I think she's been kidnapped!" Somehow a mother just knew these things. This was awful. Horrible! Unthinkable! Someone had taken the heir. "Somebody done stole Tanya!"

Indiana wasn't any more interesting than Mississippi, which was kind of sad if you thought about it. They had arrived in a small town and a police car had been waiting for them at one intersection. The police car got in front and led them to an old, abandoned factory on the outskirts. There were a bunch of Hunters just kind of chilling, looking all sorts of cool with their fancy armor and guns, just hanging around outside the crumbling old building, but Harbinger had called them a "perimeter" which Tanya filed away as an important-sounding term for hanging out.

Harbinger got out and immediately started asking questions, getting answers, and giving orders. This was a man used to being in charge, but not all blustery and yelling like the queen. He didn't need to hit anybody with a thrown shoe. They just did what they were told without arguing because they automatically knew that Harbinger was right. Since Tanya was going to be queen someday herself—if she didn't get disowned for this stunt—she filed that information away. Being all sorts of smart got you more respect than a well aimed bunny slipper.

"Anybody know what we're dealing with yet?"

"Witnesses couldn't tell. The only thing we could get from them was that it gave everyone headaches that got close to it. Tracks say quadruped with big claws, probably seven or eight hundred pounds. Lee's cross-referencing the files on that." It was a girl with dark hair and glasses that answered. "Local police have the place surrounded, but nothing's moved since we got here. We've got another problem, though. Timeline just sped up."

"Status?"

"Possible hostages. Two children, male, five and seven, were reported as missing yesterday. They were last seen playing around here. We just found kid-size footprints, but the tracks lead up to the gate and disappear. I think they're on the other side."

"That complicates matters," Harbinger muttered. "I was hoping we could just blow everything up and collect the parts. Looks like we're going in."

A group of Hunters formed a circle around them. Tanya recognized some of them. Harbinger rattled off introductions, but Tanya was so overwhelmed with all the bustle and excitement that she remembered them as Dreadlocks, Blondie, Red Beard, Glasses Girl, Limpy, and the Big Ugly One. When he was done, Harbinger turned to her. "This is Elmovarian, master diviner of the Enchanted Forest."

Red Beard looked confused. "Aren't you the princess? Toni? Tawny? Something?"

"Tanya." Harbinger looked right through her. "What do you mean, *princess*?"

"What? No . . . Me? That's crazy talk." Tanya hadn't thought through the idea that some of the Hunters might recognize her. Curse her amazing and unforgettable beauty! "You're thinking of the *other* Tanya."

"No. I remember you, too," said Dreadlocks. "Your mom hit you in the face with a bunny slipper for asking how to join MHI."

"Looked like it hurt," said Blondie.

Harbinger didn't seem happy. "Well, that explains some things."

"No . . . I . . ." *Busted.* All of the Hunters were scowling at her now. Scowling was like a default setting on these humans. "Crap. Okay, whatever. Yeah, I'm the princess. So? I'm a way super good diviner."

"Sure you are," Harbinger said. "I'm going to have some words with the queen once I take you home. I can't believe she tried to rip me off. I should have hired a gnome."

"No, you can't tell the queen. She doesn't know I ran away. I'm here on my own. This is like my dream. I want to be a Monster Hunter."

Blondie whistled. "The queen is going to be *pissed*."

All of her carefully laid plans were falling apart. "But, I can totally help!"

"It doesn't matter anyway. We're going in after those kids. You're going to sit your ass in that van and not move until we come out."

"She can't go in the van, Earl . . ." Big Ugly noted. "We've got a *you know what* in the van, and I don't really know if he'd do very good at the whole *rescue* thing. He recognizes Hunters okay, but he says that other humans kind of all look the same to him."

"He does love decapitating folks." Harbinger sighed. "Okay, leave Edward in the van. Can't have her royal highness getting sliced and diced."

"What's an Edward?"

"An Edward is somebody you don't want to mess with, and he really doesn't like elves," Harbinger stated. "Now go sit in the truck and eat your stolen Corn Nuts. I don't have time for your nonsense."

"I'm not afraid of no Edwards."

Harbinger stopped, obviously frustrated. "Edward is an *orc*." Tanya's mouth fell open in shock. She looked fearfully at the van. "You give me any more lip and I'll tell him to babysit you . . . Corn Nuts. Now."

Tanya ran for the truck.

Tanya was really freaking out. Momma was going to murder her. The Hunters were so mad that now she'd never get a job. She couldn't even show how great she was by breaking the bonds that held the *eskarthi-dor* to the world so it could float away, because there were some stupid human kids inside of it. She still had one last chance. She could try to talk her way out of this, but though that usually worked with Momma, she really didn't think it would work on somebody like Harbinger. Even though it was a long drive back, and normally her whining could wear down anyone, she had a feeling that would probably just make Harbinger angrier, and if he got too angry, he'd probably feed her to MHI's pet orc.

The worst part was that it was taking *forever*.

The Hunters had gone inside the old factory an hour ago. There hadn't been a noise out of the place since then. They'd left two Hunters on the outside: Blondie and the one with the bum leg had gone inside the factory with some bazookas and a radio. They were probably there just in case something went wrong in the *eskarthi-dor*.

There was a big radio in Harbinger's truck. She wondered if she could listen in to see what was going on. It beat being bored. She flipped it on, and luckily she didn't even need to fiddle with the knobs. It was already tuned in to the Hunters frequency.

"—say again, over." That sounded like Blondie.

"—messing with our heads—" The other side had a lot of static. "Can't proceed . . . —ve to fall back . . . —the trail, out now."

That didn't sound good. That sounded like they were running. She didn't think that Hunters ran from anything.

"This is Holly. Did you find those kids?"

"Negative. Had to retreat." The other girl was talking.

"This is Lee." Tanya hadn't heard Limpy talk before, but from the lack of static she assumed it was one of the Hunters that had stayed Earth-side. "I think I've found our creatures. Something called a mind colossus fits the description. Rare and dangerous. You need to get the hell out of there."

"—rking on it." There were a series of pops that Tanya had to assume were gunshots.

"They're telepathic." Lee sounded really nervous. "They can cause hallucinations, confusion, even insanity."

"Can we block it?"

"No known way. There's a note here that they only affect humans. Earl?"

Harbinger stopped shooting long enough to talk on the radio. "No dice. My head feels like it's gonna explode, same as everybody else. Looks like I'm human enough."

I'm not human at all.

Tanya pulled out her cell phone and turned it back on. She had to wait a minute for the phone to power back up and find a signal. She found MOMMA on her address book. The queen was probably going to be asleep or too lazy to get up to answer the phone, but she had to try. Surprisingly, she picked up on the first ring.

Momma sounded even more breathless than usual. "Tanya! Where you at, girl?"

"No time to talk. This is important. Real quick, what's a mind colossus?"

"Huh? A what? Have you been stolen?"

"No, but I need to know if a mind colossus can hurt an elf brain or not."

Momma sputtered. "Why you need to know something like that for?"

"Because there's one here right now and I need to know if it's gonna fry my brain or not is why. Jeez. Quit being so nosy."

Momma screamed at somebody in the background. "Tanya's been kidnapped by fey! Drive faster!"

Momma had *left* the trailer park? That was impossible. "Wait, where are you?"

"I'm coming to save ya, baby!"

Oh shit. The queen never left the Enchanted Forest except to go to Walmart, and Indiana was a whole lot farther away than Walmart. She was in *so* much trouble. "Uh . . . Okay . . . Cool. Now on the monster thingy, does it hurt elf brains?"

"They're called *blargs*. Fey bred them to hunt humans long time back for some war. Shouldn't hurt no elf brains, but they got claws like nobody's business, rip you right up."

The Hunters were in danger. There were stupid but innocent human kids in need of rescuing. The blarg wouldn't be able to use its magic on her, but it could still hurt her. She needed wisdom. Tanya pulled her Elvis Presley medallion, set it spinning, watched the sparkles, and asked herself, *What would the King do?*

That was easy. He'd kick some fey ass, show MHI that he was cool, be the best elf ever, and never have to live in the stupid trailer park again. So that's what she'd do, too.

She curled her fingers around the holy symbol and made a fist. "A little less conversation, a lot more *action*."

Momma was confused. "Huh?"

"Nothing, Momma . . ." She didn't know much about fighting monsters. She could probably borrow a Hunter's gun, since like all elves she could shoot good enough to poach deer, but beyond that she was pretty much clueless. The meanest thing she'd ever tangled with had been a raccoon that had somehow gotten into the trailer, and even though it had put up an *epic* fight before she'd brained it with a frying pan, this would probably be much harder. She would probably need some muscle for this . . . That thought gave her an idea, even though the idea was frankly terrifying. "Can a blarg hurt an orc brain?"

Edward was listening to both radios at the same time, Sean Hannity on one, his adopted tribe of Monster Hunters on the other, and it sounded like it was time to fulfill Gretchen's latest prophecy. Edward did not know what a mind colossus was, nor did he particularly care. It would either be something he could kill or it would kill him. Either way, it would be a glorious day to be an *urk*.

He carefully placed the leather straps over his shoulders and cinched the buckles tight. The scabbards rattled as he adjusted them to make sure his swords were perfectly placed. He was carrying two short *urkish* swords on his back, two curved daggers and six small throwing knives on his belt, a push dagger hanging from a cord around his neck, four folding knives in various pockets, and a Swiss Army knife that

Trip Jones had given him for his birthday. Edward had no use for that one, but found the corkscrew and scissors fascinating. The thing they were talking about on the radio sounded big, so Edward took the mighty two-handed war ax out of his bag and pulled the leather hood off its giant razor head. He chuckled approvingly. This would be fun.

Edward never used guns, though he'd tried. He had nothing against them, but his gifts for bladed combat just did not extend to human guns, which were all complicated and noisy. It was kind of like how Skippy could fly a helicopter but couldn't drive a car without crashing. Basically, Edward was a terrible shot.

There was a knock on the back door of the van. There were many humans present not worthy to witness *urk* perfection, so Edward reached for his mask and goggles. He didn't get to them in time before the door was flung open.

It was a girl. She saw his face and screamed. He saw her pointy ears and bellowed in surprise.

The elf regained her composure first. "Orc! Your Hunter masters need you. I summon you to battle!" Confused, Edward lifted his ax and pointed at himself, then at her. "*No!*" the elf shrieked. "Not me! The monster. Go battle the monster!"

His first inclination was to just lop off her peroxide-colored head. The clan ancestors had always taught that the only good elf was a dead elf (and also, coincidently, that dead elves made great holiday decorations), but Edward hesitated, because he did not want to upset the Harb Anger. Edward had never actually seen an elf before. He didn't know if any of his clan had. This one was kind of scrawny. Not very impressive at all, really.

"Come on, what are you waiting for?" She moved her hands about like she was trying to shoo him out of the van. "You guys are supposed to go berserk with blood lust. You call that berserk? You're just sitting there. Are you going to go into a killing frenzy or not?"

That was the idea before you showed up. He put on his mask and reluctantly got out of the van. He didn't talk much to non-*urks* because his English was rough, and Skippy was the one that was smooth and good with human words, but he tried anyway. "Me . . . Edward."

"That's more like it. Okay, cool. Now let's go kick that blarg's ass. I'm Tanya."

This was certainly awkward. *Gnrwlz*, god of war, commanded that he should kill all elves, but the Harb Anger would want him to be polite, and that meant no decapitations. Tanya was making this complicated, but at least she hadn't tried to steal his soul with her foul elf magic. If he was lucky, the monster would eat her first, then he could kill the monster. Everybody would be happy. It would be like killing two foxes with one swing.

Talking to the insane orc barbarian killer had been the hardest single thing Tanya had ever done in her life. By some miracle, he hadn't immediately cut her ears off for his elf ear necklace that Momma had taught all orcs had, so she was calling it a win. Maybe if she got lucky, the monster would get mortally wounded, *then* kill the orc. That would sure simplify matters.

She led the way into the old factory. The place was rusty, falling apart, with puddles of water standing on the concrete floor. There were huge holes in the roof that beams of sunlight streamed through. Big human machines were slowly melting back into the ground. Except for the blarg that had been hidden underneath this place forever, the only other residents seemed to be pigeons.

They found the Hunters at the far end of the building. A brick wall had been broken down recently, and behind it was a plain old door. The Hunters were gathered around that door and pointing guns in its direction so it was obvious where the problem was. Most of the Hunters were out of breath and dripping sweat, which was odd since it was really chilly in the shade of the old factory's walls. The ones that had been on the other side all looked like they were fighting an Elmo-sized hangover and rubbing their temples.

Tanya gathered up her courage. "Okay. Y'all can relax. Me and the orc have got this one. That there's a blarg nest. Its magic will screw humans up, but it can't hurt elves or orcs."

Harbinger glanced her way. "You've got to be shitting me . . . Edward?"

She looked to the orc. Edward just shrugged, as if to say, *I guess*. At least the horrific barbarian lunatic had her back. She smiled at Harbinger. "See? Told ya so."

"Those kids are still alive, Earl," the girl with glasses said. "But if she could get them out, then we can blow this place to pieces."

"No way. It's too dangerous, princess. I'm not going to have the queen yelling at me because you got stupid," Harbinger said with finality. Tanya gritted her teeth and suppressed the scream of rage. She was not used to being told *no*. Harbinger then addressed the orc. "On the other hand, Ed, you think you can get those kids out?"

The orc's voice sounded like a clothes dryer filled with rocks. "Yes . . ."

"All right. Remember the little pink fleshy ones are the *children*. Don't hurt them. The big green fucker? It you can kill. Got it?" The orc just grunted and patted the head of his giant ax tenderly. "That'll do. About two hundred yards straight ahead you'll find a clearing. Owen, open the door."

Big Ugly lifted an enormous gun with one hand and grabbed the doorknob with the other. Everybody else aimed their guns too. Big Ugly nodded at Edward then jerked the door open. Tanya gasped. According to where they were inside the building, the door should have opened into a space about the size of a broom closet. Instead she was looking at a vast, dark, scary forest. But the trees were all bulgy, with big vines hanging off them, and something was screeching like a monkey in the background. It was like looking at a Travel Channel show about jungles, only it was in a bricked-off broom closet in Indiana.

Red Beard was standing next to her. "No matter how long I do this," he said, "There's always something new and freaky."

"Clear!" shouted Glasses Girl as she peered into the jungle through a rifle scope. "Go get them, Ed."

Edward was undeterred by the sight of the mysterious jungle. Clenching his ax, he walked toward the doorway. That was one brave orc, or maybe orcs were just too dumb to understand fear, but either way Edward was about to go be a hero and Tanya was going to live the rest of her life in the trailer park.

She had to do something, and do it quick. Glancing around, she noticed a bunch of equipment cases that the Hunters had brought in. On top of one was a big bolt action rifle. It didn't look too different from the one that Elder Varty had taught her to shoot squirrels with for dinner. The rifle had a leather sling with loops filled with giant bullets. It was her only chance.

"What would Elvis Presley do?" Tanya whispered.

Red Beard had heard her. "Probably a lot of drugs. Why?"

Edward was walking into the jungle. He disappeared behind some big round leaves. The Hunters were covering him. Tanya snatched up the rifle, which was much heavier than it looked, and she ran after the orc as fast as she could. It was probably better that way because she didn't have time to think about how stupid it was to randomly cross into another dimension.

"What? Wait! Grab her!" Harbinger shouted, but it was too late. Big Ugly reached for her and snagged one sleeve of her letterman's jacket, but elves are way quicker than humans so Tanya just shrugged out of the coat, caught the rifle, and just kept on running. Big Ugly made it a few steps after her before the blarg's magic hit him in the brain like a hammer and he went to his knees with a shout.

Harbinger was yelling after her but Tanya just pushed her way through the vines and kept going. It really wasn't much worse than kudzu once she got into it, and elves were very light on their feet. Even if it wasn't for the telepathic mind attacks, there was no way a big lumbering human would be able to catch up to her.

I did it! She stopped to catch her breath. There was no sound of pursuit. She'd lost them! Then Tanya looked around, realized she could only see a few feet in each direction, that there was a giant fey creature somewhere ahead, and thought that she might have maybe bit off more than she could chew this time.

She screamed when something black materialized right in front of her. She raised the big rifle, but the black shape caught the barrel in one hand. Tanya breathed again when she realized it was Edward. The orc leaned in and put one finger to his mask and made a *shhhh* noise.

"Don't you shush me," Tanya whispered. "I know what I'm doing."

ROOOAAAARRRRR.

Tanya almost leapt out of her skin at the sound of the blarg. She hoisted the rifle and mashed the butt against her shoulder, but nothing came out of the trees to eat her. "That sounded huge!" she hissed. Edward held out his hands as far apart as they would go, like a fisherman talking about the biggest catch ever. "Yeah. That is big."

The orc jerked his head. *This way.* He was even quicker through the vines than an elf, and Tanya struggled to keep up. It was really hot inside the jungle dimension, and within minutes Tanya's shirt was sticking to her. Up ahead, there was a clearing, just like Glasses Girl had said there would be.

What Glasses Girl, or any of the other Hunters for that matter, couldn't have known was that the clearing was also the center anchor point for the entire *eskarthi-dor*. Tanya could see it, though, clear as day. This place was ancient, not like human ancient, but really ancient, like when the fey used to hunt humans for sport. This bubble was a leftover from those days, and apparently this blarg had been stuck here the whole time. No wonder it was so damn cranky.

The monster was stomping back and forth, angry as Momma after the time the pixies stole her credit card number and racked up all those long distance phone bills. However this monster was bigger than Momma, which was really saying something. It looked like a muscular human on the top half, but at the waist it turned into a giant lizard with four big lizard legs and a long whipping tail. It was bright green with black spots. The head was human-shaped, but it was hard to tell with all those other brains growing out of it. Momma said that the fey loved to stick different critters together, and it turned out they were just as gross in person as Momma had made them sound.

The blarg saw her and turned. She could feel the old magic pouring off that pile of pulsing green brains, but they had been designed to mess up humans, not her kind. No wonder the Hunters had been hurting. This thing really packed a wallop. When its magic didn't floor her, the blarg charged. Tanya hadn't even realized that she had raised the rifle. The sights were wobbling like crazy. Her arms were shaking because the gun was so heavy. She pulled the trigger but nothing happened. She pulled harder. Still nothing. She screamed in frustration as the monster galloped toward her. Tanya turned to run, but it was too late.

The monster was too fast. One lizard leg swatted her. She hit the ground hard and lay there, wondering about all the bright lights going off inside her head. Her life flashed before her eyes, but it was a pretty boring life, with the highlights being keggers, a few concerts, and that one time Cousin Buford had built a potato cannon and they wound up shooting frogs out of it to watch them hit the side of the overpass. She'd never been a Hunter. She'd never done anything like the adventurous elves of old. She was going to die, and she'd never accomplished anything. Blinking her way back to consciousness, she saw a giant claw descending toward her throat, and she screamed her pretty little head off.

But the claw came off in a flash and went flying into the jungle. Bright orange blood poured out of the stump and splattered Tanya in the face. "Gross!"

The orc came out of nowhere, swinging that giant ax like it weighed nothing. Edward had saved her life! The blarg reared back, slashing at him, but he dodged the attack and planted his ax square in the monster's soft underbelly. It fell over and Edward lost the ax, but that didn't stop him. Two swords zipped out faster than Momma's switchblade and it was a whirl of silver and black as Edward went to town.

Tanya watched in awe. Edward moved like a kung fu movie on fast forward. The monster had to be five times his size, but the orc didn't seem to care. He was positively nonchalant, and he took it apart, piece by piece. It was raining fluorescent orange blood and Edward was as cool as a cucumber. He was as cold as ice. He was as cool as *Elvis*.

But even as quick as Edward was, that was a whole lot of monster, and it finally managed to tag him with one of its human sized hands. His clothes ripped, knives went flying, and Edward was sent rolling across the dirt to end up by her sneakers. The blarg roared, one of its brains hanging off and dripping goop, and it came right at them.

This time it was Tanya's turn to save the day. She rolled over, scooped up the rifle, sort of aimed it, and pulled the trigger. Sadly, there was still no boom. "Stupid piece of—" Edward reached over and flipped the rifle's safety lever to fire for her. "Oh . . . thanks."

This time when she pulled the trigger, the gun went off with the loudest *BOOM* she'd ever heard. It kicked her shoulder like a horse on steroids. She squealed and dropped the rifle. "Son of a bitch! That hurt!" But she'd hit the monster! The blarg made it a few more feet before it toppled over. She'd blown half its head off, and judging from the mess, the outside brains just did the magic, the inside brains worked just like everything else. And since those brains were sprayed all over the clearing . . .

"Yay! I'm a Monster Hunter!" Edward gave her a thumbs-up. She got to her feet, rubbing her tender shoulder, and picked up the rifle. It had .416 Rigby engraved on the side. Whatever that was, it sure did pack a punch.

Edward got to his feet and pulled off the shredded remains of his shirt. There was a big bloody scratch on his side and he used the rags to apply pressure. "Dayum . . ." Tanya couldn't help but stare, because Edward was seriously the most buffed thing she'd ever seen. He made her favorite football players look like dainty ballerinas. He didn't just have six-pack abs, his six pack had six packs. Edward may have been an odd grayish-green color, but homeboy was *chiseled*. He went over to the blarg, yanked his ax out of its stinky guts, and caught her looking. Edward didn't so much as bat an eye. He was all, like, *This? Whatever.* Or at least that's what she figured he would have said, if he'd bothered to talk.

Damn. He was *cool*.

She snapped out of his orcish spell, darn all those distracting muscles, and got back to Monster Hunting business. They had to rescue those human brats. Edward must have thought the same thing, since he'd already spotted the hole they were being kept in. The kids were alive and whining, probably being kept around for a snack later, and Edward began pulling them out.

Tanya looked around. She could feel the impressive magic here and it was really too bad that she hadn't been able to use her skills. She could totally have wrecked this place. That would have impressed Harbinger even more than her blowing some stupid blarg's head off.

There was a sudden rumble. "What was that?" she asked.

Edward was dragging the kids along behind. He stopped and listened, then he lifted the ax. "More . . . for fight . . ." The sounds were coming from all around them now. The ground shifted under her feet and Tanya had to step back as the sleeping blargs buried beneath awoke. Mounds of dirt were shifting all over the clearing. There were dozens of them. She fumbled with the bolt handle until she managed to reload the elephant rifle.

"He-he-he . . ." Edward had a very unnerving laugh. "Pinheads." He actually sounded excited.

They could never make it through that many monsters. Green claws burst from the soil. She was going to have to use her magic to try to break the pocket dimension. This whole place was going to fall apart when she did that. She was terrified, but she needed to think of something sufficiently badass to say like a Monster Hunter totally should . . . She couldn't think of anything, though. In her defense, it was her first day on the job.

❖ ❖ ❖

Edward had a human child bouncing under each arm. He'd left his ax buried in one monster's head, left one sword in a monster's belly, broke the other over a monster's head, and had managed to run through most of his knives. If he'd known there were going to be that many monsters, he would have brought more than seventeen weapons.

The door was just ahead. The elf girl was running along behind. She kept shooting the big gun. She was also not a very good shot, but at least she was making lots of noise. Battle was always better with lots of noise. Her war cries were too high pitched though. If she was going to be a proper warrior, she was going to have to work on that.

Edward was torn. The elf hadn't died, and strangely enough, that made him happy . . . But then again, he hadn't liked humans much either until MHI had adopted his clan. She hadn't even tried to steal his soul *once*, and she'd saved his life by shooting a few monsters. *Gnrwlz* was probably displeased, but Edward had killed many monsters today, so they were even.

The door was open and sunlight was coming through. Which was good, because the little world full of monsters was coming apart and with all the trees falling down, he might not have found his way. Harb Anger, Brother of the Great War Chief, and Trip Jones were in the doorway shouting for him. There was a scream from the elf, though this one was not a battle cry, and Edward turned to see that a monster had caught her by the foot and was dragging her away.

Sadness. Edward had started liking the elf. Edward reached the door and shoved the human children at the Hunters. You know what? Edward decided that maybe he did like that elf just enough to not let her get eaten. *Gnrwlz* could suck it. Edward would save her, too. He turned and ran back through the shifting dirt and collapsing trees. He was out of proper *urk* weapons, but he still had something stabby, and that would do.

Edward leapt over Tanya, landed on the monster's wide lizard back, and scrambled up to its globular head. He drove Trip Jones' Swiss Army corkscrew deep into the monster's head, twisted it in, then ripped out a plug of skull. The monster gurgled and fell, making the Swiss Army knife one of the best presents ever. Edward jumped off, scooped up Tanya in his arms and ran for the doorway as the world around him collapsed into oblivion.

❖ ❖ ❖

"I like her," Red Beard, or Milo it turned out he was called, was saying. "She's certainly energetic."

"Crazy is more like it. Not that that's necessarily a resume killer with this outfit," Harbinger answered. "Skippy's people won't like it."

"Ed said he'd vouch for her," Milo pointed out.

Harbinger shook his head. "Hell . . . Trip hired a troll. How much worse could this be? Oh, look, pretty-pretty princess has decided to join us."

Tanya woke up in the arms of an orc barbarian. Now *that* would have really freaked Momma out . . . Orcs were like the ultimate *bad boys*, and there was something kind of exciting about that. She was on the ground and he was kneeling next to her. Edward's goggled head was tilted to the side, like he was saying, *I got you, baby. Don't worry. I'm here.* Or maybe not. It was kind of hard to tell. When Edward saw that she was conscious he unceremoniously dropped her and wandered off.

"I got a headache," Tanya said. The last time she'd felt this way was when she'd gotten into Elmo's moonshine. "So, how was that? Pretty awesome, huh?"

Harbinger sat down on the edge of an old piece of machinery and lit a cigarette. He took his time responding. "Not bad. Edward said you did okay. Were you actually telling the truth for once when you said your dream was to be a Hunter?"

"It is. It really is, I swear. I'll work hard. I want to be like you guys. I want to be *somebody*," Tanya cried. "I'll be the best Hunter you've ever seen."

Harbinger sighed. "I may regret this . . ." He took out a business card and wrote on the back of it. "This is the next Newbie class. And just because you're royalty doesn't mean you get any special treatment. Lie to me again and you're toast. Got it?"

"Serious? I can be a Hunter?" Tanya started to tear up. "I can't believe this. I've still gotta tell Momma."

Harbinger looked to the opposite end of the factory. "And speaking of which . . ."

"*Tanya!*" The whole factory shook from the power of the queen's voice and the thunder of her slippers. "*Tanyalthus Enderminon!* I'm gonna wring your scrawny neck! Comin' all the way up here, thinkin' you been kidnap stolen, and you done run off playin' Hunter!"

Momma was huffing and red-faced. This was the most exercise she'd gotten in a really long time. "Sorry 'bout this," she told Harbinger.

"It's fine. In fact, I'd be interested in hiring Tanya for some other work."

"Really?" she asked suspiciously. "Pay good?"

"Real good. I'll be in touch."

"Better be good. You pay extra for the royal line!" The queen came over and grabbed Tanya by the end of one pointy ear and hauled her up. "We're gettin' you home right now, young lady!"

"Ow! Ow! Ow! Okay! I'm coming!" Despite the aches and pains, being in torn and filthy clothing, and the embarrassment of being dragged by the ear, Tanya was happy as could be. She was going to be a *Hunter*. She still needed to talk Momma into it, but scary as Momma was, she was no monster. Elvis had smiled on her.

"You's in so much trouble." Momma dragged her out to the old Buick station wagon in the parking lot. Elmo and several other elves were sitting in the car, giving the evil eye to Edward, who had wandered back to the van. It was an uneasy truce, only because of the presence of the Hunters.

"Hang on a sec." Tanya broke out of Momma's grasp and ran over to Edward. The elves gasped, but they didn't dare make a move. Edward tilted his head to the side, confused. There was a notebook in the back of the van. Tanya grabbed a pen, wrote on the paper, then tore it out and handed it over to Edward.

"TAAANYAAAA!" the queen of the Elves screeched.

Edward looked at the phone number and scratched his head.

"Coming, Mother." Tanya flounced back to the car, only turning long enough to pantomime talking on the phone and to mouth the words, "*Call me.*" The elves piled into the station wagon and it roared off in a cloud of oily smoke. The queen could be heard shouting until the car was out of view.

Edward carefully folded the piece of paper and put it in his pocket for safekeeping.

DEAD WAITS DREAMING

This story was originally published in Space Eldritch II: The Haunted Stars *by Cold Fusion Media, edited by Nathan Shumate, in 2013.*

WHEN I WAS A CHILD, I dreamed of the stars. When I was a man, the stars stole my dreams.

A man who cannot dream becomes nothing but an empty shell, but the thing about empty shells, there's nothing left inside to corrupt. Space ate my dreams, tore them right out of my head and left a gaping hole where my soul had been living. My life ended a long time ago.

Which is why I was the only one who survived.

"What happened on Atlas?"

The question woke me up. It didn't matter. As usual my sleep was empty. I wasn't missing anything good.

"Please, Mr. Chang, we have to know what happened on Atlas."

The desperate voice was coming out of the blank wall of my tiny cell. They thought I'd been exposed to a potential alien biohazard so I'd remained in quarantine. My clothing had been burned and my body had been scrubbed, attached to tubes and machines to be monitored in every way possible, isolated from the world of flesh and imprisoned in a totally sterile environment.

The precautions wouldn't do them any good.

My words came out raspy and weak. "I don't know."

"The survivor's awake. He's talking!" She forgot to turn off the intercom. "Get the captain. Hurry."

29

"Where am I?"

"You're onboard the *Alert* in orbit over Atlas. You're safe now. Please, Mr. Chang, we need you to try and remember what happened to your colony."

I remembered, but remembering and understanding were two different things.

It began with a news report.

I didn't know at the time that this particular blurb would mark the beginning of the end of the world but I followed a lot of news. Useless talking heads, pundits, bloggers, hoaxers, malcontents, and a handful of actual experts, millions of channels streaming in from two hundred solar systems and downloaded in the few seconds whenever the gate cycled open and we were briefly connected with the rest of the universe—even if it was all months out of date—and then I followed Atlas' local streams when the gate was closed, which was the vast majority of the time.

Galaxy, system, world, or local, I followed it. War, politics, business, science, sports, entertainment, it didn't matter. I had nothing else to do, so I listened as other people actually *did*. I was a pensioner, a useless parasite on the system, popping crazy pills and streaming feeds. On more pragmatic or desperate colonies they would have recycled me. On Atlas, I wasted away in my apartment and filled my brain with other people's lives.

The local blurb had been an update on the Dark Side Dig, commemorating the sixteenth anniversary of the discovery of the ancient ruins that had changed Atlas from a backwoods mining colony to an archeological mecca. Even though the natives had been extinct for millions of years, humans had only discovered a handful of planets with life so far, so it had been a big deal, even if the odd winged cucumbers depicted in their carvings had been relative primitives compared to some of the species we'd found on other worlds.

The Dig's science team had found a new chamber to crack open. They'd dubbed it the Temple.

It should have pissed me off, because that was supposed to have been my job before a quirk of interstellar travel had ripped out all the creative parts of my mind and left me a useless, drug addled husk, but anger just got in the way of my news addiction, so I kept listening. The report closed with an interview, just some puffery with one of the newly arrived archeologists, about how the weird geometry favored in the alien architecture had given a few of them nightmares.

Nightmares . . . I would have killed for a nightmare.

Captain Hartono brought up the hologram. It showed a nearly skeletal man sitting on a slab, arms wrapped around his knees, rocking back and forth, slowly muttering to himself. "What do we have on the survivor?"

"All colonists' DNA is on file. His name is Leland Chang, contract transfer from Calhoun, been on Atlas for fifteen years." As Dr. Riady spoke, all of the pertinent tabs came up on the edge of the hologram.

The captain opened the career data. "Xenoanthropologist, supposed to be brilliant." He went back to the holo. "The guy looks awful."

"Malnutrition and dehydration mostly. The servitors found some other minor injuries, but no serious trauma."

"I listened in while the drop team lifted him out, lots of crazy babbling. Whatever happened down there drove him batshit insane. I need you to get his head straight fast."

"I don't know if that'll be possible."

"Make it possible, Doc. The evidence the drop teams have recovered so far doesn't make any sense. Command needs to know who did this and he's our only witness."

"I'm afraid Chang wouldn't have made a very credible witness even before whatever happened down there."

Hartono brought up the medical history tab. He swore under his breath. "Keziah's Disorder? That poor bastard . . ."

"It's extremely rare."

"Thank God for that," the captain muttered. "It doesn't matter. Get him talking. I don't care what you have to do. We need information and we need it now. Crack him and do a memory lift if you need to."

"That's not exactly ethical, sir."

"At the last gate cycle, Atlas was a thriving colony. Thirty days later, it's back online, we cycle through and somehow six hundred thousand colonists have gone missing and we don't know why. So right now I don't particularly give a shit about ethics."

"I can't memory lift an innocent man, Captain," Riady stammered. "That's—"

"There's no messages, no recordings, no notes, no vids. Nothing. Every AI on the planet is crashed. We've got ghost ships in orbit with their systems scrubbed. The forensic evidence doesn't make sense. There's battle damage, but no invaders. Over half a million humans vanished in *thirty* days, Doctor, and the only living thing we've found more advanced than a house plant is your survivor."

"Give me a chance," she begged.

Hartono frowned. They were stuck for now anyway. "The next available gate cycle isn't for two days. You've got one."

I was an artist once. I could take raw materials and scrape and twist them into beauty. I can still understand the fundamental techniques, but it turns out that when you are incapable of dreaming, you are incapable of creating. You can no longer reach your *full potential.*

What a blessing that turned out to be.

Before Atlas became a galactic tourist attraction—*witness the wonder of an ancient alien civilization*—it was simply the boring second planet in the Chameleon 110913-773444 system. When I got the contract offer the 26-hour days and 1.02% standard gravity made it sound pretty nice. The downside was the average temperature of 120 C combined with the 300 kilometer an hour winds made most of the planet a giant sandblaster. There was one colony and it was mostly underground, so Atlas wasn't exactly a draw for the *outdoorsy* types.

The contract specified that I would be studying the ancient inhabitants, using my expertise to reconstruct their culture. It takes a certain kind of mind to be able to imagine an alien lifestyle. I signed on. I severed my existing contract on Calhoun and embarked on a great adventure. Of course I did. This was a scholar's dream job.

Unless your scholar can no longer dream, because then he can't keep a job.

Star travel is relatively safe, considering that your frail body is being hurled across the universe through an in-between space that mankind barely comprehends, using math which shouldn't work, yet somehow does. Since our brains didn't evolve in a fashion that could handle the strange physics of null space, hypersleep was invented. They advertise that hypersleep was so that humans could travel between gates in complete comfort. Go to sleep in one system, wake up in another one on the opposite end of the Milky Way. No problem, and you especially don't have to worry about any of those pesky psychoses that all the early interstellar travelers developed.

Except that hypersleep isn't really sleep, and there's nothing hyper about it. That's just creative marketing. I used to be able to appreciate that sort of thing. Your body isn't sleeping, it's artificially shut down until it is one faint electrical impulse away from death. Space travelers are placed into a chemical coma and frozen. Everybody knows this, but nobody who has to go through it likes to dwell on it. After all, it was statistically *extremely safe*—the advertisements said so—and when you get decanted you are ready to experience life on an exciting new world.

The first humans who traveled between gates are all dead now. Back then we didn't understand that entering REM sleep while your body was in null space was a one way ticket to crazy town. We still don't know why it happens, we just know that it does. So now they practically turn you into a corpse, freeze your brain, and artificially pump nanobots through your arteries, all to keep your mind safely blank while you're flying through the space between the walls.

By extremely safe, they mean that hypersleep accidents are one in a billion. Those are excellent odds.

I should have stayed on Calhoun and played the lottery.

Dr. Riady studied the holo. The survivor's vitals were decent. Not bad considering what he must have gone through, though it appeared that he hadn't been in the best physical health to begin with. She brought up another screen. Long term poor dental hygiene, skeletal degradation, muscle mass, and cardiovascular consistent with a sedentary lifestyle, and the active scans were showing that he was going through severe withdrawal symptoms from the psychotropic cocktail he'd been on for the last fifteen years.

"How did *you* survive?" she muttered. Atlas had a small defense force, mostly made up of veterans of the Zealand Conflict, now retired from the military. Those were genetically modified, nano-enhanced super soldiers who'd fought through one of the worst guerilla wars in history, yet somehow they were missing, and an unemployed, mentally ill couch potato had lived. "Why you and not them?"

When she went back to the first display, she found Leland Chang staring directly into the monitor. "I know modesty is an outdated concept, but may I have some clothing?"

"Oh, my apologies, Mr. Chang. I'll have a servitor bring you some. We didn't intend to make you uncomfortable."

"Thank you . . . And who are you?"

"I'm Dr. Riady, medical officer of the *Alert*." He seemed rather lucid, probably due to the stimulants she'd administered. Dr. Riady decided to push forward before he descended into another incoherent funk. "I know you've been through a lot, but I have some questions."

"Why?" Chang went back to staring at his hands. "You won't believe me anyway."

"I have to believe you. I've seen your medical history. I know you have no imagination to speak of, so I doubt you'd be able to lie to me very convincingly anyway."

"That's a cruel way to put it."

"But factually true." She didn't mention that the room's biometric scanners also made an excellent lie detector of sorts. "Let me level with you, Mr. Chang. Our captain is extremely concerned, and I have no doubt that when we're able to send a burst back to Command, they will be even more so."

Chang looked up, suddenly desperate. "Don't send a message. You can't cycle the gate."

"Why?"

"It might spread."

"*What* might spread?"

"The truth."

One in a billion . . . Sounds like a lot until you realize just how many humans are traversing the stars. Keziah's Disorder, they call it, named after the first poor sucker who came out of hypersleep screaming about ambivalent squid gods and bleeding from his ears, mind all buggered up from daring to dream in null space.

You see, the dead aren't supposed to dream. It violates the rules.

The greatest medical minds of the galaxy were fascinated by Keziah. Dreaming in hypersleep had done something to his brain. It turns out that your organs begin failing after only a few months without REM sleep, so he was crazy and dying. The scientists jumped on this one. First off, dreaming while in hypersleep was technically impossible. Second, doctors love that technically impossible shit. And third, the space lines really wanted this thing cured before the news scared off too many potential colonists. Drugs forced Keziah's brain through all the stages of sleep and saved his physical body. The doctors gave each other awards. Colonists kept on paying for temporary death.

But the treatment couldn't make Keziah dream. Since science had never found a mammal that didn't dream, they couldn't realize just how important that process actually was, how every single bit of goodness in life was attached to it.

A year later Keziah stepped in front of a train.

Forty years after that, I was trapped in a metal tube, hurtling through space, dead but dreaming.

"Can you draw the graffiti symbols you saw for me, Mr. Chang?"

"I can try." One of the servitors in the quarantine room hovered over and handed her patient a stylus. Chang took it and began writing. "My memory is fine, but I can tell you now that I won't be able to convey everything. I had a friend who said their writing had nuance . . . I doubt I'll be able to do it justice."

"Because of your condition?"

"Something like that."

Dr. Riady tapped her finger on the projection. "Enlarge." She'd never seen anything like the strange letters before. They looked like gibberish to her. Making sure the intercom was off, she addressed the *Alert*'s AI. "Emma, can you read that?"

"The symbols are similar to those recorded by the Dark Side Dig archeological teams. I will translate. Processing."

Chang's hand-drawn symbols floated before her. Gradually the strange runes twisted into familiar words.

"Translation complete, however I estimate with only 87% accuracy."

From His dark house in the mighty city beneath the sands beneath the winds, He offers freedom to the living children of the pillars of heaven. The day has come to heed the call of dreams.

When you're paranoid and prone to sudden fits of violent rage, you don't collect many friends.

Thomerson was one of the few people who still came to visit me. It was probably because he felt guilty. He was a linguist, and we'd worked together deciphering the Calhoun pyramid. He'd been the one to recommend me for the Dark Side Dig contract. We'd even made the trip together. I believe his was far more pleasant.

He sat on the edge of the couch, like he was scared he'd get his pants dirty. My settlement from the space line had paid for the apartment, my treatments, and anything else I might conceivably want for the rest of my life, if I could be bothered to want anything, but I wasn't much for decorating. Or cleaning . . . Or much else really.

"You should open your windows more, Leland. You've got a marvelous view here."

I humored him. "Fine." The covers automatically lifted. My apartment building was suspended from the side of the main chasm. It kept us out of the wind, and we could see most of the undercity from here, as well as a long sliver of howling red sky.

"When's the last time you went outside?"

I shrugged. "I don't know. A few weeks."

"I could arrange a day pass to the Dig for you." Thomerson was fat, so his leaning forward conspiratorially just looked awkward. "I can even get you into the Temple. It's pretty exciting stuff. They think it might even finally answer the big question."

"What killed off all the Atlanteans?"

"I wish you wouldn't call them that. It makes them sound like a joke."

"I don't make jokes."

"I know. Never mind. But listen, Leland, this is big. All this time we've been trying to reconstruct how they actually lived. There's been glimmers of a religious philosophy here and there in their art, but nothing like this. They're calling it the Temple, cathedral, whatever, but it really *is*."

Fifteen years ago, that would have been incredibly exciting. "And?"

"This isn't just their religion, but this is their version of a doomsday cult. This is the newest construction we've ever found. It dates to the end. They were on their way out and they knew it. You know how hard their alphabet is to translate, so much nuance . . ." Thomerson sighed wistfully. "But this reeks of desperation. We never knew if they had an afterlife myth like most of humanity's various cultures, but they did! They were looking for a way out, just like primitive man."

"Fascinating," I lied.

"I know, right? We've seen that they had a god figure, we've seen it over and over again, but this is the first time that we've found an opposite. Obviously human social mores don't translate, but consider it a devil figure if you will. They knew their species was going extinct so they were making a proverbial deal with their devil."

The only reason that I hadn't killed myself yet was because part of me was terrified that what I'd seen in null space was real, and I was too afraid to find out for sure. "I'll pass on the day trip."

"They were as frightened by the mysteries of death as primitive man. The carvings said that this devil came to their entire species, appearing in their dreams and making them an offer . . ."

Even winged cucumbers had dreams . . . "Wonderful . . . It's getting late. Maybe you should—"

But Thomerson wasn't listening. He was still talking, staring off into space. Almost like he'd forgotten I was there at all. "They took his offer . . . Imagine that? An offer that an entire civilization couldn't refuse. They were a rather metaphysical lot, believing in spirit worlds nearly as much as they believed in the real world. They still believed in magic, and perhaps that's why their science lagged behind . . . Regardless, they accepted the devil's deal. The word they used translates to the Great Becoming . . . *and upon his will the world became undone.*"

"What?"

Thomerson stood up suddenly and then shuddered, like he'd begun to swoon. Flushed, he placed one fat hand on his fat cheek. "I'm sorry. I was feeling a bit dizzy. Forgive me, Leland. I've not been sleeping well."

I escorted him to the door. "Yeah, I've heard on the feeds that's been a problem out there lately. Something about the background noise keeping people awake at the Dig."

He collected his hat and cloak. "Yes. There's been some accidents. Tired workers and whatnot."

"Well, be careful then." I steered him out, then closed the door behind him. "Full secure." The locks sealed. My paranoia temporarily mollified, I walked back into my apartment. "Close view." The covers began dropping.

But not before I noticed something black and hairy, pressed against the bottom of the glass, watching me. At first I thought it was a monkey, with a face like an ugly baby, but it had the shimmering wings of a fly, and in the brief moment our gaze met, its mouth moved like it was trying to say something, with a mouth filled with all too human teeth, and then it was covered.

I rubbed my eyes. "Open view."

The monkey-fly-man-baby was gone.

I went into the bathroom and took another pill.

"Come inside, Doctor. I just got word Drop Team 2 just entered the lower levels of the city. I'm waiting for their report."

She entered the captain's chamber and saluted. "The survivor's been speaking freely, Sir."

"So what's the verdict?" Captain Hartono didn't need to ask; he could already tell by her haggard expression that she hadn't gotten anything good, but he needed it spoken out loud so her recommendation could be recorded by the ship's AI. If the Atlas event was the opening act of a new war or first contact with an unknown species, then Hartono was going to cover his ass as best as possible in case it all went sideways and Command needed somebody to hang.

Riady stopped in front of his desk. "I'm afraid I can't make sense of the survivor's story . . ."

"And?"

She gave him a look that said *do I have to?*

Hartono addressed the *Alert*'s AI. "Emma, stop recording. This is now a private conversation."

"Yes, Captain." The AI gave the audible response for Riady's benefit. "Recording stopped."

Riady was a veteran and had been a combat medic during the bloody Zealand Conflict. Being genetically modified, she was as close to human physical perfection as possible, and had been decorated for valor against the vicious alien Martor. So, frankly, it unnerved Hartono to see her *frightened*.

"Have a seat." He nodded and a chair rose up through the floor. "What is it, Doctor?"

Riady sat uncomfortably. "Chang is talking, but . . ." She rubbed her face in her hands and sighed. "I sort of wish he wasn't."

"Send me the transcripts."

She blinked. "Done."

They took him a moment to process. "This description can't be right. There are no residual signatures showing any ships coming into the system. We've checked the whole city, but there's not a bit of DNA down there that doesn't belong to a colonist of record. It couldn't have been alien."

"That's the thing, Captain . . . I don't think it was alien."

Hartono's eyes narrowed. "I'm not liking your other option."

There was a flash transmission behind one of his eyes. A drop team had found something on the bottom level. *Open live feed. Public.*

The hologram appeared on his desk between them, obviously being reconstructed in three dimensions from multiple helmet cams. It was a mangled body, or perhaps *bodies* . . . It was hard to tell. Hartono willed the hologram to rotate slowly. "What is that thing?"

The AI answered, having only needed a fraction of a second to review every cataloged organism in the universe. "The physical structures match no known entity."

"I want samples," Hartono said.

The drop team had already taken one. A strand of DNA appeared floating in the holo, listed as a *partial* match.

Martin, Eliza J.—Atlas Colonist.

Chamberlain, Harold R.—Atlas Colonist.

Geist, Terron I.—Atlas Colonist.

Names continued to scroll by. Dozens of them.

Hartono killed the feed. Riady had unconsciously reached into her uniform, pulled out a small silver crucifix, and was fingering it nervously. He hadn't known she was religious.

"Emma, begin recording."

"Yes, Captain."

"Doctor Riady, what is your medical recommendation for the lone Atlas survivor?"

"Since I'm unable to gain any meaningful intel through interviews with Leland Chang, I recommend that we perform a memory lift immediately. Let the record show that the medical officer is fully aware this procedure may prove fatal to the subject."

"*Alert* command concurs with this recommendation. Expedite."

While the gate was closed I was limited to Atlas local feeds.

Considering it was the apocalypse, you'd have thought it would have been more obvious, but my fellow colonists simply blundered toward their inevitable Great Becoming. Nobody realized that the story about the alarming increase in sleep disorders was truly that important. The Atlas Sleep Clinic blamed it on the harmonics from the wind.

I didn't go out much, but I wasn't a complete hermit. I knew most of my neighbors by name and was always as polite to them as social obligations demanded. There was a shopping mall beneath my building and I went there whenever my food dispenser told me it was nearly empty.

I'd lost track of how many days it had been since I'd last been outside. The first thing I noticed was that Atlas City Public Works was slacking. Normally the corridors were tidy, but I saw litter, and even abandoned sacks of trash left in corners. I'd not read about any labor strikes. Then I recoiled as a large black bug landed on my lips. I swatted it away, and it buzzed off angrily. *Odd.* Insect pests had inevitably followed man across the stars, but normally they were kept under tight control in a sealed colony. This wasn't the wretched undercity.

The usually busy market was remarkably dead. There were a few people standing listlessly on corners, as if unsure of what they were waiting for. I saw only a handful of shoppers, and they seemed almost furtive, keeping their heads down and shoving products into their carts, almost like they didn't even care what they were hoarding. There was a teenager leaning next to my destination's entrance, seemingly staring off into space, obliviously listening to music and watching a holo on the inside of his glasses. I went inside.

"I've come for my order. I'm Leland Chang from the two hundred and sixteenth level."

The girl didn't respond. She was focused on the screen in front of her. I thought this was a typical lazy employee, ignoring customers while she watched funny videos, but when I leaned over the counter the screen was blank. "Hello . . ." I waved my hand in front of the clerk's face. "Hello."

She blinked rapidly. "Huh? Sorry. I'm really tired. I've not been sleeping good."

"I take pills for that." The clerk handed me the compressed box of protein sludge. When food has no flavor, you simply purchase whatever keeps you alive. "Thank you."

When I walked back outside I noticed that the power light on the teenager's glasses was off. He was engrossed in absolutely nothing. A large black fly was walking around, unnoticed, on his pimply face.

The servitors had secured Leland Chang to the slab.

"What're you doing to me?" He sounded more resigned than afraid.

Dr. Riady reasoned that she might as well be truthful. "We're going to make an electronic imprint of your long term memory."

"I'm familiar with the process. I keep up on all the science reports ... It'll probably kill me, won't it?"

"I'm going to do my very best to make sure that doesn't happen, Mr. Chang."

"I don't mind, Doctor . . . I've only got one last request."

"What's that?"

"If this works, if you're able to see into my brain and record what's there, please, no matter what, don't look at the dreams I had in null space . . . It's for your own good."

The news changed over the next week. There were fewer and fewer blog posts. Social media was unusually quiet. The pundits were extra angry and dimwitted. The ADF had been called up for an unspecified reason. The talking heads pontificated that it was related to the sudden increase in property crime. A riot had broken out in the undercity but it was contained. There had been a rash of accidental deaths at the Dark Side Dig. Compared to all of this, the fact that the Sleep Clinic was overwhelmed was hardly a footnote.

The news was my anchor. I needed other people going about their lives so my lack of one was palatable. I did not like this.

Needing stimulus, I opened the window covers. The sky today was a brilliant red as mile long tornados battled above the chasm. Far below, a large fire had broken out in the city, and it was surrounded by flashing red and blue lights. I was more upset that this event hadn't even made the news than the actual reality of the event.

Flies began landing on the window, great black, hairy things. Dozens at first, and then hundreds of them. I closed the cover.

"Emma, I need to make a statement for the record."

"Confirmed, Captain."

"Dr. Riady has completed the memory lift of the patient, Leland Chang. The data is currently being analyzed. The gate will cycle in one hour and then the *Alert* will return home to report. As of this time our investigation into the cause of the Atlas incident remains inconclusive. I regret to say that our memory lift proved to be too much for Mr. Chang in his weakened condition and he has gone into a vegetative state. He's been placed in stasis in preparation for hypersleep. I'm fully aware that taking someone with Keziah's Disorder into null space may be considered torture under the Durban Accords, but I believe the urgency of our mission outweighs this so I have overruled Dr. Riady's protests."

Captain Hartono rubbed his temples. He had a splitting headache. It was getting hard to think and even harder to make good decisions, but none of them had gotten much sleep since they'd arrived.

The noise had come from the hall of my apartment. It had been loud enough to wake me from my drug induced slumber. It had trailed off before I'd come fully awake. Had it been a scream? An animal howl? A little bit of both?

I asked my apartment building's AI what had made the sound. It began to answer. Then it froze, gave me an error message, and had to reboot. It came back a moment later and said that there had been no sound and nothing was wrong.

Logic said to stay in bed, perhaps call the authorities. I am no longer capable of curiosity, so I could not even blame that base instinct, but for whatever reason, I got up, went to my security door, and listened through the port.

I heard grunting. And squishing.

I took another pill and went back to bed.

By the next morning the news feeds had grown . . . *odd.*

Most of the local stations were offline. Only a handful remained, and those were the larger affiliates with more staff. I watched as one of the news reader beautiful people rambled incoherently about the beauty of tentacles, before vomiting blood all over the news desk. She began drawing in the blood with her finger before the feed was cut. *We are experiencing technical difficulties.*

The independent sources and some of the bloggers kept on, though many of those had become garbled. The written ones struggled as well, and one popular author's feed, now filled with typos, complained that typing was difficult once your fingers began growing together.

I opened the window to the real world and watched the fall of Atlas. There were more fires in the streets below, as well as the occasional bright flash of a particle weapon. Vehicles were overturned and I could watch the people dance about them like ants.

There were still clouds of flies clustered on my window. Only now I noticed a single, greasy handprint, undeniably human, pressed there, on the *outside* of the glass on the 216th floor.

The *Alert* was prepared for the gate to open. The crew had already been placed in stasis. Captain Hartono and Dr. Riady would be the last to enter hypersleep, and after that control of the ship would be turned over to Emma until they cycled into their home system in a few months.

Dr. Riady checked on the stasis tank holding the body of Leland Chang one last time. He appeared as dead as any other space traveler, but she knew it was an illusion. Unlike the rest of them, his mind would be totally open to the sanity-breaking horrors of null space.

What would be left of this man on the other side? What did it matter, the Captain had argued, one man's sanity versus six hundred thousand presumed dead? Command needed answers, and they'd get them, even if they had to dismantle the only survivor down to his individual molecules.

Sweet dreams, Mr. Chang.

There was no more news. No feeds. No brainless chatter. The silence was deafening.

I was nearly out of meds. I called the treatment center but only got their automated message system. Even their AI would not respond.

I would have to go outside.

You do not need an imagination to be frightened. I still experience fear. Self-preservation is the most basic of all human instincts. I really did not want to go outside.

But it was preferable to remembering null space and the dreams of the dead.

The hall was empty. Some of the other apartment doors were open. The rooms inside were a mess, but I didn't see anyone alive. Mrs.

Garcia was on her couch, pistol in her lap, brains all over the wall. In Mrs. Johansen's apartment there was something odd stuck to the ceiling. At first I thought it was a green and grey sleeping bag, but it was a cocoon, made of a material like unto mucus.

The lift still came when called, which was good, because I didn't think my legs could handle the stairs.

The apartment's lobby was empty. It was the first time in fifteen years that I'd not seen another human being inside of it. The room was filthy. The air scrubbers were off. There was a wet black trail through the red dust, at first I thought it was oil, but it had a greenish tint to it. Following the trail with my eyes, I came to a steaming pile of dead skin and regurgitated bones.

The main doors were made of glass. On the other side was chaos.

The streets were filled with trash. There had to be a crack in the dome because red grit coated everything at ground level. Clouds of insects were swarming, hopping and flying, skittering about in the shadows.

Opening the doors, I stepped into the end.

The environmental systems were failing. The air tasted like metal. It was terribly hot.

There were . . . people . . . in the market. Hunched, lurching about, their bodies covered in rags that had been clothing so recently. They paid me no heed. A hulking man brushed by, not even noticing me. He kept his head down, hat concealing his face, but I saw the puckering green hole where his ear had been, and then he went down an alley where some others had gathered, feasting on the guts of a stray dog.

Focus. The nearest pharmaceutical dispensary was only a block away.

I made it half that distance before I came upon the Black Man.

He was waiting on the sidewalk. His featureless head swiveled toward me, watching without eyes.

The Black Man wasn't part of the chaos. He was above it. He'd seen it before.

He saw me and knew that I was different.

You do not participate in the Great Becoming?

I turned back toward my apartment, walking quickly.

Wait.

The Black Man followed.

Beneath the red winds, beneath the sands of Rhonoth-dur, the temple of undoing beckons. You alone decline this invitation?

I began to run.

The Black Man continued walking after me.

Unable to meet your full potential, you are broken. You have gazed upon the grandeur of the Between and have wilted. Your dreams of unmaking are not for my world. To another master they must fly.

I reached the glass doors of my building. Recognizing I belonged there, they slid open to save me.

Delicious screams.

"Help! Wait!"

"Let us in!"

There were three children running up the sidewalk from the opposite direction, terrified, reaching for me with tears streaming down their faces. There was a shadow behind them, shambling. My eyes tracked up toward the incomprehensible mass of hungry, twisted meat that was pursuing them.

Tentacles wrapped around the last child's ankles. He sprawled into the street, and was sucked back to be consumed.

I held the door open. "Hurry!"

The first child, a girl no more than ten, got past me. The next, a boy probably six or seven, ran up, and I placed my hand on the back of his head as he passed to push him to safety.

My fingers touched hard chitin.

I snatched my hand away. Beneath his patchy blond hair, the back half of his skull was a slimy black and red plate.

He looked up at me with wide goat pupil eyes.

I shoved him back into the street and forced the door closed.

The girl was inside, watching me, emotionless, as the tentacle horror dragged the boy away.

The Black Man stood outside the door.

This world is mine. You have been claimed by another.

I went back to the lift as the girl squatted in the lobby and began to draw intricate designs in the slime.

The lift doors opened. The Black Man was inside waiting.

I stepped inside and called for 216. We started up.

This world is mine, priest of another. We do not share. Your dreams of unmaking must serve another.

A few seconds later we reached my floor. I stumbled into the hall in a swarm of flies. The Black Man did not follow. Mrs. Johansen's cocoon had burst open. Something had slid beneath her couch and was breathing wetly. Mrs. Garcia's body was gone, but her bloody footsteps went to the wall and simply disappeared.

I went inside my apartment. The Black Man was waiting, standing in front of my window, watching Atlas be cleansed.

We do not share worlds. This one is mine. It has always been mine. We do not share priests. You have been marked by another. Return to He who has anointed you and awaken him from his slumber. Awaken him with your visions, so that the worlds he has claimed may hear his call.

Ph'nglui mglw'nafh Cthulhu R'lyeh wgah'nagl fhtagn.

Die again. And Dream.

The *Alert* cycled through the Mars gate without incident. Within seconds AIs had exchanged vast swaths of information. Curiously, Emma was unable to send certain bits of information because her database had somehow become corrupted.

By the time the first of the *Alert*'s crew began to thaw from hypersleep, a fleet of ships had been dispatched to Atlas to continue the investigation.

Dr. Riady, being genetically enhanced, was the first to shake off the stasis effects. She summoned a basin of water, splashed some on her face, and stared at her reflection in the mirror. As a side effect of near physical perfection, it was extremely unusual to find a pimple on her forehead. It was even more unusual that when scratched at and squeezed, to have a tiny insect pop out and fly away . . .

"Emma, is there a bug in my chambers?"

"No, Doctor. I do not detect anything of the sort."

She shook her head, blamed the hallucination on the aftereffects of the hypersleep drugs, splashed some more water on her face, and got back to work. She had a crew to decant.

Within the last of those stasis tanks, deep within the *Alert*'s quarantine, Leland Chang's eyes moved rapidly behind closed lids, as his broken mind relived visions of tormented ancient gods, trapped between the walls of reality, so vivid and imaginative that they could wake the dead.

Far beneath the ocean of the human home world, something began to stir.

And the sixteen billion humans spread across several planets, moons, and orbitals around Earth did not even realize that this was the beginning of the end.

THE THEME of this anthology was Lovecraft in space, so I was excited to try something new. I don't get to write straight-up horror very often. I use a lot of Lovecraftian elements in my Monster Hunter series, but that's more about heroes having adventures and shooting cosmic horrors in the face, than well-spoken New Englanders telling each other scary stories in the dark. Lovecraft excelled at creating a feeling of creeping doom. He wrote about academics in an age where reason and science was supposedly going to banish religion and superstition, only their quest to know the unknowable was inevitably doomed. That's the vibe I was trying to achieve with this one.

I also share a birthday with H.P. Lovecraft and Ron Paul, which probably explains a lot about me.

❖ ❖ ❖

SWEOTHI CITY

This story was originally published on the Baen Books website. It is the origin story of one of the two main characters in the Dead Six trilogy (Dead Six, Swords of Exodus, and Alliance of Shadows) published by Baen Books, co-written by me and Mike Kupari.

Sweothi City, Central African Republic.
December 15th, 1993.
1:25 P.M.

THE HOTEL had been evacuated since the government had collapsed and revolution had spilled over the countryside, but the lobby still stank of stale cigarette smoke and sweat. Random cries, crowd noise, and honking horns resonated through the windows as the seemingly endless mob of refugees surged through the streets.

The refugees did not know they were doomed. With the *Mouvement pour la Libération du Centrafricain* (MLC) rebels tearing up the Ubangi river basin, there was no escape. And from what I had seen in the last forty-eight hours, they didn't take prisoners. The CAR Army was in shambles from the coup, with half of them joining the rebels, and the other half fleeing for the Congolese border.

The lobby had become our improvised command center. Furniture, debris, and even some of the planking from the walls had been stacked against the doors to deter adventurous looters. Ramirez was on the roof, armed with an ancient DP machinegun and a radio. So far the MLC hadn't made a move against the city, but they were massing, and every escape route was blocked.

There were twenty men in the lobby, two separate groups forced together, uneasy allies with only one chance for survival. One could feel the anxiety in the air, a physical buzz, almost louder than the refugee train outside. All of them were filthy, armed to the teeth, exhausted, and aware that death was coming, and it was coming hard and fast.

SWITCHBLADE was headed by Decker, the dispassionate mercenary leader. Someone had scrounged up a chalkboard, probably stolen from the missionary school next door and he was busy drawing a rudimentary map of the city and the route that the rebel army was most likely going to use to assault it. O's were the bad guys. X's and arrows showed his plan. Each X was one of us. Each arrow was an order given in a cold, emotionless, voice.

There weren't very many X's on that map. There were a whole lot of O's.

Hawk, the weathered gunslinger, was second-in-command. The man always made me think of those gun magazines I had read as a kid, with the stories about blazing six-guns on the border. He was seemingly unfazed, even in our current situation. Cuzak sat on a barstool, head wrapped in a blood-stained rag, still in shock from the landmine that had splattered Irwin all over the rest of us. Areyh, the former Israeli commando, was squatting next to the board, memorizing the plans while he ran a bore brush frantically through a filthy Galil. Doc was our medic, and he was off to one side attending to one of the wounded Portuguese mercs. I had a feeling that Doc was going to have a long day.

And me.

And that was all that was left of the illustrious mercenary company called SWITCHBLADE.

Fucking Decker. Fuck Decker and his fucking mission. He should have listened to me. If he hadn't been so damn sure of himself, so damn proud, Irwin, Slick, and Sam would still be alive.

I hid my emotions behind a mask of mud and dried blood, and went back to dispassionately cleaning the Yugoslavian RPK that I had stolen, listening to Decker's defensive plans, but already making plans of my own.

The other half of our ragtag group of survivors was all that remained of the Portuguese mercenary company out of Angola. They had been hit worse than we were. Nobody had expected the rebels to be this well organized and equipped, but apparently the Montalban Diamond Exchange had brought in a large group of Cubans to train up the disorganized MLC. The Ports had lost most of their leadership in the last skirmish, and the only thing holding them together was a short, angry, hairball of a man named Sergeant Gomes.

"If we put up enough of a fight along these streets, then the rebels will commit their reserves. Currently that reserve is blocking here, and here. And as far as we can tell, those are the shock troops. The groups moving into the city now are the irregulars. With them out of the way, we can then retreat down Kahiba Road toward Manova-Gounda. Then it's a straight shot, fifteen clicks, to the airfield," Decker explained calmly. "The plane is fueled and ready to go, but they will not wait for us if the rebels approach the airfield. We do not have much time."

He was calm now. The Belgian was always calm. He was calm when he got us into this suicide mission. Calm when we overthrew a government and brought hell down on these people to placate a diamond company, and he would probably be calm when I put my knife in his throat. I snapped a fresh drum into the Yugo and worked the charging handle.

"It'll be tight, but we can fit in the truck, all of us," the leader of the Portuguese said, referring to the deuce and a half they had stashed in the hotel garage. His English sounded strange, and had probably been taught to him by an Afrikaner. "Who's gonna cause enough problems to get a division of rebels to concentrate enough to let us slip out though?"

"We'll need a diversion. Someone will need to cause enough resistance to stall the irregulars, here"—he gestured at the board— "long enough for them to call in the Cubans and the trained MLC. We'll need someone who can fight, and then slip away once we escape, someone who can disappear, go to ground. Stealth will be their only chance to evade capture." He looked right at me as he said it.

So he knew.

I should have kept my mouth shut after this operation went to hell. But I didn't. I violated my own rule of always being the grey man, the one that didn't draw attention, the thief in the background. I had let my emotions get the better of me. And Decker must have sensed my anger.

And over the last year, he had seen what happened to people who made me angry.

So this was how it was going to be.

"Ozzie," he nodded toward me. "I think you would be the only person who would have a chance." Decker was good, very good. He didn't display any indication that he was disposing of me. Rather, he was just the good leader, picking the best man for the job. "We're counting on you. Force them to pull their reserves; if not, we'll have to try a frontal assault, and since they have those APCs, it would be suicide in the open."

The only surviving radio in the room suddenly crackled with static. Every head in the room swiveled towards it. "This is Ramirez. Militia forces are moving into the south end of the city. Looks like they're going to burn it all."

The room was silent, then broken by a fit of coughing from one of the wounded mercs who'd caught shrapnel in the lung.

"Do you mind if we have a word about this, in private?" I asked, perfectly calm.

Decker made a show of looking at his watch. "Certainly." He gave an imperceptible nod toward Hawk. They had been around, and knew what was happening. "But we'd best hurry."

"No shit," Sergeant Gomes said, as a mortar shell exploded somewhere in the city.

"It didn't have to be like this," Decker said, as he strolled into the side room. He had his back to me. The spot between his shoulder blades and the ALICE suspenders was an inviting target, and I could feel the heavy weight of the combat knife on my hip. But Hawk was trailing behind me, and as fast as I was, I knew that Hawk was that much faster with that big magnum revolver.

"It is what it is," I replied, too damn tired to try to put on any sort of act. "We killed the president. We caused this. The diamond exchange used us, and you let them."

"How long have you been with SWITCHBLADE?" he asked, already knowing the answer. "A year, yes, a year. And honestly . . ." he finally turned to face me, his eyes sad, his spirit injured by the events of the last two days. "I saw great things in your future. You were nothing but a common thief when you joined us . . ."

"I was an *exceptional* thief."

He ignored that. "But I saw a leader, a man that could make a difference. I could see you taking over, and running this organization." Decker was sincere, at least. That I could tell, but sincerity doesn't make a rattlesnake any less venomous.

"If you haven't noticed, half your organization's dead, because you screwed up."

"I know . . ." Decker said, his voice cracking, the pain obvious. "This is the end of SWITCHBLADE. Even if we make it out, the diamond exchange will have us hunted down like dogs. I'm sorry about the men. They . . . they were like family to me." I could hear the creak of gun leather as Hawk shifted behind me.

Also true, but it didn't make me hate him any less right then.

"And I know that's why you're going to do your best to slow down these rebels. Because I know that Ramirez, and Doc, and Cuzak are like brothers to you, and you won't let them down," Decker said simply.

"True," I answered.

"You had better hurry." Decker put his hand on my shoulder. "I'm sorry," he said. And I believed him.

And that was the only reason I decided not to kill him.

The refugees were panicking now, turning from individuals into a deadly entity, discarding and crushing bits of itself underfoot. Screams filled the air. In the distance could be heard the boom of mortars and sporadic automatic weapons fire. The boards that had been blocking the front door flew into the street in a spray of dust as I booted them hard and pushed my way into the street.

It was hot. Muggy, sticky hot, and sweat rolled down my back and soaked my camouflage. The air stank of oil and smoke and fear.

The group had been low on ammo after two days of furious combat and retreat, but I had still commandeered every piece of hardware that I could carry. I had the RPK in hand, our last RPG slung over one shoulder, Cuzak's Ithaca 37 over the other shoulder (he was in no shape to fight anyway), a Browning Hi-Power on my belt, and every spare round of ammo and frag grenade that I could scrape up. Any more munitions and I wouldn't be able to move. Tsetse flies kept landing on my face to probe the dried blood patches.

Doc had tried to stop me. He understood what was happening, that

I was a threat to Decker, and therefore expendable. I just shook my head and made him promise to get the wounded to safety. Cuzak hadn't said a word, but he shook my hand solemnly, knowing what I was about to do. If I had one weakness, it was that when I occasionally made a friend, I was too damn loyal.

And it was about to kill me.

Decker gave me a brief nod. Hawk tipped his hat in my direction. Areyh spit on the floor.

So this was the end of SWITCHBLADE.

The others exited, fanning out, forming a perimeter around the hotel, where they would hold until Ramirez, acting as our spotter, could see that the road was clear. If I failed, their only choice was to attack straight into the Cubans and try to break through to the airfield. They would never make it. I walked away, the deadly mob of women, children, and old men parting before me like water, leaving the last year of my life behind, and knowing that I was probably going to perish in the next few minutes. The terrified Africans moved out of my way, my anger like an invisible plow.

The CAR was a blighted land. Torn by war for generations, poor beyond all comprehension, and I knew that probably half of these refugees would be dead in the next ten years from AIDS even if they managed to somehow survive the machetes of the approaching rebels. And we had come here, paid in blood money, to topple their corrupt government and install another corrupt government that the diamond exchange liked better. And even then, the exchange had sold us out.

What a waste.

Then there was someone pushing forward with me. Sergeant Gomes, the Portuguese mercenary, appeared at my side, his burly form cradling the Port's PKM machinegun. A stubby Steyr Aug was tied around him with a discarded web belt serving as a sling. His oddball camouflage was ripped, blood-stained, and every exposed patch of skin was covered in caked-on mud. He looked hideous.

But happy. "Let's kill us a bunch of these rebel sons of bitches," he grinned, his beady eyes narrowing dangerously.

"What're you doing?" I shouted over the chaos.

"My men? They're in no shape to fight. So I figure, nothing I can do for them," he shrugged. "You could use the help. Might as well go fight."

I couldn't argue with that.

He stuck out his hand. It was calloused and strong. "Call me Carl."

I had been going by Ozzie for the last year, but I knew that I couldn't go back. Even if I lived through this battle, it would be best if I disappeared. I knew that the diamond exchange could not afford to allow any of SWITCHBLADE to survive, knowing the things that we knew. And if they didn't get me, then Decker might very well try, just to tie up loose ends. It was time to start over, to disappear, to become grey again.

I said the first name that popped into my head.

"Lorenzo . . . My name is Lorenzo."

Sweothi City, Central African Republic.
December 15th, 1993.
2:15 P.M.

THE CROWD thinned out enough for the two of us to break into a run, counterintuitively, toward the sound of gunfire. Normally I was the type that liked to plan, but there was no time for that.

This part of Sweothi City was rougher than the rest. Half the buildings were the stacked mud-brick type, but compressed between them was a maze of shanties built out of things like chicken wire, packing crates, and old tires. Some of them were already burning.

Carl grabbed me by the arm and pointed down the street into the emptying marketplace. Black smoke was rising from the neighborhood behind it. "The irregulars will come through here."

"How do you know?"

"I've been fighting in Africa since my people lost Mozambique. They'll come through here because they're stupid rabble and it's obvious. They'll want to loot the shops, rape the stragglers." He swept his hand to the right, and pointed down the other intersection. "When the Cubans come, they'll move up this street, and then try to flank us through the shanties on the north. That's how those commie bastards will do it."

I nodded quickly, trying to burn the layout into my mind.

"Stick and move. Don't let them pin you down. Most of these shit birds can't shoot, but they shoot a lot." Carl hefted the massive PK. "Always attack. Make them react. Got it?"

"Got it."

My pulse was pounding in my head as I turned and headed into the market and toward the rising smoke plumes of black tire-fueled smoke. The 75-round drum in the RPK was heavy and pendulous at the balance point as I let the muzzle lead the way. I moved in a crouch, Carl slightly behind me, gun shifting toward every sudden flash of movement. Several scrawny dogs ran past, tails between their legs.

Then I saw the first of the rebels. I raised my fist, signaling contact. We both crouched low and moved into the shadows beneath a meat stand. A thick black cloud of flies covered the hanging goats and chickens. A can of generic bug spray was under foot, surely used to spray the meat down to keep the flies off.

The first of the MLC were making their way through the bazaar, kicking over stands, and picking up anything left that looked shiny. They really were rabble. Nothing like the disciplined troops we had fought earlier. Most of them were scrawny, malnourished conscripts, wide-eyed with fear or barely coherent on khat. I hunkered down, waiting for more of them to come into view before I opened fire.

Then there was a scream to the side. A woman. Carl and I both jerked toward the noise, just in time to see two of the rebels dragging a young girl by the hair from one of the brick houses into the street. She was hysterical, with tears running down her dark cheeks.

Carl's machinegun shifted toward the two men, but I grabbed his arm and shook my head. The rebels hadn't seen us yet. I jerked my thumb toward myself, made a slashing motion across my throat, and then pointed at the two would-be rapists. Carl nodded and trained his weapon back at the rebels collecting in the market. We only had one belt for the machinegun, and needed to make the most use of it.

I put the RPG, RPK, and Ithaca on the ground, as quietly as possible, and drew the Vietnam-era Air Force knife from my belt. I slid under the booth and crawled through the dirt, brushing between hanging meat and half-gutted chickens, using every shadow and piece of cover. Luckily my Rhodesian camouflage was so crusted with filth that I was the same color as the earth. I covered the thirty feet to the first rebel in a matter of seconds. This was my element. No one could move quieter or faster than I could.

The men were distracted. The first had shoved the girl down and was trying to rip her clothes off as she thrashed and screamed. He was obviously inexperienced at this whole pillaging thing, and the girl was wailing on him.

The second man got tired of waiting, lowered his machete, and pushed the younger man aside. "*Ashti sangha m'baka*, dummy."

I moved in a blur, my knife humming through the air. I hit the first man in the base of the neck. The knife jabbed in under his ear, and out in a flash of red. The second man had time to turn, shock registering on his face, just as I kicked his knee cap backward. He went down on top of the girl. I grabbed him by the hair, jerked his head back, and slashed him across the jugular.

Neither man was making noise now, but both were thrashing, spraying arterial fluids everywhere. They would be dead in seconds. The girl looked up at me in shock as I grabbed the rags that served as her assailant's shirt and hauled him off of her.

"Run."

She heeded my suggestion, leapt to her feet, and bolted, trying to hold her torn clothing closed. I heard motion coming from the open door of her house, and quickly moved against the hot brick wall, dripping knife held in a reverse grip, close to my chin.

Another rebel walked out of the house, AK in one hand, dangling uselessly; the other hand was holding some gaudy, cheap necklace up to the sunlight. He was grinning from ear to ear, pleased with his plunder.

Enjoy it, motherfucker.

He paused, realizing that his two friends were the source of all that blood, just as I grabbed him by the top of the head, jerked it back, and rammed the combat knife straight down, just above the junction of his neck and sternum. I used the knife against his ribs like a lever to force him to his knees as I sawed through his aorta. I yanked the blade out and let him thud, lifeless, to the ground. I wiped the knife on his pants, sheathed it, and grabbed his AK. The whole thing had taken less than twenty seconds.

Carl was staring at me in slack-jawed wonderment as I slithered back through the hanging meats.

"*Filho da Puta . . .*"

"Yeah. I get that a lot," I muttered as I slung the RPG tube and the shotgun. I now had a Kalashnikov in each hand. This was getting kind of extreme.

"Contact right," Carl hissed.

Sure enough, there was the main body of the irregulars. Now they were clustered in the marketplace, fighting like dogs over the scraps of a ruined civilization. There were at least thirty of them, armed with everything from meat cleavers to grenade launchers, and they were not in the least bit worried about resistance.

"On three," his voice was a whisper as he slowly extended the PKM's bipod. "One mag, then run like hell back to the intersection."

"One." I proned out behind the AK, using the magazine as a monopod, and centered it on a knot of men. They were less than one hundred meters away.

"Two," Carl hissed as he took up slack on the trigger.

"Three," I moved the selector to full.

BBBBRRAAAAAAPPPPP . . . BBBBRRAAAAAAAPPPPP . . .

The PKM was horrendously loud as it cut a swath through flesh and bone. Whole knots of the rebels disintegrated in clouds of red as the 7.62x54R tore into them in great piercing blows. As Carl was swinging the reaper's scythe, I tried to pick out anything he was missing. I centered the front sight on a running rebel, and cranked off a burst.

The wall three feet to his side exploded under the impact.

"Damn it!"

The sights on this thing were so far off that aiming was useless. I held the trigger down and swept the muzzle across the market, emptying the magazine in one burst. I let go of the AK and let it flop to its side. I was to Carl's left, and the steel cases from the PK hit me with brutal impacts. I scooped up the RPK and prepared to cover his withdrawal.

Carl was saying something repetitive in Portuguese with every burst. In seconds, our hundred-round belt was gone. "Moving!" Carl shouted as he jumped up from behind the smoking beast.

"Move!" I answered as I scanned for threats. Carl ran for the intersection while pulling the Aug from its makeshift sling. The market was a mess, with the dead and dying spread everywhere. The rebels were in disarray, but that wouldn't last long. Already there was movement as more came in from the south. I sighted in on one charging man, and stroked the trigger. The Yugo barked, and the man pitched forward into the street. At least *this* one was sighted in.

"Go!" Carl shouted as he took up position behind a brick wall.

I sprang to my feet and leapfrogged past him, sliding into a position behind a bank of broken cinderblocks. The RPG on my back made it hard to maneuver, and damn near impossible to get low.

Several of the very brave, or very stupid, moved out into the open. In African warfare, you could often get away with this, as the fundamentals of marksmanship were not really known or taught by very many people here. For Carl and me, however, marksmanship was apparently not a problem. The rebels went down in a quick hail of gunfire.

The street was silent.

We had bloodied them, but I didn't know what it was going to take to get those Cubans' attention and get them off that damn road.

"Give them a minute to get puffed up, get over the shock, and then they're gonna charge. Then it won't stop until we're dead, or they're dead. So let the dumb ones get popped in the open, and then we'll fall back into the houses and alleys"—he jerked with his head in one direction— "and counterattack. When we hear the commies' vehicles, move so we can hit the intersection."

And then it was *on*. Rebels poured through the marketplace. Some ran straight at us, firing from the hip; others hung their guns around corners and blazed away. It was chaos. None of them could shoot worth a damn, but they made up for it in volume. Bullets tried to fill all the empty spaces. The cinderblocks around me exploded into powder and clouds of dust, and I swear some of those guys must have been shooting black powder from all the smoke. I fired at everything that moved and put rounds through anything that looked suspicious.

"Reloading!" Carl shouted as I hammered a line of impacts through some shanties. "Move to the buildings! Go! Go!"

The whole world had gone insane. I was up and moving as fast as I could, hot lead all around me, sounding like angry bees. The RPK sparked hard and spun from my hands, torn nearly in half. The hot muzzle smashed me in the face and my feet flew out from under me. I crashed into the gravel as gouts of flame tore all around.

"Technical!" Carl shouted as he lumbered past me, grabbing me by the straps of my LBV and pulling me up. This particular technical was a red Toyota pickup with a massive 12.7 DhSK machine-gun mounted on the back. I hadn't heard it roll up behind us in the intersection.

The huge gun tracked over us, spitting bullets past, and into the soldiers on their own side. Carl shoved me through an open doorway and into the cool darkness.

I lay on the floor, breath coming in ragged gasps. It was actually quiet. Or I think it was quiet. It was hard to tell over the ringing in my ears.

"Are you hit?" Carl shouted as he quickly poked his head through the door.

"I don't think so," I answered.

"Good." Carl pulled back, just as the doorway exploded into mud fragments. The DhSK was seeking us again, probing for us with bullets bigger than my pinky finger. "*Fodas!*"

Now it was brighter as sunshine streamed through the fresh new holes in the wall. This home was a simple, one-room dwelling. There was a back door. I crawled toward it, rolled over, yanked Cuzak's 12-gauge, and kicked the simple plywood door open. Leaning out, I could see that the door led into an alley. I scanned the other direction and—

CRACK!

"Damn it!" I screamed as the bullet flew through the plywood and past my face. I fell into the dirt alley, right at the feet of a rebel. He looked down at me in surprise as he tried to work the bolt on his Mosin Nagant. I smashed the Ithaca's steel buttplate into his groin. He stumbled back as I rose and smashed his skull with another butt stroke. I brought it down twice more in rapid succession, each impact a meaty thud. He slid slowly down the wall.

Someone else appeared around the corner, and I raised the shotgun without thinking, front bead centering on his head. I froze, as the unarmed old man raised his open hands and begged for his life. My trembling finger had almost pulled the trigger.

"Get down!" I shouted at the old man as the DhSK raked through the house again, with the bullets passing through multiple walls and into the alley. The old man vanished back around the corner.

I had to take out that machine-gun. Now. I sprinted down the alley in the direction of the noise. I could hear Carl breathing hard as he tore after me. The alley was long, and twisty, with each mud house having a back door. "Watch our back!" I shouted as I thought about all those openings behind us.

The Aug barked twice. "On it!" Carl answered.

There was movement ahead, one of the plywood doors flew open, and the muzzle of an SKS snaked through. The rebel stepped through the doorway and I blasted him in the face with a round of double aught, pumped it, and swung around the door. The little house was packed with soldiers. Packed.

They looked at me. I looked at them. That one second stretched into eternity.

Then everybody moved.

Cuzak's gun was the old style with no disconnector, so you just held down the trigger and pumped and it kept shooting. It also had an extended magazine, but I didn't stop to think about those facts at the time.

BOOM BOOM BOOM BOOM BOOM BOOM click.

"*Meu Deus,*" Carl gasped as he viewed over my shoulder.

I reached one shaking hand into my pocket, pulled out some more buckshot, and started feeding them into the loading port.

"We've got to keep moving."

2:22 p.m.

Sweothi City, Central African Republic.
December 15th, 1993.
2:35 P.M.

"WE NEED TO KILL that technical!" Carl shouted into my ear as the walls exploded around us from heavy machinegun fire. Whoever was manning that DhSK was just working it back and forth across the houses. They didn't know which house we were hiding in, or we would already be dead.

"Ya think?" I screamed back.

This was the third home we had leapfrogged into after the shotgun massacre. The area was covered in rebels now, shooting at anybody who didn't look like they were from around these parts. Carl and I sure didn't look like locals.

"You gonna use that thing" —he gestured at the end of the RPG launcher sticking above my shoulder like a psychotic blunderbuss— "or just carry it around all day?"

I flipped him the bird and pulled the heavy tube around in front of me. "Head for the alley so the backblast don't kill you."

He nodded once, rolled over, and low-crawled for the back door. I knew once I opened that front door, I would have a clean shot at the intersection, but every scumbag in a three-block radius was going to zero right in on us. I wouldn't have much time.

I made sure the rocket was fully seated, the hammer cocked on the launcher, and push button safety deactivated. This was it. I stood, risked a quick peek through one of the approximately fifty-caliber holes through the wall, and spotted that damn little Toyota, parked in the middle of the road about ninety meters away. The tube settled heavy on my shoulder.

The plywood door flew open with a bang, powered by my boot and a whole lot of adrenaline. I centered the front sight through the lowest aperture and focused on it, with the Toyota a blur behind.

But then something caught my attention. I don't know if it was the rumble of the heavy engines, or the crunching of debris under its tires. The RPG dipped slightly as I turned toward the lumbering thing coming from the direction that, sure enough, Carl had predicted the Cubans would use.

"BTR!" I screamed, as I pivoted toward the massive Soviet armored personnel carrier. It was all angles and armor, ugly, and swarming with Cubans. I aimed the RPG at the new, deadlier threat, and yanked the trigger. The tube boomed against my face and years of dust billowed from every surface inside the tiny African home. The rocket streaked to its target. It was deafening and awe-inspiring.

The front of the BTR seemed to shiver for a brief instant before the grey steel tub belched flames in every direction. Several quick, massive blasts shuddered through the hulk, and I could see figures tossed, windmilling and spinning through the air.

I had not seen the second BTR enter the intersection. But it had seen me. Its cannon swiveled toward me. I turned and dove back into the house.

Suddenly the world was white. Brilliant flashing white. Up was down, and the ground was somehow now far below. It came up to meet me, very quickly.

Then nothing.

2:37 P.M.

Bob looked grim when he walked out of the hospital room and into the hallway. His eyes were red, puffy from crying, and at that moment he looked aged far beyond his seventeen years. My heart broke when I saw him, because Bob was our rock.

"Mom's on her way," I said quickly. She had been hysterical on the phone.

My older brother put one massive hand on my shoulder, using me to steady himself on wobbly legs. He towered over me, intimidating in his size and mass, though he never meant to be. "Dad wants to talk to you," he croaked. Bob then let go of me and seemed to melt, as he slid down into one of the waiting-room chairs. "You better hurry." He put his head down and started to sob.

Several members of the hospital staff were clustered nearby, watching us. It was a small town and everybody knew my foster father. They were all stunned by the senseless act of violence that had ripped our little community. I gathered up my courage and headed for the door.

There was only one bed in the room. A bank of archaic instruments were beeping and clicking behind it. Doctor Smith nodded at me, placed his clipboard down on a small table, and silently left the room. The doctors had done everything they could, but the thugs that had attacked my father had been thorough. If Gideon Lorenzo lived, it would be a miracle. Tubes and mysterious bags descended from the ceiling. Through the tangle, I could make out my father.

"Dad?"

"Hector . . ." he wheezed. His bandaged head tilted slightly in acknowledgement.

I moved to his side. He looked bad, with great dark circles around eyes so laced with blood that I couldn't help but blink in sympathy. Always an amazingly strong man, it was shocking to see him in this state. I felt like someone had punched me in the throat. He was a good man, an honorable man. The idea of him being mortal had never entered my mind.

"I've got to tell you something . . ."

I waited, hot tears streaming down my face. This was the man that had taken me off the streets. This was the judge that sent the miserable wretch that had been my real father to prison. The Lorenzos had taken me in, welcomed me into their happy home, let me know what real family and loyalty was like. And now he was dying.

"What, Dad?"

"I'm worried about you . . ." His voice was barely a whisper. "I see things . . . in your future. Bad things." I wiped my running nose on the back of my hand, and leaned in close. His red eyes were open wide, staring right through me. "You have a streak in you. You're good, but you have . . . an evil inside. Don't let it out. Please, whatever you do, don't let it out."

"I won't."

I flinched involuntarily as his hand clamped onto my arm, suddenly strong.

"Don't avenge me. Leave it to the law, boy," he hissed. "*Don't let the evil out . . .*"

Then he was gone.

I stumbled back, crashing hard into the wall, instruments scattering across the floor, the strength gone from my legs. The machines began to scream and nurses rushed into the room. The wall was hard against my back, and the floor was cold beneath my legs. Bob was a hulking shadow in the doorway. A doctor began to pump his hands up and down on my father's chest. I heard a wailing as Mom arrived, her hands pressed to her mouth, but the noise still coming through. I wanted to move to help her, but my body wouldn't respond. Her scream was the word no, over and over.

My ears were ringing.

2:38 P.M.

My ears were ringing.

Where am I?

"Lorenzo! Come on!" Someone slapped me in the face. Hard. "Move, damn it!"

I woke up, and everything hurt. I was on my back, at an awkward angle, the Ithaca under me, stabbing me in the kidneys. It was hard to breathe and the air was choked with dust and smoke. I raised my shaking hands in front of my face and saw that they were covered in blood. I had no idea if it was mine.

"What the hell was that?" I blurted, sitting up and feeling something grate unnaturally in my chest.

"The Cubans are dropping mortar rounds right ahead of their advance."

"They can do that?" I quavered as Carl pulled me up.

"Apparently. Good thing they missed. Can you move?"

"I think so." Pain was shooting through me, but everything seemed to be connected. The house that I had been hiding in was . . . gone. "That was a *miss*?"

The area was now overlaid in swirling dust and smoke from the burning BTR. That mortar round had raised a mess. I could see flashes of movement through the fog, but I was lucky to see ten feet. This was our chance. We had accomplished our mission and gotten the Cubans to abandon their post. "Carl, head for where the technical was. Let's hitch a ride."

"Good idea," he coughed as he inhaled a lungful of particulate. He pulled a black bandana out of his pocket and quickly tied it around his face like some bandito. *Nice.* I started toward where I thought the intersection was. Carl grabbed me by the shoulder, turned me 180 degrees, and shoved. I had really gotten turned around.

It hurt to move. It hurt more to breathe. I was confused and disoriented, but I would be damned if I was going to die in this forsaken hellhole. I hefted the shotgun and ran through the rubble and over the occasional body. This dust screen was going to settle fast.

It was like something out of a nightmare. Shapes appeared only to fade away through the haze. I slashed my leg open on a protruding piece of jagged rebar, scattering red droplets that disappeared into the ground like it was covered in sawdust, but I couldn't even think of slowing down. A rebel materialized in front of me, and I instantly shot him through the heart with the 12-gauge. More men were moving to the side, and I fired at them as I sprinted past until the firing pin landed on an empty chamber.

Then we were out of the cloud, but we were in the open, running down the middle of a dirt street. My eyes gritted in their sockets, locking onto the technical, now only twenty meters away. A rebel was charging straight at me, a machete held high overhead, spittle flying from his lips. He was screaming something.

I tossed him the Ithaca. He caught it, looked at it in surprise, and then I crashed into him with my shoulder, bowling both of us to the ground. My combat knife was already coming out of the sheath as we hit. He screamed as I drove it between his ribs, but he still struggled to bring the machete into play.

Carl stepped past me, Aug shouldered, and opened fire on the Toyota. There were two men in the back, and both of them shook as the angry Portagee put bullets into them. The driver's window shattered as Carl shifted targets.

The rebel and I rolled across the ground, locked in a dance to the death. I blocked the machete with my forearm. It cut deep, but he didn't have the room to swing it. I pulled the knife out, and slammed it in again, and again, and again. Finally, he quit moving.

"Lorenzo, quit screwing around!" Carl shouted, as he scanned the wall of dust and flames. "We've got to go."

I rose, panting, and sheathed the still-bloody knife. Angry bullets whined past my head as more rebels saw us. "I'll drive."

"No, I drive. Nobody can catch me," Carl answered as he opened the Toyota's door, grabbed the dead driver, and hurled him out. "Get on that gun!"

I vaulted over the side of the pickup bed, landing on a pile of hot 12.7 brass. Carl revved the engine. Then the smoke wall opened and a great screaming beast roared through, muzzle flashes erupting from its machinegun.

"BTR!" I screamed as the APC rolled over a knot of rebels. But Carl was fast. He slammed the Toyota into gear and put pedal to metal. I slipped on the brass, and bounced off the truck bed walls as Carl cranked the wheel and took us through the rubble. I looked up in time to see an unlucky rebel bounce off the front fender and fly through a scrap-wood shanty.

Bullets puckered through our technical as we tore down the street and right through the militia. The remaining windows shattered. Carl bellowed in rage and pain as something struck him. I crawled up to the DhSK, but it was empty, with the feed tray cover locked open. I yanked the Browning 9mm from my holster and fired at the rebels one-handed, the other holding onto the rollbar to keep from being tossed out.

We seemed to be going unbelievably fast.

The BTR was right behind us. For being so big, damn that thing was quick.

"Get on that gun or we're gonna die!" Carl yelled, as he cranked the wheel and we took a corner far too fast.

THOOM!

The 37mm cannon round flew past and most of the marketplace disappeared. The shockwave rocked the little technical onto two wheels, and then back. I spotted a big, green, ammo can and opened it. There were the huge 12.7 rounds, linked in a rusty, metal belt. I hoisted it out, put the belt in place, slammed the cover down, and yanked back on the charging handle.

I swiveled the DhSK around, but the BTR hadn't followed us around the corner.

But there were plenty of other targets.

I opened fire on random MLC rebels as we drove by. The muzzle blast from the big Russian was like a mushroom cloud. The recoil shook the Toyota down to its suspension. Carl took another corner, trying to head south, out of the city, but the streets were a maze.

Suddenly the brakes locked up, and we slid to a halt. I had the gun trained to the rear, and craned my neck around to see what the problem was.

The road was on fire.

For a good thirty feet, the road was nothing but a blazing oil slick, with flames taller than I was. This had been the source of the great pillar of smoke that we had homed in on to get to the marketplace. It must have been some sort of gas station before the rebels had blown it up. There was no other way past.

I turned back. The way we came from was swarming with rebels, looking like ants. A bullet sparked off the Toyota's tailgate. Ants with AK-47s.

The taillights lit up, signaling that we were in reverse. Another bullet smashed one of the lights. We started back toward the pile of rebels.

"Carl? What are you doing?" The only remaining taillight shattered. Another round cut a chunk from my ear.

"We need a running start."

"You've got to be kidding me . . ." I laid on the DhSK like it was the hammer of Thor, sweeping it across the street. It ain't pretty what one of these things does to a human being. I held the trigger down, the concussion so deep that I could feel it vibrating the jelly in my eyes.

Carl stopped, ground the transmission, and floored it.

I dropped down, threw my arms over my head, and tried to think happy thoughts.

Fire. Everywhere. Holy shit.

It was hard to explain. I opened me eyes and could see it, like it was a living thing, coming up over the edge of the truck, leering down at me, hungry and angry. The heat hit like a sledgehammer, evaporating all of the moisture from my skin. I held my breath, but could feel the poison crowding up my nostrils. It wanted to eat me.

Then we were through.

I jumped back up. The DhSK's wooden spade grips were on fire. I smothered them with my shirt. The Toyota's paint was burning; the wind quickly beat it out.

Carl turned back around and looked at me through the shattered rear window, beady eyes gleaming through a layer of soot over his bandito mask, and said, "Hey, Lorenzo, your hair's on fire."

Well fuck me. I rubbed it out.

This road seemed to lead to the edge of town. I could see down it, a straight shot, and in the distance was open country and room to run or hide. Carl shifted gears and we continued to accelerate.

Then I saw it.

The BTR was running parallel to us. It was one street over to the right, separated from us by a single row of mud houses and shacks. The grey hulk was going to intercept us. The Cubans inside opened up through their firing ports. Most of the rounds smashed into the buildings, but at each gap, some passed through. Tracers stabbed a dotted line across the road.

Two could play that game. I grabbed the smoking handles and swiveled the DhSK.

"Hey!"

"Yeah!"

"BTR on our right. Will 12.7 pierce their armor?"

"Hell yeah! They're light plate."

I wasn't going to try to time it between the houses. We were almost out of town, and I didn't want to square off with this thing in the open. I mashed the butterfly trigger down.

The DhSK roared. Homes disintegrated as we played tag to the death with the Cubans at fifty miles an hour. The mighty 12.7 rounds crashed into the monstrosity, zipping right through the armor and through the crew inside.

The BTR swerved hard toward us, smashed through a house, actually got some air, and careened onto our street. I kept the DhSK on it the whole time, stitching it from end to end, opening it like a teenager shooting a pop can with a .22. The BTR continued on at an angle and smashed through another house and disappeared onto another street.

"I think I got him!"

"No." Carl pointed out the window. The BTR was now traveling down the street to our left. The 37mm cannon was rotating toward us. I cranked the DhSK back around and opened fire, bouncing wildly as the Toyota careened down the rutted road. Carl stomped on the brakes. I flew forward and smashed into the cab as the cannon bloomed flame. The round narrowly missed us and a pile of shanties exploded into flames and shrapnel.

I spit a mouthful of blood onto the roof and shoved myself back onto the machinegun. The BTR was slightly ahead of us on the next street over. Carl suddenly accelerated. Somehow I knew exactly what he was doing. I cranked the DhSK around toward the front.

Carl swerved, crashing us through a fence made of sticks and cardboard. A pile of chickens fell victim to the Toyota, and suddenly birds and feathers were flying everywhere. We seemed to be airborne for a brief second, then the tires struck earth, and we were behind the speeding BTR.

I mashed the spade grips, the sight lined up on the rear end of the BTR. The muzzle brake reverberated painfully off the Toyota's roof. Carl stuck his fingers into his ears, and steered with his knees. Round after round ripped through the armored vehicle from end to end, and it careened wildly to the side and crashed into a ditch, flames suddenly licking out of its ports.

Carl pulled his fingers out of his ears, put one on the wheel and one on the gear shift, and hammered the little Toyota forward. We zipped past the now-burning BTR and toward freedom. A hot wind struck my back as it exploded behind us. Another black, oily cloud was rising above Sweothi City as we sped onto the highway and past the sign pointing toward the Congolese border.

2:52 P.M.

The man looked up at me in fear, as he thrashed against the duct tape that held his wrists to the heavy chair. The old warehouse was deserted and I knew that nobody would hear him scream. "Please, come on, man, don't do it!"

I held the syringe up to the flickering fluorescent light. "You know what this is?"

"No, please, come on, I'm begging you."

Did my father beg? No, of course not.

"It's heroin. Mostly. The rest is drain cleaner. The heroin is to make this plausible. You're just another scumbag junkie, got some bad stuff, had an overdose. There won't even be an investigation. The drain cleaner is so this will hurt. A lot."

"You can't do this. T-Bone will kill you. He'll kill you, man!" the thug screamed.

Did my father threaten violence? No. I'm sure he hadn't. He was a man of peace and justice.

"T-Bone's dead. I got him already. He fell out his apartment window. Landed on one of those pointy fences. Real nasty." I gave a fake shudder. "The others are dead too. Ice got shot in a drive by shooting this morning. Little Mike is floating in the river. He fell in, couldn't swim. Especially with those cinderblocks I tied to his legs."

His eyes were wide. I could smell the fear. "Who are you?"

"A year ago, you were passing through a little place outside Georgetown. You beat a man to death. He was a good man. Why? Why did you do it?"

"I don't know, man! I don't remember . . . He had a nice watch or something. Come on, man, he was just some dude! We didn't mean to kill him. Just mess him up, take his shit."

I stabbed the needle into his arm and smashed the plunger down. I tossed the now empty syringe aside. He began to convulse as I cut the tape and stuffed the evidence into my pocket. He fell to the floor as I walked away. I shut the lights off on the way out and left him in the dark to twitch and foam. I started walking, and didn't look back. I was sixteen years old.

The thing is, when you let the evil out, it's hard to put it back.

Sorry, Dad.

Ten Kilometers east of Banti-Guonda, Congo
December 16th, 1993.

DREAMS of home. So very long ago.

I woke up sore when I heard the sound of the airplane. The stitches on my arm, back, and legs were tight and itchy. Carl did good work. He was already awake, cleaning his Aug while leaning in the shade beneath a crumpled tree. He had a bandage wrapped around his torso, over the carpet of black hair that was his body. The ruined Toyota was hidden in the bushes.

He squinted at me with beady eyes. "Bush plane's coming in. You think we can trust this guy?"

I yawned. "Yeah. He's good people . . . Phil specializes in helping people move valuable things. He owes me a favor. So, Carl, you think about what you're going to do now?"

"I don't know." He shrugged. "My company's gone. Most of us died in the coup. I don't even know if my men made it out."

"They're with Decker. They made it." I answered truthfully. As much as I hated the man, he was extremely good at what he did. "You know, I'm now out of work myself." I pulled a black bag out of my pocket and tossed it to Carl.

He caught it absently, opened the drawstring, and shook some of its contents into the palm of his hand. He whistled.

"SWITCHBLADE had a few simple rules. The leader always got a double share, and he was the only one that has access to the Swiss bank account. Since the diamond exchange crossed us, I'm pretty sure nobody got paid. So we looted some of the treasury while we were in the palace. The six still gets a double share."

Carl's hand was filled with diamonds.

"I took the liberty of lifting Decker's shares. And to think he called me a *common* thief. I'm pretty sure he'll be massively pissed when he finds out. Good thing he thinks I'm dead." I knew that was for the best. I would gain nothing by tracking Decker down. It was time for the evil to be put away once and for all.

"Not a bad haul," Carl said, as he poured the diamonds back into the bag. He started to hand it back.

"No, that's your share. I've got mine."

"Serious?"

"Yeah, I've been thinking . . ." I said as the bush plane approached the runway, landing gear extended. "I'm going to go on my own, form my own team. Be my own boss. But I'm going to need help. Have you ever thought of stealing stuff for a living?"

"Can't say I have," he answered. "Unless you count twenty years of plundering Africa, but I'm sick of this place."

"Well, I'm thinking about only robbing bad people. They've got all the money anyway, and screwing with them is a lot more fun."

The little plane touched down with a squeak of tires. Carl chewed his lip for a moment, then extended his hand.

I shook it. "Carl, I think this could be the beginning of a beautiful friendship."

SWEOTHI CITY was one of my earliest short stories, but I still really like it because Lorenzo is one of my favorite characters to write. Plus, I originally wrote this story aimed at an audience of online gun forum members, so I got to turn my gun-nuttery up to ten and break off the knob. I love writing giant gun battle scenes.

The novel *Dead Six* originally started as an online fiction serial called *Welcome Back, Mr. Nightcrawler*, written by Mike Kupari. He would post a new scene every few days. I didn't really know Mike, I was just another reader, but I loved his story, and asked if he minded if I wrote a scene from the perspective of one of the minor background characters. He said go for it. People liked my addition so we kept writing the serial together. At the time neither one of us had published a thing and were complete newbs at writing fiction. We made it up as we went, yet by some miracle it actually turned out surprisingly good.

Years later we polished that story and Baen released *Dead Six*. It turned into a trilogy that I am really proud of, and now Mike Kupari has launched his solo writing career with the excellent sci-fi novel *Her Brother's Keeper*, also from Baen.

THE BRIDGE

This story was originally published in Champions of Aetaltis *in 2015 by Mechanical Muse, edited by Marc Tassin and John Helfers.*

LAVRO could have sat in the shade of a nearby tree, but Droth had blessed this day with miserable heat and a merciless sun, so he gave thanks for his sunburn and discomfort, and remained standing in the middle of the bridge.

He did loosen the straps of his armor a bit, so he wouldn't boil in his own sweat. Droth taught through suffering, but it would be difficult to fulfill his guard duty if he became delirious from heat exhaustion. Summer in the Free Kingdoms was nothing like the northern wastes where his clan wandered. This place was green instead of grey. The water in the river below wasn't choked with ice. It was a good thing this land was so plagued with perpetual warfare, otherwise those who lived here would be in danger of becoming soft.

This portion of the Serenth River was sluggish. The shores on both sides of the bridge were mud and reeds, so Lavro was continually bitten and stung by hungry insects all day. At night, it was cool, but that was when the beast men liked to sneak up and try to murder him.

Praise Droth.

It had been many days since he had spoken to anyone, not that Lavro cared much for speaking even when there were others around. Most things a Drothmal wanted to communicate were better shared with steel than words. He had been all by himself since the rest of the mercenaries had fled.

Lavro the Drothmal did not flee. He had accepted a contract and would fulfill his duty until relieved or killed. Mercenaries had been hired to hold this bridge because one petty lord was feuding with another petty lord, and someone somewhere had seen this crossing on a map and decided it might be of strategic importance. Sure, they'd camped here for weeks without seeing so much as a single refugee, in a forsaken part of the Free Kingdoms abandoned by civilization and reclaimed by nature and monsters, where they had been neglected, unsupplied, and forgotten . . . but a promise was a promise.

So, long after the others had left, Lavro continued guarding the bridge. He slept beneath it so that he would wake up should anyone attempt to cross. The hardest part of this duty was foraging for food in the reeds while still keeping an eye on the crossing. It was hard for a three hundred-pound Drothmal to find sufficient nourishment in such a small area. He was very tired of eating frogs. If he never ate another damned frog again, that would be fine by him. Especially these miserable, stinking swamp frogs that tasted like mud.

Praise Droth.

Boredom was just another form of blessed suffering, but Lavro couldn't help but hope that if the war was over, eventually someone would remember to tell him.

Could it be? Lavro lifted a hand to shield his eyes from the glare of the setting sun. Someone was approaching his bridge. At first he thought it was just another vicious beast man, coming to throw rocks at him, but this one wasn't running on all fours or howling for his blood. It walked like a normal, boring, civilized traveler.

The man was tall for an Atlan, but still tiny compared to Lavro. He wore simple, baggy clothing, a straw hat, and carried a large traveling pack. Despite looking like a farmer, the man wore a pair of swords through an orange sash on his waist. The stranger also had a confident walk. He certainly didn't carry himself like a refugee. Lavro knew refugees. You couldn't work as a mercenary in the Free Kingdoms for long without becoming very familiar with the look of refugees. They were always either shocked, skittish, or defeated. This man was confident and walked with purpose.

Excited, Lavro adjusted the straps of his armor and dusted off his steel breastplate so that he would look respectable. Since he'd been wallowing in mud and insects for a month, that wasn't very respectable at all, but Lavro put his great sword over one shoulder, drew himself to his full seven-foot height, and tried to be as intimidating as possible.

"Hello," said the man.

"You will not pass!" Lavro bellowed.

"Oh . . ." the man stopped and looked around. There really wasn't much to see, except for a rickety old bridge and a whole lot of mud. He lifted the straw hat and wiped his face with one sleeve. Lavro was not good at guessing atlan ages, but this one was no longer young, but not yet old, though his long hair was turning grey. "Why?"

"I have orders to hold this bridge. Only the forces of Lord Wainbrook may cross here."

"I don't know who that is." He pointed at the Donarzheis Mountains on the other side of the river. "I need to go there."

"Well, you can't cross here," Lavro said with grim finality. "If you try, I will bleed you."

"Bleed? Interesting choice of words."

"Whether you live or die is the will of Droth. But when I hit somebody with this sword, they usually die. More often than not."

The man nodded thoughtfully. "That would be terribly inconvenient. Do you mind if I have a seat while we debate this?"

"There is no debate. Those are my orders." But the atlan had already taken off his heavy pack, placed it in the dirt road, and sat on it. As long as he didn't try to cross, Lavro didn't mind the company. "Fine."

"What a miserable day." The atlan paused to swat a mosquito on his neck. "Normally, your people are as deathly pale as your tundra. I didn't know you could get so red in the sun. May I ask your name, Drothmal?"

"I am Lavro, son of Ulm."

"A pleasure to meet you. I am Decimus." He held out his straw hat. "If you let me use your bridge, in trade, I will give you my hat. It would make that sunburn far more bearable."

"We learn through suffering," Lavro muttered, though he wished he'd brought a hat. He'd been so bored he tried making one out of reeds, but given up when he discovered his large fingers were no good for weaving. "There is another bridge ten miles that way." He nodded downstream, toward the village of Korval.

"I'd rather not. I am on an important quest."

Lavro didn't care. A contract had been made. "No."

"What if I were to offer you a real bribe? I have money. I could probably pay you more than you accepted to guard this bridge, just to look the other way for a moment."

It wasn't about money. Lavro shook his head.

"I suppose I could swim across."

Lavro shrugged. His orders didn't say anything about intercepting swimmers. He'd only seen a couple of scaled gillcutters swim by the entire time he'd been here, so he might even make it.

Decimus looked at the river suspiciously. "Or I could just fight you and get it over with. Only killing you over something so trivial seems like a waste. I will take the middle path and beat you soundly. I will do my best not to kill or maim you, and this way you will learn a valuable lesson about etiquette."

The Drothmal snorted. The little atlan could try. Life was cheap in the Free Kingdoms. "Come on then."

"Very well, Lavro, son of Ulm." He stood up. "It is nothing personal, but I really do have important things to do." He didn't even bother to draw either of his little swords as he started across the bridge. Decimus didn't seem intimidated. In fact, he seemed rather calm about the whole thing.

"I'm not kidding, atlan."

"You don't strike me as the joking type, Drothmal." Decimus stopped a few feet away, bent at the waist, and bowed respectfully. "Shall we begin?"

Lavro lifted his sword high overhead, roared his battle cry, and brought the blade crashing down with the fury of an avalanche.

Decimus moved aside and let the blade embed itself deeply into the wood. *Nobody's that fast—* Before Lavro could tug his sword free, Decimus stepped on the steel with his sandal and trapped it. Lavro didn't even see the punch coming, but the small man hit him in the chest so surprisingly hard that Lavro found himself sailing back through the air. He landed flat on his back several feet away.

The Drothmal clambered back to his feet. The knuckles of the atlan's fist had left dents in the steel. "What manner of magic was that?" he snarled.

"No magic. Just focus . . . You lost your sword." Decimus grunted as he pulled the heavy blade free. "This isn't a proper sword. This is a log splitter some delusional smith welded a handle onto." He lifted it in both hands and tossed it toward Lavro.

Lavro caught it by the grip, and spun the sword to show that he meant business. "I was not ready. Now I am ready."

"Good. It's hard to tell what a Drothmal is thinking with such a catlike face, but I thought you remained unconvinced. Let us try this again."

It angered him that Decimus hadn't even bothered to draw his own blade. That seemed incredibly insulting. Lavro roared and swung his sword, this time from the shoulder, so fast it whistled through the air. Decimus ducked beneath it. Lavro recovered and brought it back around, hacking at the atlan's legs, but this time Decimus jumped over it.

"Fight me, cowar—" but Decimus stepped inside the next swing, caught Lavro's wrist with a grip as hard as iron, and somehow, the next thing Lavro knew he was flipping through the air. This time when he hit the bridge, it knocked the air from his lungs.

Praise Droth, that hurt, Lavro thought as he desperately got back to his feet, gasping.

"I find your fighting stance fascinating. I will call it Lumbering Ox style," Decimus said. "May I be on my way now?"

Lavro didn't bother to respond, he just hurled himself at Decimus, counting on his extra mass and weight to crush the atlan. Decimus caught his arm again and rolled Lavro over his hip, using his momentum to hurl him across the bridge again. He hit in a clang of metal and a rattle of chain.

"You do not give up easily, do you?" Decimus asked as Lavro got up again.

"Easily? I do not give up period."

"It's only a bridge," Decimus said.

"It is my duty." Lavro was wary this time, and he led with the tip of his sword. He would use his reach advantage to impale the obnoxious atlan. He thrust, and was glad to see that Decimus actually had to move back. Lavro had him now.

Decimus snap-kicked his sword aside. The next kick hit him in the thigh, which caused his leg to buckle, and the next spinning kick hit him in the teeth. For just a moment, Lavro saw a cloud of spit and road dust floating in the sunlight, but then he was somersaulting through the air again. The Drothmal found himself facedown on his precious bridge, bleeding onto the wood.

"Now may I pass?"

Shaking, dizzy, Lavro got up and looked for his sword. "No." He couldn't find his damned sword. Decimus offered it to him helpfully. Annoyed, Lavro snatched it. "You will have to kill me."

"I respect your dedication," Decimus said as he drew his sword. It was a simple, thin blade. The atlan could have just run him through while he was dazed, but he waited for Lavro to collect himself. "Are you sure you want to do this?"

Lavro was young, but he was no stranger to war. He'd survived many battles. He'd fought monsters, dark beasts, and other soldiers, but he'd never fought anyone this skilled. There was no doubt Decimus would kill him.

He attacked anyway.

Decimus moved effortlessly around the blow. His counterattack stung Lavro's arm. Lavro crashed forward, desperate, and Decimus slashed him in the neck. The Drothmal gasped in pain and flinched away, touching one hand to his throat. It came away clean. Both times Decimus had struck him with the flat of his blade. "Are you trying to mock me?"

"I'm trying to convince you to step aside."

"I'll be convinced when I'm dead." Lavro brought his sword up, but Decimus smacked it aside with his smaller blade, and with his other hand stabbed two fingers hard into Lavro's wrist. The great sword dropped from his suddenly numb hand. Before he could do anything else, the tip of Decimus' sword was pressed beneath his chin. He could feel the steel against his jugular.

He was doomed. "Praise Droth," Lavro whispered, totally prepared for his spirit to move on.

Decimus frowned, stepped back, and sheathed his sword. "Fascinating."

"Aren't you going to kill me?"

"I'll decide in the morning," the atlan muttered as he walked off the bridge and returned to his traveling pack. Decimus pulled out his bedroll.

"What are you doing?"

"What does it look like I'm doing? Making camp here for the night. Or is that against your arbitrary rules as well, Drothmal?"

"Just keep it on that side of the bridge and I don't care what you do, atlan."

The food Decimus was cooking smelled much better than the raw frogs and berries Lavro had eaten for lunch. Because of the visitor, he'd not been able to leave his post long enough to forage for supper. His stomach ached with hunger.

Praise Droth.

Decimus squatted next to his small fire, checking the trio of small animals roasting on spits. "Are you hungry, Lavro?"

"It is not unbearable."

"Oh, do all Drothmal stomachs rumble so loudly they can be heard from ten feet away?"

"It is not safe to travel these roads alone, atlan. These little kingdoms are always at war, but this part is worse than most. Your fire will surely attract monsters. Only a fool would be alone here."

"You're alone. Are you a fool?"

Probably. But Lavro dismissed those thoughts of weakness. "I am mighty Lavro, son of Ulm, hired to guard this bridge, and I will not shirk my duty. Why are you here?"

Decimus ignored his question. "I've got plenty of food. I caught these rabbits along the road earlier," he said as he turned the sticks.

The atlan had no bow or sling. "How?"

"By hand," Decimus said. "It is easy, really. You just need to be faster than the rabbit."

Lavro had a hard enough time catching the damned frogs. "Where I am from, we use spears. I am a great hunter of mighty beasts . . . delicious, tasty beasts."

Decimus took one of the rabbits from the fire and tossed it to Lavro. The Drothmal caught it, fumbled, and managed to burn his fingers.

Praise Droth.

He thought it might have been the best meal he'd ever had.

After supper, Decimus sat cross-legged, straight-backed, and eyes closed for a very long time. Lavro thought it was some sort of strange manner of prayer, but Decimus had called it centering, and then politely shushed him, saying he needed to focus. Lavro watched him carefully the whole time, to make sure this wasn't some manner of trick.

However, once Decimus had finished his centering, he'd gotten into this bedroll, wished him a good night, and promptly gone to sleep. The man snored like an Orog. He thought about bashing his head in while he slept, but that seemed dishonorable. So Lavro went about his duties, lighting torches of sticks wrapped in dried reeds on both sides of the bridge, so he could see anything coming. Then he grudgingly sat and rested his back against a wooden bridge support, great sword resting across his legs. He would stay awake as long as it took for this strange man to leave him to his duty.

A few hours later, the beast men attacked.

Lavro had broken his vow and nodded off, but the instant their bare feet whispered across the wooden bridge, he woke up. The beast men should have known better. The bridge had become his whole world, and he had not patience for trespassers. As Lavro lumbered to his feet, the beast men who'd intended to quietly slit his throat realized they'd been seen, and a cry went up. The noise was answered from the reeds and surrounding trees.

He'd only ever faced a few at a time before. There were a lot of angry bellows all around the bridge. This time they'd brought their whole tribe.

A huge number of the creatures rushed, screaming, from the darkness.

They were misshapen, hideous things, dressed in rags and filth, armed with sharpened bones, sticks, and rocks. As they climbed over the edge of the bridge, Lavro swung his great sword and embedded it in the boards. A severed arm landed at his feet, and the beast man splashed into the mud with a scream.

"This is my bridge," he warned the approaching mob.

They came at him in a rush of jabbing sticks and hurled rocks. Lavro split one in half.

In the heat of the moment, Lavro had forgotten his annoying visitor. The strange atlan was probably already dead. He risked a quick glance, and sure enough, the improvised camp was covered in blood and swarming with beast men.

But then he realized all the blood was from the monsters. Decimus was spinning through their midst, sword in hand, turning and cutting so incredibly fast Lavro couldn't believe his eyes. Each strike was precise, dropping another beast man. It was like Decimus was dancing between their attacks. He had been holding back when they'd fought earlier. The sword flashed back and forth, so quickly that the blade seemed to glow.

Quicker and quicker, Decimus took down the beast men. The stupid creatures never even realized what was happening. He used their momentum against them, guiding them into each other's weapons simply by shifting his stance. Every single movement dispensed crippling injury or death, all while Decimus wore a mask of serene calm.

Lavro was fascinated by the display, but he had to pay attention to the monsters swarming the bridge. His technique was much simpler than the atlan's. Be stronger than your opponent. Hit harder. It had worked well enough for most of his life, and sweeping his sword in a wide arc swept several monsters over the side and hurled them down into the mud.

It had worked well before. Only he'd never been attacked by so many of the terrible things at once before. It wasn't working nearly as well while surrounded. A club splintered over his shoulder, and another slammed into the back of his leg. Lavro roared in pain as he cleaved through a beast man's chest.

For each one he knocked down, two more took its place. Lavro tripped over corpses. Thrown rocks clanged off his armor. One split his lip. A bone dagger pierced deep into his hip. It was incredibly painful. *Praise Droth.*

Since his sword was stuck in a beast man's ribs, he grabbed the beast man who'd stabbed him by the hair, and slammed his skull against a bridge support. He was surrounded by screeching, chattering nightmares. More beast men hit him around his legs. One leaped from the rail and landed on his back, scratching at his eyes with its filthy, diseased fingernails. Lavro took that one by its pointy ear, yanked it off, and hurled it into the night.

But then he was hit with several more stinking bodies. Off balance, the mighty Drothmal found himself on his knees, being beaten with rocks and sticks as the monsters cackled and jabbered.

Lavro wasn't afraid of dying, but being eaten by beast men while guarding a bridge to nowhere was embarrassing. It was good that his clan would never know about this.

A white light was coming toward him, spinning across the bridge. Lavro realized it was the sword of Decimus just as the atlan lifted the glowing blade high overhead, then slammed it point first into the wood of the bridge.

The flash was blinding.

It was late in the morning, and already miserably muggy and hot when Lavro, son of Ulm woke up with a throbbing headache. Every muscle in his body hurt. It felt like he was covered in bruises. It had been a very educational combat.

Praise Droth.

Sitting up took a few tries, but he managed. There was wood beneath him. He was still on his bridge. He reached up, and found that someone had bandaged his head.

Decimus sat cross-legged on the road, running a rag across the blade of his sword. "I wouldn't dignify evil with a proper burial, so I pushed all the bodies into the river and let the current take them. I didn't think it was wise to leave them out to attract scavengers."

"Fish must eat too," Lavro muttered. Maybe someone in the village of Korval would get curious as to why there were so many beast men corpses floating past, and someone would remember he was still here. His throat was parched, but when he went for his canteen, he discovered it had a hole in it from a beast man spear. "Blast."

"I apologize for stepping onto your bridge last night, but I did not think you would mind, considering the situation." Decimus got up, went to his pack and found a wineskin. He carried it to the bridge, but politely stopped before stepping onto the boards. He tossed it the last few feet so that it landed in Lavro's lap. "There you go."

Lavro glared at the wineskin suspiciously. Suffering was a blessing, but he couldn't fight again if he was dehydrated. He took it and drank greedily. The wine was much better than swamp water. He tossed the skin back when it was empty. "You saved my life."

Decimus squatted at the edge of the bridge. "Don't worry. I'm passingly familiar with the beliefs of your people. I didn't intervene until I thought you had suffered everything you could on your own. I didn't want to deprive you of the experience."

"Thank you . . ." It was rare to hear such wisdom from an outsider.

"I don't worship any of the Enaros, but I can respect them," the atlan continued. "Especially the one who gave the gift of challenges to this world. I'm told Droth believes in trials. My school taught that we are the sum of our trials. I spent most of my life preparing and training, then testing myself and correcting my assumptions, all to become what I am today. We're probably not that different, you and I."

Disturbingly, Lavro thought that might actually be true. "Why didn't you cross while I was unconscious?"

"That seemed dishonest."

"I have never seen anyone fight like you." It is said that the Enaros and their servants sometimes walked among the mortal world in disguise. "Are you an avatar?"

"I'm only a man."

"Then you are a wizard?"

"I am Kinjatsi."

Lavro had heard of them, mostly whispered rumors of the mystical atlan warriors who could disappear into one shadow and come out of another, or ride the winds, or stop a heart with a touch. "You don't look like you eat children."

"I haven't heard that one for a while!" Decimus laughed. "Some of our schools are more secretive than others, but I'm afraid there's nothing lurid about the source of our power, Lavro, son of Ulm. It comes from here." He touched the side of his head. "If you train hard enough, and learn to center yourself sufficiently, you can call upon energies that most warriors will never understand."

"You are an assassin." The very concept offended Lavro. Killing should be done face to face.

"Me? No. That isn't my path. It is doubtless, though, that some Kinjatsi are the deadliest assassins on Aetaltis, but there are also those who study the way of the open hand, the fist, or those who follow the path of the sword like me. There are as many styles as there are teachers now. Before the destruction of the world gates, the Atlan Alliance crossed many worlds, and we could pass freely between them. The Kinjatsi were the ones who studied the various martial traditions we came across. We collected the best and made them our own. Kinjatsi was the pure distillation of the arts of conflict."

"Sounds impressive."

"It was." Decimus sighed. "It was said that through mastering the one true path, a Kinjatsi could overcome any obstacle. Sadly, all of our grand masters and many of our practitioners were killed during the cataclysm. Techniques, feats, whole schools were lost. We have been rebuilding ever since. There have been disagreements between schools as to the true path. It has been . . . fractious."

"Your schools fight each other?"

"Too much. Pride has become a distraction from our search for enlightenment." Decimus didn't seem to want to talk about that further. "You should rest, Drothmal." The atlan began walking toward the forest. "I will find us some more food."

Not that he wasn't starving, but that act of kindness begged the question, "Why are you helping me?"

"Because you will need to be at your best when I try to cross this bridge."

The atlan was a strange one, but Lavro was glad for the company. Decimus spent the next few days hunting—he was rather efficient at it—and practicing with his sword. The Kinjatsi techniques were unlike anything Lavro had ever seen before. Instead of brute strength and wild attacks, they were about speed, grace, and anticipation. He would move through hundreds of complex movements, stances, and attacks, all from memory, without ever seeming to think about it.

The last straw was when Decimus took up handfuls of grass, tossed them into the air around him, drew his sword, and then cut every individual blade before any could touch the ground.

Lavro finally swallowed his pride and asked, "Could you teach me to fight like that?"

"I can teach, but I don't know if you can learn."

"I am smart."

"It isn't about being able to think, Drothmal, it is about being able to *not* think. Before we can reach our true potential, a Kinjatsi must be able to clear his mind and truly think about nothing. Only then can you begin to understand everything."

"Fine." Lavro was already sitting on the bridge. He wasn't flexible enough to cross his legs, but he closed his eyes, like he'd seen Decimus do when he'd been centering, and then he thought about absolutely nothing.

He opened his eyes an hour later. "Was that sufficient?"

Decimus had gone back to working on his shelter. "Seriously? You cleared your mind of all thought that whole time?"

"Yes." Honestly, Lavro didn't see what was so difficult about it.

"Hmm . . . that is unexpected. It seems there is much I could learn from the Drothmal." Decimus actually seemed impressed. "Stand up. Let's work on your footwork."

"My feet are fine. I want to learn to sword fight better."

"Your stance is fine for your current style, such as it is, but Lumbering Ox is insufficient to learn the way of the Kinjatsi. Now shut up and do what I do."

After a week of training, Lavro was just beginning to understand how little he actually understood about the fighting arts. The Kinjatsi had taught him much, but it was obvious his teacher was becoming impatient. The bridge was Lavro's world, and now Decimus was his only friend. Soon, his friend would need to kill him so that he could continue on his mysterious mission. That seemed like a particularly profound method of suffering.

Praise Droth.

Now they built the campfire at the edge of the bridge. Lavro trusted Decimus, and knew he no longer needed to physically block the way, but it made him uncomfortable to stray too far from his duty.

The normally serene Decimus seemed sad tonight. "You are healed from your wounds, you're no longer weak from hunger, and you have improved greatly."

"You are leaving?"

"I've procrastinated too long already. Tomorrow I must continue on my way."

"You intend to cross the bridge?"

Decimus nodded as he stared into the fire.

He could have easily gone on to the next crossing. In the time he'd wasted here, he could have already reached the Donarzheis. But Droth had brought them both to this bridge for a reason.

"You have never spoken of this important quest of yours, Decimus. Why do you have to go to the haunted mountains?"

"I swore to avenge the murder of my teacher."

That was a worthy quest. "You do not seem to be in much of a hurry to get your revenge."

"That's because it was my sister who murdered him."

"Oh . . ."

Decimus placed another log on the fire. The smoke kept away the mosquitos. "A Kinjatsi master has a duty to his students, and the students to their master. A rival school desired a forbidden technique from an old world. Our teacher refused to share it . . . It is a long story. Just know there is no greater crime than treachery . . . I am the last of my school, and though they're all gone, my duty remains."

Lavro was a warrior. He understood perfectly well what that meant.

Which was why he was prepared to die in the morning.

Praise Droth.

He centered his mind and thought of nothing.

At first light, Lavro opened his eyes.

"I know now why you atlans clear your heads. It isn't just for battle. After there is no noise, it is easier to think."

Decimus was already packing his gear. He didn't look pleased to be doing so, but a promise was a promise. "That's true," he agreed. "Clarity helps in all aspects of life."

Which was why Lavro had an idea. "What will you do after you get your vengeance?"

"I don't know if I'll survive. Aurelia was always the better student."

"But say you do . . ."

"In that unlikely event?" Decimus paused as he rolled up his blanket. "Too much has been lost as it is. Kinjatsi should be a force for good. I would rebuild my master's school."

Lavro stood up, took one of his unlit torches and stuck it into the remains of their fire. The dried reeds quickly caught. Decimus watched him curiously as Lavro carried the burning torch over to the bridge.

"Then I will be your first student."

As the two Kinjatsi walked downstream toward the next crossing, the burning bridge collapsed into the Serenth River.

AS A PROFESSIONAL WRITER who also has a reputation of being a role playing game nerd, I get requests to write in various game settings from a lot of different companies. However I don't have time to take on most of them, but when Marc Tassin approached me about writing something in the Aetaltis game setting, I asked for a copy of the sourcebook. The background of the world turned out to be really interesting, so I agreed to take a shot at it.

Writing in somebody else's world is always a challenging experience, in that you are limited by the rules and conventions they've established, but it can be really rewarding too. In this case, all the authors invited to the anthology got a big list of possible topics to pick through, so we could claim our turf and not step on anyone else's toes. On that list, one of the races, renowned for their stoic, stubborn outlook, worshipped what was basically a god of suffering and that was an intriguing idea—*praise Droth*—and then there were these dimension-hopping sort of Romans who had mystical warrior/ninja/Jedi/monks who had competing schools like something from a kung fu movie. It turned out that neither of those two ideas had been developed much.

Luckily for me, neither of those had been claimed by the other authors yet. Good stories are all about making up interesting characters and then having them collide, and there were two perfectly good voices right there. Sometimes an author hears an idea, and our imagination just runs with it. That's when writing in other people's universes gets fun.

As a result *The Bridge* is a pretty straightforward little fantasy story that I had a lot of fun with it.

THE GRIMNOIR CHRONICLES: DETROIT CHRISTMAS

This story was originally published in 2011 on the Baen Books website. It is set in the Grimnoir Chronicles universe and is a prequel to the novel Hard Magic. *My goal with Jake Sullivan was to write a character who would feel right at home inside a Raymond Chandler story (or at least if Raymond Chandler had been writing contemporary urban fantasy about magical superheroes).*

December 25th, 1931

DETROIT. One of the greatest cities in the world. The crossroads of industry and commerce. The American Paris, the City of Champions, Blimp Town, Motor City, call it what you want, it's one crowded place. Nearly two million people live in Detroit, but as far as Jake Sullivan was aware, only a few of them were trying to kill him at that particular moment in time.

Sure, there might have been others in Detroit that were gunning for him, as he wasn't the type of man that made a lot of friends, but judging from the volume of gunfire pouring through the windows and puckering the walls . . . *Six*. There were only six shooters.

He could handle that.

"Enough! I said enough!" The gunfire tapered off. One last angry bullet bounced off his cover with a *clang*. "You still alive in there?"

The seven-hundred-pound chunk of steel plate he'd picked up to use as a shield had worked better than expected. Sullivan checked his body for holes, and finding no more than usual, shouted back, "Yeah, but your boys ain't. You ready to surrender yet, Johnny? The cops will be here any minute."

"You'll be an icicle before then."

The temperature was dropping fast, which meant that Snowball was out there too. Both Maplethorpe brothers were Actives, which was just his rotten luck. Sullivan's teeth began to chatter. He had to finish this before the Icebox could freeze him out. At this range, a clean shot could freeze him solid, but behind cover . . . even a really powerful Icebox wouldn't be able to steal more than ten degrees a minute from a room this big, but it had already been cold to begin with. That didn't leave Sullivan much time.

"Kidnapping, murder." He needed to goad them into coming after him. It was his only chance. "You boys been busy."

"Throw 'em on the list. They can only send me to the gas chamber once," Johnny Bones shouted back through the broken windows. "Are you the Heavy? Is this the legendary Heavy Jake Sullivan, J. Edgar Hoover's pet Active?"

Sullivan didn't dignify that with a response.

"Heard you been looking for my crew. How'd you find us? I thought you Heavies was supposed to be stupid?"

"Even a blind pig finds an acorn once in a while, Johnny." Sullivan picked up the giant Lewis machinegun from the floor with one shaking hand. It was a good thing he'd already been wearing gloves or he would've left skin on the freezing metal. "You ready to go to prison?"

"You know all about that from what I hear. So how's Rockville this time of year?"

The infamous prison for actively magical criminals was in Montana. Sullivan had been an inmate there for six long years. "Cold. Very cold." Some of Johnny Bones' men were going to try to flank him while they were talking. He knew because that's what he would've ordered if their situations had been reversed. Sullivan picked the most likely window, pointed the Lewis at it, and waited. "You'll get used to it. Your brother will be nice and comfy, though."

"We can make a deal," Johnny shouted, trying to keep Sullivan distracted. "It don't have to be like this, with you all blue and frozen stuck to the floor. How about I let you walk out of here, pay you enough to make it worth your time? We'll call it my present to you. 'Tis the season and all that jazz. I'm in a giving mood. What do you say?"

Someone moved on the other side of the window. Sullivan held down the trigger and let the Lewis roar. Bricks exploded into dust and glass shattered. The man on the other side went down hard.

That left five.

"I'd say you gotta do better than that."

Johnny Bones Maplethorpe ordered his remaining men to open fire and bullets ricocheted off the steel plate. Jake Sullivan was pinned down in a room that was rapidly turning into a walk in freezer by a gang of hardened criminals led by a vicious Shard. It was one hell of a way to spend Christmas.

Two Days Earlier

"SO, MR. SULLIVAN, you got any plans this Christmas?"

Sullivan finished counting out the January rent money and passed it over. It was the last ten dollars he had to his name. Paying work had been sporadic lately. "Nothing in particular, ma'am."

"I see," Mrs. Brooks said. His landlord owned the entire building and the diner downstairs. It was obvious the old woman didn't like her tenant much, but Jake Sullivan always paid his rent on time. "I don't want any loudness or carrying on. I know how you Irish get during the holidays with the devil drink."

"Why, Mrs. Brooks, alcoholic beverages are illegal."

"I know all about your disdain for the law, Mr. Sullivan." Mrs. Brooks eyed him suspiciously, then glanced around the office, as if expecting to see a distillery hidden in a corner. Instead there was only a battered secondhand desk, a couple of sturdy wooden chairs, a bedraggled couch, and a few book shelves. "It's only my strong upbringing that's allowed me to forgive your horrific criminal history and your unseemly magic."

The landlord talked a big game, but both of them knew that she'd rent to anybody who could pay in these tough times, and that included convicted felons, less popular types of Actives, or anybody else for that matter. The old lady would rent a room to the Chairman himself if he had ten dollars ready on the twenty-third of each month. "And I won't forget it," Sullivan said.

Mrs. Brooks stepped back and examined the words painted on his door. "Why would someone like you go into this kind of business anyway?"

"I like puzzles . . ." Sullivan said honestly. "Anything else I can do for you, ma'am?" and before she could even answer he was already closing the door on her. "No? Wonderful. Merry Christmas. Good bye."

The sign on the door read SULLIVAN SECURITY AND INVESTIGATIONS. His last security job had been intimidating the union strikers at the UBF plant. Good work that, standing around earning money because you had a reputation for being able to crush a man's skull with a thought. It had paid well, too, but that had been months ago. The last investigation job had meant confirming to an angry wife that her husband liked prostitutes. The final bit of money from that one had just paid the rent.

There was other work out there. There always was for a man with his skills, whether physical or magical, but Sullivan was an honest man, and he preferred honest work. There was a difference between being a felon and being a crook, and Jake Sullivan was no crook.

Then there were the government jobs. . . . The monetary payment on those was meager, but completing them meant he got to stay out of Rockville. Sullivan sat behind his desk and reread the recent Bureau of Investigation telegram. It was a bulletin on the notorious Maplethorpe brothers. Their gang had recently gotten shot up in a robbery in Albion, and it was believed they were hiding in Detroit. A Shard and an Icebox, with Power to spare, armed, and extremely dangerous, wanted for bank robbery and murder. The telegram said a BI representative would be in touch if it was felt his services would be needed.

The terms of his early release specified that he needed to assist in the apprehension of five Active fugitives. He wondered idly if the Maplethorpes would count as two. . . . As long as the government's terms hung over his head, he would never truly be free. Sullivan crumpled the telegram and tossed it in the waste basket. Nothing usually came of the telegrams.

❖ ❖ ❖

The first client for the month of December arrived just before noon on the 23rd. Sullivan had been reading a *Popular Mechanics* article about a British Cog named Turing and his controversial attempt to build a mechanical man capable of reasoning, when there had been a delicate knock on the door.

Like all Gravity Spikers—or Heavies as most folks insisted on calling magicals of his type—Sullivan's Power enabled him to manipulate the forces of gravity. He was just much better at it than everyone else. A quick surge of Power enabled him to see the nearby world as it really was, shades of mass, density, and force, and it told him that there was a single body in the hallway, approximately one hundred and twenty pounds.

Hopeful that it might be business related, he quickly saw to it that both he and the office were presentable before answering. He stubbed out his cigarette and hid the magazine in his desk. Sullivan checked the mirror, fixed his tie, and ran a comb through his hair. He was built like a bull, had the face of an anvil, and wasn't particularly well-spoken, but that was no excuse to not present well.

The lady in the hall certainly knew how to present well. She was good-looking, mid-twenties, brunette, and petite. She was wearing a blue dress, ten minks' worth of coat, and shoes that cost more than all of Sullivan's earthly possessions combined. "I need a private detective," she stated, having to crane her neck to see since he was over a foot taller than she. "Are you Heavy Jake Sullivan?"

"That's me." He didn't much care for the nickname, but it would do. At least that meant she knew he was an Active and was okay with the fact. It wasn't the kind of thing you advertised to most respectable clients. The general attitude was that Heavies were good for lifting things and that was about it. "Please come in."

"Thank you, Mr. Sullivan." Her blue eyes were red from crying. Her manner was resigned and tired.

He closed the door behind her. She was graceful, like a dancer, as she walked in and took a seat. He went to the other side of the desk and settled into his massively reinforced chair. Sullivan weighed far more than he appeared to, a byproduct of his magical experimentation, and he'd gotten tired of breaking chairs.

"So what brings you to this neighborhood?"

"You came highly recommended." The lady glanced around the room. There was a single light bulb wired into the ceiling and the whole place seemed dingy and small. It was times like this that he wished he could afford a real office instead of this rotten dive. Judging by her getup, she could hire whoever she felt like, but apparently she was undeterred by the shabbiness of her host or his office. "I need your help."

"Sure," he answered. "I'm afraid I didn't get your name."

"Emily Fordyce. I'm here about my husband."

So it was another jilted wife case. The rock on her wedding ring was huge, but in his experience the size of the rock seldom corresponded to a husband's loyalty. "I'll be glad to help, Mrs. Fordyce. What's wrong with your husband?"

"He's missing," she answered with a sniff. "He was abducted."

Sullivan perked up. His day had just become far more interesting. "Really?" She was obviously money, so he asked the logical question. "Has there been a ransom demand?"

"There's been no ransom, and the police say that he's certainly dead."

Sullivan urged her to start from the beginning. Arthur Fordyce had not returned from his office days ago. Yesterday his automobile had been found in a ditch just outside of the city, where it had been hidden by the snow. A great deal of dried blood had been found on the seat. The car was otherwise undamaged.

Emily became increasingly upset as she spoke. Sullivan offered her a smoke to calm her nerves, but she turned him down. He took one for himself. "Your husband have enemies?"

"Oh, no. Everyone loved Arthur. He was a sweetheart."

"He gamble? Owe anyone money?" She shook her head in the negative. Those minks didn't buy themselves. "What did he do for a living?"

"He was a Healer."

Sullivan stopped, match hovering just below his suddenly forgotten cigarette. "A *Healer*?"

Emily nodded. "He's an Active and very skilled. He works freelance, fixing anyone that can afford his services. The finest families in the city have used him."

Healers of any kind were rare; Active Healers with significant amounts of Power were especially so. They were talking about somebody who could cure any illness or mend any wound with a touch. Someone who was literally worth *more* than their weight in gold. "I've never actually spoken to a real live Healer . . . Who were your husband's recent clients?"

"Arthur didn't speak about many of them. You see . . . sometimes influential people need to be discreet. . . ." *Rich guys with syphilis,* went unsaid. "I know he did do a Healing for an unsavory man recently who may be some sort of criminal. His name was something Horowitz."

That was a bad sign if it was who he was thinking of. Abraham Horowitz was a local legend amongst the bootleggers, but it did give him a place to start. Sullivan spent the next hour learning everything he could about the last days of Arthur Fordyce. When he'd exhausted his questions and Emily looked like she would begin crying again, Sullivan decided that she needed to get home.

"Yes, that's probably a good idea, but we've not yet talked about your fee. . . . Whatever it normally is, double it. I'm prepared to write you a check in advance."

He'd need operating money, but his pride didn't like taking money for work unperformed. "That's not necessary, ma'am."

"I've got more bank accounts than husbands. Just find him."

"All right, then. I'll do my best, Mrs. Fordyce," Sullivan promised.

Emily pulled a handkerchief out of her purse and dabbed her eyes. "I know you will, Mr. Sullivan. You came highly recommended."

Sullivan certainly hadn't performed many jobs in her neck of the wood. The Fordyces lived over on mansion row in Woodbridge. "Who recommended me?"

"Arthur, of course."

Sullivan didn't know what to make of that response. "Your missing husband . . ."

"I'm sorry, that must sound rather crazy." His expression must have confirmed the idea. "Not recently obviously. No, it was because of a newspaper article several months ago. It said you helped the government capture some Active madman."

"I know the one." He had gotten a brief mention in the papers after he'd helped the BI arrest Crusher Marceau in Hot Springs. There had been no mention of Jake being a recently released convict, thankfully, because that would have sent J. Edgar Hoover into an apocalyptic fit.

"Arthur knew right away who you were and said that if we ever had need of a private detective, then you would be the only man for the job because you didn't know the meaning of the word *quit*. You see, he had a lot of respect for you. Arthur was in the First Volunteers during the war too, Mr. Sullivan. I believe every survivor of the Second Somme knows who you are."

Sullivan was humbled. His respect for Arthur Fordyce had just grown tremendously. Very few Healers had bothered to join the Volunteers. "Men like your husband saved a lot of lives over there."

"Arthur led me to believe that you saved even more, Mr. Sullivan. . . . Now please do it again, and if my husband has been . . ." She choked on the word, then couldn't finish. Sullivan came around, but he didn't know the first thing about how to comfort a grieving woman. Luckily, she waved him away. "I'm fine . . . I'm fine. I'll be going."

Sullivan opened the door for her. Emily stopped, and her voice grew unexpectedly hard. "If Arthur is *gone*, then I don't want the men who did it arrested, I want them *gone* too. Do you understand me, Mr. Sullivan? If they hurt him, I want you to hurt them right back, and if you do so, I will double your fee again. I want you to do to them what Arthur said you did to the Kaiser's army."

Sullivan closed the door behind her. Rage at the men who might have made her a widow notwithstanding, Emily didn't know what she was asking for. He wouldn't wish the fate of the Kaiser's army on anyone.

It was snowing when he left the office.

Arthur Fordyce's automobile had been towed to a police lot. A quick phone call to a Detroit P.D. officer who owed him a favor got Sullivan inside for a quick look. The car was a ritzy '29 Dusenberg roadster. The paint gleamed with tiny flecks of real gold. Ostentatious, but fitting for a Healer. The only thing that spoiled the perfection was the gallon of blood someone had left to dry on the leather seats. Most of the blood was on the driver's side, like it had pooled around a body. No wonder the law was assuming it was a murder instead of a kidnapping.

Sullivan was still poking around the Dusenberg when there was an angry cough from behind. He turned to see Detective Sergeant Ragan. "Afternoon, Detective."

"What're you doing in there, Sullivan?"

He'd cultivated a decent enough relationship with many of the local cops, but not all of them. Ragan was in the latter category. An old-fashioned, hard-drinking tough guy, Ragan didn't like magicals, and he especially didn't like ones with reputations for having *accidentally* killed a law enforcement officer, even if the officer in question had been a murderous piece of work. "Mrs. Fordyce hired me to find her husband."

"Find her husband's *body* is more like it . . ."

"Who do you think did it?" Sullivan asked, still going about his business.

"Whole case is fishy. I'm thinking the wife had him popped, just to get the insurance money. Fellow like that's bound to have a hefty life insurance policy."

Sullivan snorted. "That's rich."

"Why am I even talking to the likes of you? Get out of there! That's evidence." Sullivan climbed out of the car, quickly hiding the handkerchief he'd used to wipe up some blood. "You can't be in here. Who let you in?"

"Nice fella. Forgot his name. About this tall . . ." Sullivan held his hand out about shoulder height then moved it up and down six inches.

"You private ops are a pain in the neck. I ought to have you arrested for tampering with evidence."

That would never hold, but Sullivan definitely didn't want to spend Christmas in a cell. It was time to go. "My apologies, Detective." Sullivan tipped his hat and walked away.

Sometimes prejudices make life harder than it needs to be. Sullivan was fairly certain that if Ragan was running the official investigation then there was no way in the world that he'd resort to consulting a Finder. Ragan distrusted magic, and besides, any clues divulged through magical means wouldn't be admissible in a court of law. Sullivan didn't have those issues. He just wanted to find Arthur Fordyce and get paid.

To be fair, it wasn't just about the money this time. Fordyce was a fellow veteran of Roosevelt's First Volunteer Active Brigade. Sullivan had never associated with any of the unit's Healers, other than to dump wounded soldiers onto their tables. The valuable Healers had been kept as far from the front as possible, while the dime-a-dozen Spikers were always where the bullets were flying. Healers were officers, Sullivan had been an enlisted man, but despite those differences, they'd both shared a little slice of hell in the biggest battle in human history, and that made them brothers.

Sullivan would have done his best no matter what, that was just his single-minded nature, but Fordyce wasn't some anonymous victim. He was First Volunteer, and that made it personal.

The fourth best Finder in Detroit lived in a humble home in Brush Park. Sullivan couldn't afford the other three. A reliable Finder demanded a premium wage. Finders existed in that nebulous grey area of Active popularity. The public considered them useful but scary. At least Finders were far more well-liked than their more powerful cousins, the Summoners. Most religious types simply wouldn't tolerate them or their alien Summoned.

It didn't help that Finders tended to be a few bricks shy of a wall. Talking to disembodied spirits all day tended to do that to a person. Bernie was all right though . . . usually.

Sullivan knocked and only had to wait a minute to be let in. Bernie was a pudgy, unshaven, wild-eyed fellow, and today was wearing some pajamas that had seen better days. "Sullivan! Good to see you, my boy."

"Nice hat, Bernie."

Bernie's head was wrapped in a tin foil cone. "Keeps some of the voices out," he explained. "I picked up a screamer this morning. Poor thing won't shut up. You know how it goes."

"No. Not really."

"Come in! Come in!" Bernie dragged him inside. The interior of the home was filled with stacks of newspapers and at least a dozen mangy cats. Bernie kicked stray felines out of the way as he led Sullivan to the living room. "Did you bring me a present?"

"I got you a sandwich." He passed over a paper sack. Bernie had a reputation for forgetting to eat when he was on a Finding, and Sullivan needed him focused. Sullivan then pulled out the red-stained handkerchief. "And this."

Bernie took the handkerchief. "Oh . . ." He sounded disappointed. "I meant a Christmas present."

"Sandwich isn't good enough? Well, if you Find me the body that blood came out of I'll give you fifty bucks. This is a rush job."

The Finder studied the stain. "Half up front . . . and you still owe me a present."

"Fair enough." Sullivan had cashed Emily Fordyce's generous advance check already and he counted out the bills. "What do you get for the man that's already got everything?"

"I'm almost out of tin foil." Bernie shoved a particularly ugly cat off the couch and took a seat. He placed the handkerchief on the stack of newspapers that, judging from all the dirty plates and dishes stacked on it, served as his table. "Rush job, eh? I've got just the spirit for you. Strongest thing on her plane. I call her Mae, 'cause you know, she kinda reminds me of this poster of Mae West I got. Bringing her in burns up all my Power for a few days, but she works real fast. I'm warning ya, if this body ain't close, it could take time."

Sullivan leaned against the wall. His overcoat was black and he didn't particularly want to cover it in cat hair. "If you can do a Finding for me today, I'll get you *two* rolls of foil."

Bernie rubbed his hands together greedily. "You got a deal, but lots of things can go wrong. If the body is buried real deep, takes time. If the thing I'm Finding is behind iron . . . If it's been cut into little bits and scattered, or if it's been burned to ash, or if—"

"Just do your best, Bernie." Sullivan settled in to wait. He knew how erratic this method was, but when it worked, it worked really well. They'd used the disembodied creatures of the Finders as scouts during the war. Nobody knew where the creatures came from exactly, they tended to be flaky, but they could cover a lot of ground and see things a person couldn't.

Bernie concentrated on the handkerchief, scowled, confused, then cheered up as he remembered he was wearing a hat. He took the tin foil off and went back to concentrating. "That's better. Here comes Mae."

The lights flickered and the house shook. Stacks of newspapers tumbled. Cats screeched and ran for cover. At first Sullivan thought that they were having an earthquake, but then the wind hit, sending the curtains billowing across the room. Sullivan stumbled back as his fedora was blown off.

"Ain't she a good girl? Yes, she is. Mae's my good girl."

Bernie hadn't been lying. This one was a doozy. Sullivan had been around many Summonings, but this was the first time he'd actually been able to see the shape of the vaporous creature, even it was only for an instant. The thing hovered in the center of the room, a weird conglomeration of winged hippopotamus and six-legged porcupine with four glowing eyes, and then it was gone as quickly as it had appeared.

The curtains and blowing trash settled. Sullivan picked up his fedora and brushed away the cat hair. "Impressive critter . . . though I don't see the resemblance to Mae West."

Bernie put his tin foil hat back on. "Beauty's in the eye of the beholder, Sullivan."

Mae had told Bernie that it was going to take awhile. Arthur Fordyce wasn't close, which meant she needed time to roam. Sullivan was still holding out hopes that Fordyce was alive, he was a Healer after all. Despite the volume of blood, he could only assume that Healers could fix themselves like they could fix everyone else, provided he was conscious or had Power enough to do it. Hopefully the demon-hippopotamus-porcupine ghost would come back with good news.

In the meantime, Sullivan had another lead to follow.

Abraham Horowitz ran with the Purple Gang, and the Purple Gang ran most of Detroit. Predominately Jewish, they were strongest on the east side, but there wasn't a criminal activity in this city that they didn't have a piece of. Mostly they stuck with bootlegging, tried to limit their killing to competitors, and kept the petty crooks under heel well enough to keep the law happy. They were tough enough that even Al Capone knew it was easier to just buy from them than to go to war.

If you saw a boat on the Detroit River with gunmen on it, then it probably belonged to the Purples. Nobody brought Canadian booze across the river except for the Purple Gang, and if you got caught trying it, you'd get boarded, robbed, and sunk . . . And swimming is difficult with a .45 slug in your chest. The locals called them the Little Jewish Navy, which meant that Abraham Horowitz probably held the rank equivalent to admiral.

The snow had gotten worse and the worn-out tires on Sullivan's old Ford didn't get the best traction, so it took him awhile to get across town. Horowitz's base of operations was at a sugar mill on the river's edge. The mill was legitimate. The hoodlums hanging out in front of the business office obviously were not.

Sullivan stopped the car and got out. The sun was going down and taking the last bit of warmth with it. He threw on his scarf and gloves, but left his coat open in order to get to the .45 automatic on his hip. He knew some of the Purples' muscle since they'd also worked the UBF strike, so wasn't expecting any trouble, but with these types violence was always in the air.

Three men were loafing on a bench at the top of the steps. To the side, the rollup doors to the sugarhouse were open and two burly men were throwing burlap sacks onto the back of a truck. He didn't even need to activate his Power to know they were like him. The way that each of them was effortlessly lifting four or five fifty-pound sacks at a time told him that the workers were fellow Spikers. A bunch of guys were sitting around smoking while Actives did all the work . . . *Figures.*

The Purple thugs got off the bench when they saw him coming up the stairs. The lead tough intercepted him before he could reach the door. The kid was barely old enough to shave, but had already developed a street swagger, but everyone was tougher when they had two buddies standing behind them. He tossed his cigarette into the snow. "Whadda you want?"

"I want to talk to Mr. Horowitz."

"You got an appointment? You don't look like you're here to buy sugar."

"Tell Mr. Horowitz it's about a mutual friend, Arthur Fordyce."

The three thugs exchanged a look that told him they recognized the name, but the kid didn't budge. "Who're you supposed to be?"

"Jake Sullivan." He looked over the group. Unfortunately, he didn't recognize any of them. "Isadore Lebowitz around? He can vouch for me."

"Buddy, Izzy got put in the ground weeks ago. He ain't vouching for nobody ever again."

"I hadn't heard."

They were starting to fan out around him. "He got shot in the teeth. If you was his friend, you shoulda knew that," said the second thug as he walked behind Sullivan. The sharks were circling.

"Mr. Horowitz said no visitors," said the last, this one with the bleary eyes of someone on the weed. "Not till the bone man leaves town."

"Shut up, idiot," hissed the second.

Sullivan didn't have time for intergang nonsense. "Why don't one of you guys go *ask* Mr. Horowitz if he wants to talk to me."

The kid snickered. "Yeah? Well, he's busy. You should come back . . . oh . . . never." His buddies all had a good laugh at that. "Now beat it 'fore we beat you."

Sullivan's magic was collected in his chest, just waiting. He'd saved up quite a bit. He activated the Power, using just a bit of his reserves, and tested the world around him. The weed head had something dense enough in the small of his back to be a pistol. The leader had something metal in his pocket. The Spikers loading the truck both stopped and looked over his way, having sensed the subtle flux in gravity.

"I'm not leaving until one of you asks Mr. Horowitz if he'll talk to me."

The leader glared at him and the look in those cold eyes said that he'd seen a fair share of blood spilled in his young life. "Last chance to walk away," he said.

Sullivan took his time taking out a cigarette, putting it to his mouth, and striking a match. The thugs watched him light up, incredulous as he took a puff, held it for a moment, then let it out. "Last chance to get your boss."

He had to hand it to the kid. He was fast with that straight razor. It came out in a silver flash. "You know what time it is now, big man?"

Sullivan shrugged. "Can't say I do."

The kid held the razor low at his side. "Now's the part where you say you don't want any trouble."

"Does that ever work?"

"Nope."

The kid lunged. The razor zipped out like a striking rattlesnake. Sullivan grabbed his Power and twisted gravity. When in a hurry, there was no time for finesse. A small piece of the world *broke*. Up was down and down was up. The kid's feet left the ground as he tumbled, surprised, toward the overhang. He slammed into the sheet metal cover overhead. Sullivan let him hang there for a moment, just so that he could know he'd barked up the wrong tree, before cutting his Power. The kid hit the concrete in a shower of dust and snow.

Sullivan turned just as the weed head went for the gun under his coat. He had plenty of Power stored up, and it never hurt to make an example of idiots, so Sullivan drastically lessened the strength of gravity around his target before he slugged the punk square in the face. Weedy left the ground, flew back to the end of Sullivan's range, then fell and bounced down the steps. A little nickel-plated pistol went skittering off into the snow.

There was one Purple left. He was just standing there, too flummoxed to move. Sullivan removed the cigarette from his mouth and pointed at him. "Like I said . . . *I'll* wait here while *you* go tell Mr. Horowitz."

The punk jerked open the doors and ran for his life. Sullivan looked over to see the two Spikers coming his way. One of them had picked up a length of pipe. "Brothers, you don't want to try me. I may be like you . . ." Sullivan let a bit more of his Power slip so they could feel the obvious surge. Gravity distorted. Falling snow stopped and hung in midair. The workers looked at each other, surprised at the display of control. Sullivan cut it off before he wasted too much precious Power. The snow resumed falling. "But I've got *way* more practice."

The Heavies returned to their truck, but they kept an uneasy eye on him. The punk at the bottom of the stairs was moaning about the condition of his face. The kid with the razor was out cold. That's what they got for picking a fight with someone who'd survived Second Somme *and* Rockville. Sullivan took a seat on the bench and finished his smoke.

Two minutes later the door opened again. This time four Purples filed out and they all trained shotguns on him. "Mr. Horowitz will see you now."

Abraham Horowitz sat behind a giant oak desk, thick arms folded, and prepared to listen to Sullivan's request. The bootlegger was a steely-eyed killer, past his physical prime now, but this was a man who'd grown up busting heads and collecting protection money. This was not somebody to short change, so it was probably wise to start with an apology. "Sorry about your boys downstairs, but I didn't do anything until the kid tried to carve me a new smile."

"Well, they should have asked me first. There was no need to be impolite to guests. Bad for business." Horowitz grunted. "From your rep I'm surprised you didn't just kill 'em all. You're a living legend. Way I hear it, you got an early release 'cause you're so good at it . . . You cut a deal with the enemy to take down dangerous Actives, right? You wouldn't happen to be here on the government dime, are you, Mr. Sullivan?"

"No, sir. Far as I'd tell anybody, you run a sugar mill, that's all. As for the enemy, any man would make a deal with the devil to get out of Rockville. It's a hard place. I just do what I've got to get by, same as anybody."

"I'd appreciate it if no Purples ever show up on your list, Mr. Sullivan, 'cause that could be *unpleasant* for everybody."

If one of the Hoover telegrams had a member of the Purple Gang on it for him to help catch, Sullivan would make damn sure he had plans to get the hell out of Detroit real quick afterwards. "I'd like that very much too, sir."

"Respect . . . Let me tell you, I wish you woulda taken Isadore's job offer after the UBF strike. A Heavy like you could make a lot of money working for the Purples. My Heavies down there said you're downright frightening how much Power you got."

Of course he was good; he'd done nothing but practice the entire time he'd been in Rockville. "You honor me, Mr. Horowitz, but I'm just a simple man," Sullivan said.

"Isadore said you were a whole lot smarter than you talked, too. My people appreciate an educated man, especially a self-educated man such as yourself. Izzy, may he rest in peace, said you read books like some sort of professor."

"Reading's my hobby. Keeps me out of trouble."

"Seems like a man who's avoiding trouble wouldn't end up in the middle of it so often."

"Just curious I guess . . . Like I'm curious about Arthur Fordyce. His wife hired me to find him."

Horowitz chuckled. "I liked old Arthur. You're probably wondering how we knew each other. Well, let's just say that Arthur didn't care much who he Mended as long as their dollars were green. Last time I used him was 'cause I'd started losing my vision and couldn't feel my toes. He fixed me up good as new and told me to quit eating so much sugar. Ha! Not with this sweet tooth." Horowitz pounded one meaty hand on the desk, then he paused and frowned. "Well, shit . . . Now that he's gone I might have to cut back . . . Arthur did other things for the Purples too. If one of my boys got shot and I needed him back in action quick, I'd go to Arthur. He was good at pulling bullets out but not asking about who put them in, if you get what I'm saying. Son of a bitch charged an arm and a leg, though."

"You know who might have taken him?"

The gangster shrugged. "Lots of folks. Maybe somebody who needed something fixed couldn't afford to pay an arm or a leg. Sick folk can get mighty desperate."

"These are desperate times," Sullivan agreed. Detroit was better off than most of the country, but even here there were tent cities growing on the fringe. Lots of people were out of work, hungry, and hurting.

Horowitz made a big show of studying Sullivan for a long time. "Maybe not just sick folks get that desperate . . . Come to think on it, maybe I know somebody else who couldn't afford a Healing, but might need a Healer real bad . . . Maybe I could tell you something that would help us both out of a jam."

He was looking for an angle, but men like Horowitz always were. "I'm listening," Sullivan said.

"You ever hear that old saying, kill two birds with one stone? You got to find somebody and I don't get to eat sweets because the only Healer in Detroit is gone . . . and maybe, just maybe, I know somebody who might have taken poor old Arthur. Maybe there is this crew mucking around in my area, robbing banks where they shouldn't be, but maybe this crew have been muscle for another group that the Purples don't want to mess with. Maybe this crew works with the Mustache Petes . . ." Sullivan knew that the Mustache Petes were the Sicilian-born gangsters that ran New York. The word was that Purple Gang had an uneasy truce with them. "Maybe this crew was caught robbing a bank and got themselves shot to bits by policemen over Albion way. Maybe they'd be desperate enough to steal a Healer . . . Maybe this is something I'd like to take care of myself, but my hands are tied on account of business reasons. What do you say to that?"

That's a lot of maybes. The last BI telegram had said the Maplethorpe Gang had gotten hit in Albion. They certainly wouldn't be above kidnapping. "That's very . . . forthcoming of you, Mr. Horowitz. If this crew was to get rolled up by the law, they'd be out of your hair."

"You find your man, this other crew goes away. Two birds, one rock. Bam. As long as you never said where you heard it from . . ."

"Of course. How about you let me know where this crew is and I'll go get your favorite Healer back?"

"Doubt it. Johnny Bones enjoys killin' too much, likes to cut on people so they die slow, and his brother Snowball's damn near as mean. The second he got his crew Mended, Arthur probably died. Let me put the word out. As soon as I know where that crew is, I'll be in touch."

Sullivan knew when he'd been dismissed. Horowitz didn't offer to shake on their deal. As far as the gangster was concerned, selling out Johnny Bones was like taking the garbage out to the curb for pickup. Sullivan stood to leave.

"One last thing, Mr. Sullivan. When you come up against Johnny, you're gonna have to kill him fast. Shoot him, squish him with your Power, whatever you got to do. Don't try to talk to that crazy Shard. He's sly. He'll cut you to pieces or his crazy brother will freeze you just to watch you shatter like glass. Mark my words. Take them fast or you'll regret it."

Sullivan debated his next move. Mae was still coming up with nothing. If Horowitz was right, Arthur Fordyce was probably already dead. Until he got a lead on where the Maplethorpes were holed up, he was at a dead end. If Horowitz was wrong, he was wasting his time.

Well, not exactly wasting . . . Which was why Sullivan's last stop for the evening was at the Detroit office of the Bureau of Investigation. Horowitz wasn't the only man that liked to kill two birds with one stone.

The BI office was near the Fisher Building. The giant art deco skyscraper was impressive, even if they were turning the lights down at night to save money now. It was late, the snow was still falling, and most everyone had gone home for the night, so Sullivan left a note for the agent in charge of the manhunt to contact him.

He got home around eleven. Sullivan's mind was too spun up to go to sleep, so instead he found himself pulling out a book he'd purchased last year on the history of the First Volunteers. He'd found it a fairly accurate, yet rather dull account of the events in question. To be fair, it would be rather difficult for some academic historian to chronicle the unrelentingly bleak meat grinder of the trenches, the sheer mind-numbing spectacle of Second Somme, or the final march into the blackened-ash wasteland that had been Berlin.

Even though Sullivan had been the most decorated soldier in the unit, there was only one picture of him, and it was a group shot of some Spikers taken somewhere in France. All of them were tired, dirty, starving, cold, suffering from dysentery, wearing their rusting Heavy suits, carrying their Lewis guns, and lucky to be alive. The book only had two pages about the Gravity Spikers. That was it. All that fighting, all those sacrifices, condensed into *two* lousy pages, and sadly one of those pages was mostly about his own exploits. He didn't deserve his own page. He'd just been lucky. Of the men in the photo, only ten percent had come home alive.

But it wasn't bitter reminiscence that had caused Sullivan to open the history book. There were photos for most of the officer corps and Sullivan was looking for one in particular. When he found Captain Arthur Fordyce's entry, at first Sullivan thought that he'd found the wrong picture . . . He checked again, just to be sure, and it was correct. Fordyce certainly didn't look like what he'd expected.

Fordyce had to be in his sixties in the picture, and it had been taken back in 1916 . . . Fifteen years ago . . . *Has it really been that long?* Sullivan had been so young that he'd had to lie about his age to enlist, and he was quite a bit older than Emily now. For that reason Sullivan had been expecting a younger man. That was not such an odd thing, especially for a man of Arthur's success, to have such a young beautiful wife.

Too damn young to be a widow.

He fell asleep after midnight, which made it Christmas Eve.

Sullivan checked on Bernie and his cats in the morning, but still nothing from Mae. Bernie said that was a very bad sign, meaning that the target was not in an easy-to-find state, as in aboveground or in one piece. Since he was actually a little worried about Bernie's health, Sullivan made sure to drop off another sandwich.

The BI agent in charge of the manhunt had Sullivan come into the office to talk. Most of the G-men tolerated him, a couple respected him because he was very good at his job, and a few openly despised him for being an ex-con. But like it or not, when it came time to arrest somebody who could bend the laws of physics, Sullivan was damn handy to have around.

The head of the Detroit office was a weasel named Price. He was a ticket-puncher, a man who existed primarily to get promoted. Price loved getting in the papers. Hoover didn't like sharing the spotlight with his underlings, but Sullivan had no doubt that Price would end up in politics as soon as he got an arrest big enough to make headlines.

The agent in charge of the manhunt was a homely fellow by the name of Cowley, fresh off the morning dirigible from D.C. Apparently he was one of Hoover's personal favorites. Which inclined Sullivan to dislike him automatically. Sullivan briefed the agents about what he'd heard, though he was careful never to mention the Purple Gang.

Despite looking like he'd be much more comfortable behind a desk, Cowley had listened intently enough that Sullivan had come away suspecting that the agent might actually have a clue about being a decent cop. He also didn't seem dismayed to find out that Sullivan was an Active. Cowley's primary concern was that if Arthur Fordyce was alive, he be returned safely. Price was mostly worried about how the arrest of the Maplethorpes would play in the news, but rescuing a Healer . . . Sullivan could see the wheels turning there.

Cowley showed him sketches of the members of the crew. He memorized the names and faces, but since none of them were Actives, he wasn't as worried about them. Kidnapping was a local matter, not a federal crime, but both Maplethorpes were on the most wanted list, so it was agreed that if Sullivan helped capture them it would count as two against his quota. He made sure he got that in writing.

The rest of the day was spent chasing leads to nowhere. Nobody had heard anything, and if they had they weren't talking. He placed a telephone call to Mrs. Fordyce to inform her that he was still looking, but had no real progress to report. He'd tried to sound encouraging but failed.

When darkness fell, Jake Sullivan returned to his office to prepare. His magic was ready, Power built up in his chest, just waiting to be used to twist gravity to his will. But Power burned quickly, and once it was gone, it took time to replenish. So that meant guns.

One of the Lewis Mk3 machineguns he'd brought back from France was kept hidden under the floorboards of his office. He dragged the huge weapon out, cleaned and oiled it, and loaded the huge drum magazines from boxes of military .30-06 ammunition. Twenty-six pounds of lethal steel, the Lewis was big, ugly, and effective, sort of like Sullivan. It was a lot of gun, but the BI hadn't specified that the Maplethorpes needed to be taken alive.

He'd fought his whole life. He was good at it. As a soldier for his country, as an inmate for survival, and now as a . . . *what am I?* Somebody who didn't know anything else? A slave to the G-men? *No.* It was better if he told himself that he was doing this one for a young widow and to avenge another First Volunteer. It seemed more pure that way.

The Lewis went into a canvas bag. He went downstairs, ordered a late dinner, and waited. Burning Power was like hard physical exercise, so he treated himself to a real good meal in preparation. Mrs. Brooks was glad for the business and didn't even enquire about why the usually frugal Sullivan suddenly seemed to be Mr. Big Spender. A ten-year-old serving as a Purple Gang runner showed up while he was polishing off his coffee, gave him a note, and took off.

Sullivan read the address, finished his drink, put out his smoke, and left a generous tip. It was time again to go to war.

The address was for an auto parts factory on Piquette. Like many other businesses in the area, it had recently been shut down and the workers laid off. He parked a block away and went in on foot. Between the lousy weather, the fact that most of the surrounding businesses were closed, and it was late Christmas Eve meant that there wasn't anyone around. Regular folks were eating hams, singing carols clustered around the fire, or some such thing, not spying on an abandoned factory through a hole in a fence.

After an hour of miserable cold, a blue Dodge rolled up to the back door and a man got out carrying grocer's bags. The lights of the city reflected off the snow clouds enough to give him plenty of pink light to see by. He recognized the lean, broad-shouldered fellow making his way to the back door from one of the sketches Agent Cowley had shown him as one Bruno Hauptmann, a German immigrant and member of the gang. This was the hideout, all right. Hauptmann was walking with a bad limp. He knocked on the back door and a few seconds later it opened and he disappeared inside.

Location confirmed, he debated calling the BI. There was strength in numbers, but the only person Jake Sullivan trusted was Jake Sullivan. The G-men would probably just get in his way, but at the same time, if he got killed, he didn't want the kidnapping trash to escape. Finally, caution won out and he hurried back to the phone booth he'd parked by. The switchboard put him through to Cowley. He gave them the scoop, then reminded the G-man to make sure the rest of his boys knew not to shoot at him. The cavalry was on the way.

But he'd never been the type to wait around for cavalry. Sullivan removed the Lewis gun from his car and headed back to the factory.

They might be watching through the long row of windows, so best to move quick. He reached the fence, and using just enough Power to lighten himself, leapt cleanly over the barrier. The door was solid by any measure, but not built to withstand someone like him. Not even pausing, Sullivan lifted one big boot and kicked the door wide open. The interior was dim, lit only be a single shielded lantern. Hauptmann and another man with one arm in a sling were caught flatfooted just inside, stuffing candy bars in their faces.

Sullivan leveled the machinegun at them. "Hands up."

"Cops!" The stranger went for the revolver stuck in his waistband. Sullivan moved the gaping round muzzle over and simply shot him dead. The body hit the cold concrete without so much as a twitch.

The .30-06 had been deafening against the metal machinery surrounding them. Ears ringing, he turned the gun back on Hauptmann. "Your friend was an idiot. Let's try that again." Terrified, the kidnapper reached for the ceiling. "Better." Sullivan looked down the rows of darkened machines, but there was no sign of anyone else inside. He picked up the lantern and lifted the cover, filling the space with light. Sullivan walked around a big hydraulic press. There were several mattresses and blankets on the floor, but the rest of the gang was out.

Damn. "Where's Fordyce?"

"Who?" Hauptmann asked.

"Don't play stupid." Sullivan concentrated. Using Power in big bursts was easy; fine control took more concentration. He gave Hauptmann another two gravities. The German grimaced and stumbled against the wall. "Talk. Where is he?"

"I don't know what you're talking about!"

"You wanna end up a pancake?" Sullivan dropped one more gravity on him. Hauptmann screamed as bones creaked. "Don't be a baby. I do pushups in that." The kidnapper was surely feeling it. "Where's the Healer?"

"I don't—" Hauptmann's head sprayed red as the window behind him shattered.

Sullivan instinctively flung himself to the floor. A muzzle flashed outside as someone worked a Tommy gun across the glass. He needed cover, fast. There was a thick steel plate leaning against the hydraulic press. With no time for finesse, he grabbed the plate, surged his Power so hard that it felt light as a feather and jerked it around to use as a shield.

Sullivan cursed himself for turning up the lights. *Dummy.* The others must have returned and seen them inside. Bruno Hauptmann was a few feet away, missing a chunk of skull, just staring at him while his brains leaked out. At least that guy's kidnapping days were surely over.

The bullets kept on hitting the plate in a seemingly never-ending stream of hot lead. They'd get tired soon. Sullivan checked his pocket watch. Cowley's men should be here any minute. Then he noticed the time.

Well, Merry Christmas to me.

The BI rolled up, ready for a fight. They just hadn't expected the fight to be ready for them. The first car to arrive was hit immediately. Bullets pierced the radiator, the windows, but luckily not the two agents inside, who bailed out, took cover behind their vehicle and returned fire. A Detroit police car arrived from the opposite direction thirty seconds later. It, too, took fire from a member of the Maplethorpe Gang armed with a stolen BAR. Within a minute two other cars had arrived, and the street collapsed into a chaotic gun battle that the morning papers would describe as the Detroit Christmas Massacre.

However, Special Agent Sam Cowley was not thinking about how this would play out in the media. That was his bosses' job. Cowley was too busy being pinned down behind the rapidly disintegrating engine block of his car as an automatic weapon poked holes in it. The Maplethorpe Gang had a reputation for using overwhelming force during their robberies, which is what made them such high-profile targets. Most of them were vets of the Great War—from both sides—and they knew how to work together. The responding officers were outmatched as the gang moved out of the factory's parking area, using the low brick walls for cover, taking turns shooting while the others moved or reloaded.

A nearby officer cried out and dropped his pistol. The gun metal gleamed with ice crystals. Cowley gasped in pain as he was hit with a surge of unbelievable cold. Snowball was attacking. Cowley rolled out from under the car but couldn't spot the Active. He got a bead on one of the gang and emptied his .38 at him. He couldn't tell if he'd struck the man or not since he ducked behind the factory wall and disappeared.

There was an unholy scream. Cowley turned to see that Johnny Bones had flanked them. The Shard ripped his claws free from an officer's belly, then he came at Cowley, grinning, his skull flowing and twisting under his skin. Terrified, the agent broke open his revolver, punched out the empties, and tried to reload with numb, shivering fingers. Johnny Bones aimed his Thompson at Cowley.

Then it was as if someone had thrown an invisible lasso around the Shard and yanked him sideways. Johnny flew through the air and collided violently with a light pole. The Tommy gun clattered away. The Shard got up slowly as his bones returned to their normal shape. "Kill the Heavy!" he ordered.

The parolee, Sullivan, burst through the window and rolled through the snow as a wave of force tossed the criminals every which way. Sullivan rose, cutting down his enemies like an avenging angel, wielding a giant black rifle that ripped an unending stream of thunder.

"The big one's on our side!" Cowley shouted.

Sullivan ducked. The wall above him was instantly frosted over. Even from across the street Cowley could see the ice particles striking the Heavy, but the Icebox was behind cover and he didn't have a shot. But cover didn't matter to Sullivan. Grimacing through the frostbite, he focused in on the Icebox's position and Snowball Maplethorpe *fell* into the sky. Sullivan calmly shouldered his machinegun, like a sportsman shooting waterfowl, and blasted the Icebox out of the air.

"*Mikey!*" Jonny Bones shrieked as his brother was riddled with bullets. Sullivan must have cut his Power, because Snowball dropped back to the Earth, to lay crumpled, staining the snow pink. "You son of a bitch!" Bones took a few steps forward, then realized that the rest of his gang was in a bad way. The Shard turned and ran down the street.

Sullivan dropped his now-empty machinegun and took off after Johnny Bones. Cowley closed the cylinder on his Smith & Wesson and aimed at the fleeing Shard. "Stop," Sullivan ordered, and as the big man ran past, he said, "We need one alive."

He'd fought a Shard in Rockville once. Just another punk with a chip on his shoulder, thinking that if he could off the toughest guy on the block that would somehow make him king. Sullivan had ended his life, just like all the idiots before him, and all that came after, but it had been a valuable learning experience.

Shard magic worked on a biological level. Their skin was remarkably tough and elastic, their bones could change shape and density as they desired. They were rare, and loathed by the public, considered disgusting freaks . . .Sullivan felt bad for them, but that was still no excuse for kidnapping. Disfiguring magic or not, Johnny Bones was done.

A police car roared into the next intersection, sirens blaring. Johnny slid to a stop in the middle of the street. He looked around, but there was nowhere left to run. He saw Sullivan coming with .45 raised in one hand. Desperate, Johnny spread his arms wide. "I ain't got no gun. You gonna shoot me down like a dog in the street, Heavy?" His breath came out in a cloud of steam.

"Where's Arthur Fordyce?"

"You killed my brother!" Johnny struck himself in the chest. "Come on, finish it. I ain't going to Rockville and I ain't going to the chair."

Sullivan's Power had just been burned too hard for him to do anything fancy with it. He didn't dare try the trick he'd done to Hauptmann. He'd probably just accidently splatter Johnny all over Detroit. "Tell me what you did to him."

Johnny Bones started walking toward Sullivan. "If you don't got the balls to shoot me down like a man . . ." The Shard's fingers were suddenly twice as long as normal and ended in points like needles. "I'll just take you with me."

Sullivan sensed that there were G-men coming up behind him. "Hold your fire and stay out of this," Sullivan ordered, and even though he wasn't in charge of these men in any way, when he used his sergeant's voice, men knew not to question. None of the cops said a word as Sullivan put his Colt back in the holster. "I'll kill you clean, Johnny, but not until you tell me what I want to know."

The Shard swung. His Power-fueled body was a killing instrument. Sullivan ducked away, narrowly avoiding the claws. Johnny slid sideways as Sullivan twisted gravity, but his own Power was overheated and scattered. It lacked force, and Sullivan couldn't risk giving him a good spike without killing the man. Sullivan raised his fists and the two Actives circled, looking for an opening.

Johnny came at him with a flurry of potentially lethal jabs. It would have been intimidating to anyone else. Calm, Sullivan timed it, cocked his fist back, and slammed the Shard square in the face. Johnny's entire skull seemed to squish to one side. He reeled away and Sullivan saw his chance. He slugged Johnny again and again. The Shard wasn't the only one with a magically hardened body, but Sullivan's came from years of exercising in increased gravity until his bones were dense as stone, and now he used them to beat Johnny *down*.

He pressed the attack and drove a fist deep into Johnny's guts, knocking the air right out of his opponent. "Not used to somebody who can fight back, huh?" When Johnny went to his knees, Sullivan circled, came from behind, wrapped one arm around Jonny's throat and used the other to pin the Shard's elbows to his side. Sullivan hoisted the much smaller man into the air and choked the shit out of him. "*Where's Fordyce?*" he shouted in Johnny's ear.

There was a sudden piercing heat through Sullivan's left forearm. He grunted and let go, stepping away as the bone spike pulled through his muscle. Blood came gushing from the wound and splattered the snow. Johnny raised his arm. A narrow shard had extruded from Johnny's elbow and it was painted red. Sullivan looked at the hole in his arm. "Haven't seen that before."

"You killed my brother, you bastard . . ." Johnny gasped, blood running freely from his nose and down his shirt. He charged and Sullivan struck him square in the throat. Johnny hit the ground with a gurgle.

"Yeah. Your Power don't do much for the soft bits. . . . Where's Fordyce?"

Johnny Bones' face was purple as he staggered to his feet. "I don't know who you're yappin' about. You keep saying that name. Means nothing to me."

"The Healer you kidnapped."

Johnny stopped and started to laugh like Sullivan had just said the funniest thing ever. "Him? You think I took *him*?" The laugh grew harsh and desperate. Johnny knew his time was up. "You been played, Heavy. Check my boys. We ain't had no Mending . . ."

The man he'd shot in the factory . . . His arm had been in a sling. Hauptmann had been walking with a bad limp. This crew had never had a Healer . . . Sullivan had played the chump.

People had come out from somewhere into the street to see what was going on, kept back only by the circle of lawmen. They stood there, two Actives, having fought like gladiators for the crowd. Sullivan surveyed the cops and the witnesses, sighed, and let his injured arm hang limp at his side.

The Shard faced him, eyes desperate, seething with Power as more stabbing chunks of bones stretched his skin. Nothing left to use, he was going to burn it all. Misshapen and jagged, Johnny no longer looked human.

"Stand down, Shard. It don't have to be like this." Sullivan drew his .45.

"Maybe before you used my brother as skeet . . . Ain't got nothing to live for now."

Johnny Bones bellowed as he charged. Sullivan extended his hand and fired three times.

Sullivan gave the BI his statement. He got read the riot act by Special Agent in Charge Price, who was more upset about having to talk to the bloodthirsty press than he was that three police officers had been severely wounded. It was going to take some spin to say that a running gun battle in the streets was a good thing, but at least he did have a pile of dead gangsters to show for it. Surprisingly, Agent Cowley stuck up for Sullivan, said that they'd been unprepared for how much firepower the Maplethorpes had brought to bear, and that they shouldn't have driven right into a bullet storm.

Sullivan was kicking himself for calling the BI to begin with—he should have just handled it himself—but he was even angrier that he'd been set up. They plugged the hole in his arm and wrapped it in a bandage. Just a new scar to join the constellation of old scars . . . There would be no fancy Healings on the taxpayers' dime for some dumb Heavy.

Cowley had come up to him at one point and thanked him for saving his life. Sullivan wasn't used to gratitude from official types and didn't really know what to say in return. The exhausted agent took a seat across from him. "Sure has been one heck of a night. Not just for us, but all over town . . . Sounds like one of your local gangs decided to clean house, too. One of them Purples got hit. Abe Something-witz."

"Horowitz?"

"That's the name. Tough guy from what I was told. Had to be an inside job since they got him at home. No sign of forced entry, so he let them in. Pow. Single bullet right in the back of the head. Found him in the kitchen with a bottle of wine open and a glass in each hand."

Sullivan clammed up on the topic. Cowley thanked him again for saving his life and left to send a report to his superiors. Then after another few hours of answering the same questions over and over again, Sullivan was free to go.

About damn time. He had questions of his own that need to be answered.

"Mae found your body. You owe me twenty-five bucks and a present."

Sullivan was in a phone booth not far from the police station. "Dead or alive?"

"Not just dead, but sliced into pieces dead," Bernie answered. "That's why it took Mae so long to find him."

Sullivan groaned and rested his forehead on the cold glass. It had all been for nothing. "Where?"

"All over the city. Five, maybe six different places so far. Maybe more she hasn't found yet, but I told her that was good enough. Mae found the first piece in a deli uptown. She says most of him had already been eaten."

Chopped into pieces and . . . "Did you say *eaten?*"

"Yeah. Of course. People ate him."

What kind of sickos was he dealing with here? "Bernie, you're telling me somebody chopped up Arthur and *ate* him?"

"Yeah . . . Why's that so weird?" Bernie chuckled. Sullivan didn't see what was so damn funny, since there was a gang of cannibal lunatics on the loose in Detroit. "Huh . . . Arthur. That's a funny name for a porker."

"Porker?" Fordyce hadn't been fat.

"Porker. Pig. You know, oink oink, pink with a curly tail . . . Oh . . . Wait . . . Mae says he was one of the white with brown spots kind."

The blood in Fordyce's car . . . He hadn't given Bernie any details about the case, just asked him to find the body that the blood had come from. "Thanks, Bernie," Sullivan mumbled as he returned the earphone to the cradle.

The Fordyce home was the nicest one on a very nice street. The sun hadn't been up for very long when Sullivan arrived, left arm bandaged and throbbing, to bang on the door. The butler tried to shoo him away, but Sullivan pushed his way inside and told the man in no uncertain terms what would happen if he didn't get Mrs. Fordyce. The butler threatened to call the police. Sullivan said good.

After being escorted into the study, he took a seat on an overstuffed couch and waited, reading the spines of the hundreds of books on the walls. The collection made him envious. Emily Fordyce joined him a few minutes later, still tying the waist sash of an oriental silk robe. Her hair was undone and hung to her shoulders.

"Late night?" he asked.

"Yes, I've just been so worried." But they both knew that's why she hadn't gotten much sleep. "Have you any news?"

Sullivan shook his head. "You're a real piece of work, lady."

Emily stopped. "Why . . . whatever do you mean?"

"You can drop the act. I know I'm not the one that did *all* the killing last night. So how long have you known Horowitz? Must have been long enough that he wasn't scared to turn his back on you."

"I don't know what you're talking about."

"You sent me to Horowitz. He sent me to Bones, who was such a rabid dog that you figured there was no way he'd be taken alive for questioning. Horowitz wanted him gone and Bones was as good a scapegoat as you'd ever find. Then you shot Horowitz because the only way two people can keep a secret is if one of them's dead."

The shocked expression that briefly crossed her lovely face said that he'd gotten close enough. She tried to play indignant. "How dare you accuse me!" She pointed at the door. "Get out!"

Sullivan stayed planted on the couch. "Why the pig blood?"

"How—" She caught herself too late. Emily's arm fell. "If you knew Arthur, you'd know that the pig was appropriate. Well, I do say . . . You are smarter than you look."

"Just a bit," Sullivan said. "I'm assuming you had Horowitz stage the crime scene. You don't strike me as the type that likes getting your own hands dirty."

Resigned, she walked around behind the ornate desk and flopped into Arthur's wide rolling chair. "Not usually . . . The authorities had to declare that Arthur was dead before I could collect his insurance. I wanted to be elsewhere at the time for an alibi."

Sullivan looked over at the giant painting of Arthur Fordyce hanging over the fireplace. "So, where's your husband?"

She shrugged. "Argentina, I think. He's run off again with one of his many mistresses. *Again.* The man's seventy-five with the libido of an eighteen-year-old sailor. He does this all the time. He'll be gone for weeks, sometimes months, before he crawls back, begging forgiveness."

It was actually more surprising that he was alive than that he was a philanderer. "But why make it look like he was dead if he's coming back?"

"Timing, Mr. Sullivan, timing. I had to be ready to act as soon as he ran off again. Arthur is declared legally dead. I get the insurance money, which is significant—let me tell you—I clean out the accounts and I leave the country. The jerk comes home to find out he's dead and broke. Serves him right."

"If you hated him so much, why didn't you just leave him?"

"I married that old fool for his money. I just didn't realize how awful *long* a Healer can stick around." She rolled her eyes. "I divorce him, I get nothing. It's hard to poison a Healer slow enough to make it look natural. They just keep making themselves better. Believe me, I thought about just shooting him in the night and blaming it on robbers. The kidnapping was Abe's idea."

"How'd you know Horowitz?"

Emily was looking around the desktop for something, suddenly she swept aside a book to reveal a small revolver hidden beneath. "Aha!" she shouted as she reached for it. She'd shoot him, say it was self-defense or something . . . but Sullivan's Power had recovered from last night's escapade. He slammed multiple gravities down on the little gun. Emily tugged on it, grunting and pulling, but she couldn't budge it. "Damn you, Heavy!"

"Unless you're secretly a Brute, you're not going to lift that piece . . ." He took out a smoke and struck a match. "So how'd you know Horowitz?"

Red faced, she gave up. "I was a dancer in one of his joints. That's how I met Arthur . . . Arthur met lots of girls through Abe. I was just the first one sharp enough to catch him. Ugh . . . I can't believe I'm admitting that."

"I can see why. You do put on a great show."

"Five years later, the old bastard was still kicking so we hatched this little plot . . . Timing was perfect, Arthur left again, and there was a crew that Abe wanted gone anyway, to blame. Plus they were too stupid to get taken alive, and even if they denied it, nobody would believe a filthy Shard. Should have been perfect."

"Arthur didn't recommend me at all. Horowitz did."

"Sure, you and Arthur were in the same unit, but he didn't know you from Adam. Abe couldn't tip the cops off without implicating himself. He said you had a killer's rep and you were motivated to keep the G-men off your back. Two birds, one stone, he said." She gave the revolver one last pensive tug. "So what now?"

"I decide what do with you."

Emily was thinking hard and that was dangerous. "Abe got greedy, but once the insurance comes in, I've still got his share." She rose from the seat and walked over to Sullivan while untying the sash on her robe. Stopping in front of him, she let the silk hang open, revealing that she wasn't wearing much of anything underneath. "Poor little me . . . Defenseless against a big strong man like you. Oh, have mercy, Mr. Sullivan . . . I can make it worth your time."

"I bet you could. . . ." Sullivan blew out a cloud of smoke as he examined the dancer's body. Emily waited, smirking. This was a woman who was used to getting what she wanted. He stood up, gently took the edges of her robe in hand, appeared to think about it for just a second, and then covered her back up before stepping away. "But that would've been more tempting if you'd tried to seduce me *before* you tried to shoot me."

"You no good—"

Sullivan looked toward the ceiling. "Mae! It's time to go." There was a sudden blast of wind as something stirred in the room. Emily's hair whipped wildly and she had to struggle to keep her robe shut. The fireplace popped and sparked as something flew up the chimney and disappeared.

"What was *that*?"

"That's Mae, a disembodied spirit. I brought her with me. Sweet girl, considering what she looks like. I had her record our talk and she'll be able to show it to anybody with a Finder."

"But . . . No judge will allow that. No jury is going to take the word of a demon, you idiot. You've got nothing. I'll deny this whole thing. You're a felon and a stupid Heavy. I'm somebody now. Nobody will believe the likes of you!"

"I'm not going to show it to the law, girl. I sent her to the *Purple Gang* . . ." Those two words hung in the air like the smoke from his cigarette. "I'm sure they're mighty anxious to know who murdered their admiral."

"No . . ." Emily sank to her knees. "Oh no."

"I'll be keeping your advance because I did solve the case." Sullivan paused briefly on his way out the door. "And if I were you, I'd start running. Considering those Purple boys, you're gonna want a head start."

Outside, he could still hear the screams of frustration and the breaking of furniture but the sounds faded as he walked down the steps to his automobile. He needed to get some sleep, but first he owed Bernie some tin foil.

The snow had really cleaned the air. There were kids running in the road, pulling each other on the sleds they'd just found under the tree. The people next door had built a snowman. It was a beautiful morning. Sure, he'd been tricked, lied to, stabbed, and had killed several men, but they'd had it coming, and he'd knocked two more off of J. Edgar Hoover's to-do list. So all in all, not too shabby . . .

As far as Christmases went, he'd had worse.

THE GRIMNOIR CHRONICLES: MURDER ON THE *ORIENT ELITE*

This story was originally written as an Audible exclusive. This is the first time it has appeared in print. It is set in the Grimnoir Chronicles universe and takes place a few years after the novel Warbound. *So, spoiler alert, you might want to save this story until after you finish that trilogy.*

Casablanca, Morocco
August 1st, 1937

"**ARE YOU** Jake Sullivan?"

That was his name, but it wasn't the name he'd been going by in this country. He took his time looking up from his drink. The bartender was standing in front of him, wiping out a glass with a grey rag. Sullivan had never been very good at undercover work, but that was his own fault for being so big. He stood out, especially in polite company, where even a casual look could confirm that he was the toughest man in any given room. He glanced down the bar, but the place was packed and a piano was playing, so he doubted anybody else had heard the name.

His lack of response told the bartender a story. This was the sort of establishment where business you didn't ask questions about was conducted. "Sorry, friend. I must've got the wrong giant, scarred-up American, built like a Heavy."

Sullivan finished off his whisky. If it was the Grimnoir trying to find him they'd have just contacted him through his magic ring. If anybody else was looking for him here, it was either for something important, or to set up an ambush. Either way, his cover was blown, so it was time to move on. There was no need to keep on pretending to be a low rent thug looking for work. He'd been hoping to be approached by the gang of Active criminals tearing up the countryside, but there was no chance of that now.

"How'd you know I was American?"

The bartender lowered his voice conspiratorially. "We get lots of expatriates here. Your fake Irish accent isn't very good."

"And this whole time I thought I sounded just like my old man." Sullivan chuckled as he slid his empty glass across the bar. The bartender surprised him by pulling out a bottle of the good stuff. "Easy there, pal. I'm not made of money." That was a lie. Nowadays he had access to more funds than he knew what to do with, but once a man had been truly poor, he never again felt rich.

"Word's got out. We were told to be on the lookout because Heavy Jake Sullivan's in town tracking down some Active slavers. If you're really Jake Sullivan, there's no way you're paying for drinks in this establishment," the bartender explained as he poured. "We may be at the edge of nowhere, but we still get the news. Late, but we get it. A big damned hero shouldn't ever have to buy his own drink."

"Thanks."

Most of the really interesting things he'd done had never showed up in the papers, so the bartender had to be a supporter of Actives or a magical himself. Either that or he was secretly an Imperium spy, or a Soviet agent, or one of a dozen other groups with a grudge against him . . . And the booze would be poisoned, but the bartender had an honest face, so Sullivan picked up the whisky and took a drink. *Smooth.* That really was the good stuff.

"So who's looking for me?"

"Some big shot out of Shanghai. They call him the Alienist."

"Aw hell . . ."

The note that had been passed around the criminal underworld of Casablanca would look like gibberish to most people, but for its intended target, the designs were obviously part of a communication spell. The Alienist—Doctor Wells to his acquaintances—had gotten better at spellbinding since the last time they'd worked together. Sullivan had gone back to the privacy of his hotel and scratched the design into a small mirror he'd purchased from the bazaar. Experience had taught him that glass usually worked better than sand or salt, especially since the coast of Africa was a long way from Shanghai.

Wells' magical formula was good, but Sullivan took the runes and added a few improvements of his own design. Nobody was better at spellbinding than Sullivan, and he got the spell to work on the first try. It didn't even take that much of his Power to make the connection. He must have overestimated the distance.

Dr. Wells appeared in the mirror. He was sitting behind a dark wood desk in a fat red chair, surrounded by shelves full of books and a gigantic grandfather clock right behind him. There was an ornate elephant rifle hung on the wall. The view was as clear as looking through a window. The slim man hadn't changed much. His hair was a little thinner, but other than that he looked as calm and unthreatening as ever. Considering Wells was what the Rockville Prison head shrinkers had called a sociopath, and he'd manipulated and murdered his way to the top of the Chinese underworld, he sure didn't look like much.

"Hey, Doc."

"You appear hale and hearty as ever, Sullivan. Rumors of your demise were greatly exaggerated. What's it been since we blew up half of Shanghai? Four years now?"

They both knew Dr. Wells knew exactly how long it had been, down to the minute probably, because the man had a brain like a Turing machine. "Something like that."

Though he was gifted with a rare physical type of magic, specifically being a Massive capable of altering his density, Wells was a true intellectual. He'd been a psychologist before growing bored and turning to crime. The man was brilliant, but Sullivan didn't trust him as far as he could throw him. And since Sullivan's own magical ability was related to the manipulation of gravity, so he reckoned he could hurl Wells a considerable distance.

"I'd heard that they'd made you one of the leaders of the Grimnoir Society. Good for them. Though I always thought the Grimnoir Elders were the type to issue orders from an office, where they had their secretaries take memos to send to men like Talon or that surly German to carry out. You seem a bit too *hands-on* for their style. It wasn't surprising when one of my sources said you were poking around Casablanca looking for fights to pick. Forgive my interruption. I'm certain you are very busy exposing some conspiracy, righting wrongs and whatnot. Let no one ever say that Jake Sullivan isn't a man of action."

"Get to the point, Wells."

The Alienist smiled. "Oh, come on, Sullivan. It's been a rare treat in my life to have someone worthy of matching wits against. Haven't you missed our verbal sparring?"

"No."

"Not even a little bit?"

Sullivan shook his head in the negative. The more words you gave to Wells, the more he learned about you, and the more he learned about you, the more he would eventually use against you. Once a snake, always a snake, and even though this particular snake had been really helpful in defeating the Pathfinder, that didn't mean he wasn't still an extremely poisonous snake.

"Down to business then. I need a favor. There's a mystery in need of solving and I believe you to be the man for the job."

With a normal person, he'd have asked what exactly the favor entailed, but since this was Doctor Wells they were talking about . . . "I'm predisposed to tell you to buzz off."

"But you won't, because you're by nature a very curious man. Since you are now a leader of a secret society of do-gooders spread across the entirety of the globe, I'm assuming you are also a very well informed man. You know of my current social status?"

"Crime boss?"

"Someone needed to clean up the mess we'd made." Wells waved one hand dismissively. "I'm now a successful businessman who has diversified into the gambling, tourism, and entertainment industries of the Far East. But surely, you are wondering why somebody with access to my resources would be asking you for help. Come on, Sullivan. Work it out like the old days."

Sullivan yawned.

"Fine." Wells seemed honestly disappointed that Sullivan wouldn't play his guessing game. "Time is of the essence and I have no associates close enough to deal with this particular problem, or at least any associates smart enough not to muck up everything. I'd handle it myself, but I'm in Shanghai. Luckily, it turns out you are in the right place at the right time, were once a rather capable detective, and I know for a fact you don't have any problem squishing evildoers."

As much as he'd love to hear Wells' interpretation of what qualified somebody as evil, he really wasn't in the mood for his brand of crazy today. "What's the problem?"

"As part of my legitimate business concerns . . . Don't snicker, I'm serious. I secretly purchased a shipping line. We recently took possession of a new luxury passenger vessel, one of the finest airships to ever come out of UBF. It cost me a fortune. Tell your little friend Francis that he really outdid himself this time. The *Orient Elite* is on its maiden voyage, circumnavigating the world and making stops at all of the finest establishments along the way. Gambling, entertainment, beautiful women, it is a once-in-a-lifetime sort of adventure, all very expensive and prestigious, you know, so I had society's finest practically murdering each other for a ticket."

"Darn. I missed it."

"Your invitation must have been lost in the mail. You have my apology. Let me make it up to you. I've already arranged your ticket. Luckily, my ship just left Paris and will be stopping in Casablanca before crossing the ocean to Buenos Aires."

"Why?"

"I believe there to be a saboteur aboard, planning on blowing up my expensive new airship with all of those wealthy potential investors on board. It might only be a troubling rumor, but I can't afford to cancel this voyage. These are not the sort of clients who like to be disturbed over mere rumors, and my passenger list also includes some elements of society who would not like entangling the authorities. I do not wish to alarm anyone. Best case scenario is you take a luxury cruise, nothing more. An industrious man such as yourself, why I'm sure you could use a vacation. I simply prefer to be cautious. It is probably nothing."

That was doubtful. Wells wouldn't talk to the Grimnoir if it wasn't serious.

"Who's behind it?"

"I don't know who the saboteur is or what their nefarious motivations might be. I have extremely important passengers from twenty nations onboard—"

"Imperium?" If anybody was up to no good, it would be those bastards.

"Obviously. I am a neutral party in the Cold War between East and West. The passengers are mostly businessmen, diplomats, celebrities, not to mention a few high-ranking members of . . . well, let's be honest and say major criminal organizations. Don't judge me, Sullivan. I'm only trying to make friends, I promise. You know how messy politics can be. Regardless, I'd like to prevent a horrific tragedy."

"You expect me to believe you're actually worried about the passengers' safety?"

Wells snorted. "Protecting the innocent is your thing. When I said tragedy, I was thinking about what this would do to my reputation, not to mention that my insurance costs will go through the roof should the *Oriental Elite* turn into a giant fireball. But if it helps you make a decision, there are five hundred souls aboard."

His case here was at a dead end, and Wells seemed to be telling the truth, or at least as much truth as somebody like Wells was capable of. *I'm such a sucker,* he thought to himself.

"Here's the deal. I do this, you owe the Shanghai Grimnoir a huge favor."

"I'm sure young Master Zhao will be overjoyed to hear that."

"I want every bit of information you can think of. I want all the details, and have your people have a copy of the passenger manifest ready for me. By the way, when I say favor, I mean if Zhao wants your gangs to storm the Imperial Palace, they'd better sing a song while they do it."

"You have a deal, Sullivan. I'll alert the captain that you'll be joining—"

"Alert nobody about nothing. Book me a place in steerage under a fake name."

"Ah, that's very wise of you. However, I don't think you understand the nature of my ship. There is no *steerage*. The *Oriental Elite* is first class all the way. On that note . . ." Wells sniffed disapprovingly. "Is that your best outfit?"

"Yep." Sullivan looked down at his suit. By his standards it was downright fancy. "All the bullet holes have been patched and they're even the same color."

"I can't believe you actually pal around with billionaires. That won't do. The *Oriental Elite* lands in six hours. That's time enough for you to be fitted for a proper tuxedo."

Shoot. When he'd agreed to this he hadn't known he'd have to wear a penguin suit.

Wells' original clue that something was wrong had come in the form of a bomb found stashed in the cargo compartment of the *Oriental Elite*. It hadn't been a very big one, but on an airship it was all about *where* you stuck the explosive rather than the quantity of the payload. Sullivan didn't have the exact details, but it had been big enough to make a mess of things. But the timer hadn't been set; the bomb was wrapped up and hidden to be used later. Sadly, the captain had been in a hurry to get the bomb off his ship and had tossed it over the side *after* disturbing the scene enough to tip off the saboteur. If they'd just left it there, Sullivan could have simply watched and waited for his target to show to retrieve it.

After binding a few spells that he thought might prove useful, picking up some uncomfortable new duds, and sending a message on to the Society and his wife about his side trip—Akane was used to this sort of thing from him—he'd gone to the Casablanca air station to catch his ride. The *Oriental Elite* was a long tri-hull, built for comfort and stability rather than speed. She looked like a whale compared to the sleek *Traveler* that Sullivan had come to know so well. The *Oriental Elite* was a huge ship, impressive as all get-out, and cast a considerable shadow over the city.

Now he just needed to figure out how to keep some maniac from crashing her.

Wells hadn't been exaggerating about his ship or his clientele.

The *Oriental Elite* wasn't *Kaga* or *Tokugawa* big by any means, and it certainly didn't have any Tesla super weapons aboard, but it was a really impressive feat of engineering nonetheless. Not only because it was seven hundred feet long, but because Sullivan had never realized something could fly with this much furniture in it. The airship he'd spent the most time on, the *Traveler,* had been sparse in comparison, with an interior that was all grates, pipes, and no-frills business. The *Oriental Elite* was all frills. This thing probably had twenty tons of red carpet onboard. Some of the stairs were real marble. What kind of lunatic put a bunch of rocks inside his airship? If it wasn't for the view out the main glass dome revealing that they were a few thousand feet over West Africa, he could have imagined he was in a casino in Atlantic City . . . only there wasn't anything in Atlantic City this plush.

Sullivan stood on a balcony overlooking the main casino floor and watched the crowd, trying to pick out the various players. In a way it reminded him a little bit of Shanghai, and not just because of the decorations. Shanghai had seemed to collect adventurous types at the ragged edge of the civilized world, and Wells had captured that vibe. Since he'd boarded, he'd heard Chinese, Japanese, French, German, Russian, English, and some other languages he couldn't place. Every sign was in multiple languages, though he noted English was on top. Wells had probably just done that to poke the Imperium.

From what he'd seen so far, the *Oriental Elite* was like one big snooty party, with rich folks rubbing elbows, drinking expensive booze, and telling each other how brilliant they were. It wasn't his thing. Sullivan had never been much for socializing, especially with the moneyed crowd. Francis would have been far better suited for this job. According to the manifest, most of the passengers had bought a ticket in one city and then got off at the next stop. Very few had the time or money to do the whole leisurely round-the-world trip, but those that did would have bragging rights, and it seemed that in this crowd bragging rights were everything.

The balcony was loud. A big band was playing at the far end of the main hall, and Wells hadn't skimped on the talent. They were good. The casino itself was filled with dozens of conversations, loud laughter, boisterous shouting, and the chatter of spinning roulette wheels. That was probably why he hadn't heard the man approach. It wasn't until he sensed the subtle shift in gravity that he realized he wasn't alone.

Getting sloppy in my old age. Sullivan exercised a little bit of his Power so he could feel the world around him as it really was, broken down into its component bits of matter, density, and forces. His visitor massed nearly as much as Sullivan did, was carrying some dense metal under one armpit that could only be a pistol in a shoulder holster. But then, suddenly, gravity shifted as the newcomer exercised his own magic and Sullivan was pushed back into the normal world. He was dealing with another Gravity Spiker, and a talented one at that.

"Turn around." It wasn't a request. Bossy and with a Japanese accent. That more than likely meant Iron Guard.

Sullivan stayed leaning on the railing. "Don't feel like it."

"Very well." The Jap put his elbows on the railing, leaned next to him, and pretended to watch the casino. Now they were only a few feet away from each other. He was far younger than Sullivan, probably just out of their academy, but was a solid block of muscle. They were dressed the same, as in black and fancy, only the Jap was sporting the blue sash of the Imperium diplomatic corps. Though there wasn't much diplomatic about his approach.

"Don't try anything stupid. I know who you are."

"I doubt it." His ticket said that he was Fred Smith, a successful tool and die maker from Detroit, and Mr. Smith had no problem with these jokers and their schemes for world domination.

"Do not play games with me, Grimnoir," the Iron Guard snarled. "All of us know who you are, Sullivan. We are shown your photograph in training."

Their two groups currently had an informal peace, but it wasn't much of one. Sullivan had gotten the tux tailored so he could still conceal the big .45 on his belt, but if an Iron Guard was looking for trouble, then Sullivan wasn't going to use bullets. These bastards took too damned long to kill that way. Calm, Sullivan gathered up his considerable Power and got ready to smash the Iron Guard through the balcony.

"There is no need to be impolite," the Iron Guard warned as he sensed the magic building. "You are safe for now. Toru Tokugawa has declared that Jake Sullivan and his family are off limits."

"Well, that's mighty nice of him."

"I do not like it, but you are not to be targeted. I do not understand his reasoning, but I will obey his orders to leave you alone."

"It's a respect thing. You wouldn't understand."

"*Unless* you are to meddle in Iron Guard affairs, then your life is forfeit."

"Toru was always pragmatic like that."

It was obvious that the Iron Guard was itching for a fight. He was too young to have served in Shanghai, and probably thought the stories of Sullivan's battle there were exaggerated. Different culture, different country, different army, but hard cases like this were always the same. The youngster was cocky and wanted a shot at the title.

"Why are you here?" the Iron Guard demanded.

"Gambling, pretty ladies, good music, the usual."

What was an Iron Guard doing on this ship? Sabotage would have been a Shadow Guard assignment, and he'd never see one of them coming. This was a pleasure cruise, and from what he knew of the Imperium elite magical troops, they weren't big on relaxation. Their idea of pleasure was burning villages. Sullivan kept scanning the crowd until he noticed a distinguished older Japanese man sitting at one of the blackjack tables, only his eyes were on the balcony rather than his cards. Another Japanese tough guy who also had that Iron Guard look about him was stationed near the old man.

"So who's that fellow you're protecting?"

"He is none of your concern. " The young Iron Guard leaned in close and sneered, "I do not know why you are here. Cross us and you will die. Interfere with my mission and I will personally end your life, and then the lives of your traitorous woman and your half-breed children. I will—"

Sullivan moved so fast that when the back of his big fist connected, it flattened the young man's nose. All Iron Guard were masters of hand-to-hand combat, but nobody reacted well when they got their nose broke. He stumbled away, surprised.

Sullivan adjusted his coat, and then went back to leaning on the railing. He didn't so much as raise his voice. "Mention my kids again and you'll get more of the same."

It didn't matter how tough you were or how many healing spells you had carved on your body, a sucker punch to the snout was always unpleasant. It had been so sudden that the Iron Guard just stood there for a moment, blinking, as blood came rolling out of his nostrils to splatter his sash. This would now go one of two ways . . . Luckily, the young soldier had enough presence of mind not to turn this into a full-on fight to the death without getting permission first. He looked across the casino toward the old man—he'd apparently watched the whole thing—but he frowned and shook his head in the negative.

The kid was mad and wanted to fight, but these guys were big on following orders no matter what. "I will not forget this insult." His voice sounded funny with the flat nose. The Iron Guard took out a handkerchief and pushed it against his bloody face, then turned and fled the balcony.

Sullivan checked his surroundings. None of the other passengers seemed to have noticed the altercation. *Good.* He cracked his knuckles. Maybe this rich folks' party wouldn't be so boring after all.

Sullivan had found one of the serving girls who spoke English, given her a bribe, and found out that the old fellow the Imperium elites answered to was named Professor Nishimura. The name was familiar. Toru's fancy battle armor in Shanghai had been made by a Cog by that name, and he'd also invented the Imperium *gakutensoku*, their version of the mechanical men that they'd taken to calling robots in America. If the professor was the same man, it would explain why he rated an escort of multiple Iron Guards. Nishimura was no Buckminster Fuller, but a Cog of that skill level was worth way more than his weight in gold.

As much as he hated the Imperium, Sullivan had to set aside his personal bias and admit it was unlikely that the Imperium would be trying to blow up a cruise ship with one of their most valuable geniuses on board. Since his goal was to stop a saboteur, not break the Grimnoir's fragile peace with the Imperium, Sullivan had spent fifty bucks and had the girl deliver a bottle of apology scotch to the professor for breaking his man's nose.

Most of the passenger cabins were on the floor beneath the casino, and Sullivan returned to his to plan his next move. His Grimnoir ring warned him that he was being observed by a disembodied spirit. Either the Imperium had a Finder or a Summoner keeping an eye on him, or he'd attracted somebody else's attention. He didn't even know why he bothered asking for a fake name on his ticket, since in the world of clandestine magical business he was downright famous.

He paused in the hallway. Now that he knew it was there, he could sense the invisible demon floating above him. His initial reaction was to banish it, but come to think of it, if there was a Summoner on board they could easily find the saboteur. A disembodied scout could be a real help. It was worth a shot.

Sullivan cleared his throat. "I know you're there." A small breeze moved through the hall as the demon began to flee. "Hold on, little fella. Tell your boss if he wants to know what I'm up to he can come face me like a man. I'll be in the galley in two hours." Then Sullivan went into his cabin and used his pocket knife to scratch some runes in the doorframe to keep the little demon away so he could have some privacy.

It was time to figure out who else might want to blow up the *Oriental Elite,* but first he needed to find out why Doctor Wells had lied to him.

It was easy to find the room he was looking for. It wouldn't be the nicest cabin, because he wouldn't want the attention, but it would be close. It would need a view of the action and it would be easy to secure. His own cabin was nicer than his house, but there was first class, and then there was *first class,* and one set of rooms was on the observatory level between the gas bags. So he'd gone poking around the top decks, picking rooms that had glass walls overlooking the casino. Security was heavy on this deck, so he'd narrowed his search based on what type of goon was guarding which doors.

You could put a suit on a gorilla, but it still looked like a gorilla. The gang tattoos poking out the edges of their sleeves were a dead giveaway. He didn't even have to beat up the two Chinese mobsters because they had seen him coming and got out of the way.

"So, he's been expecting me?"

The thugs stepped aside as they held the door open for him and didn't utter a word. Another thug inside gave him a nod, then disappeared to get his boss. Sullivan entered the dark office that he'd seen earlier through the mirror. He pulled up a comfy red chair in front of the big desk, and waited for his host while listening to the *tick tock* of the grandfather clock and admiring the gold encrusted Holland and Holland .800 Nitro Express rifle mounted on the wall. Now *that* was a hunting gun fit for a rich guy—who also happened to have magic that made him immune to recoil that would kill a normal man.

The thug reappeared, leading two of the ship's attractive female *entertainers* out of the suite. Wells came in a minute later, wearing a robe and a frown. "Sullivan. I'll admit I'm not too surprised to see you here."

"Hey, Doc. I thought you said you were in Shanghai."

"I must have misspoken."

"Nice wall hanger." Sullivan nodded at the gun.

"Yes. I purchased it when I decided to include Africa on this trip. I had visions of hanging from the side and shooting at elephants and rhinos as we crossed the plains."

"That don't sound very sporting."

"The captain told me it wasn't safe to cruise that close to the ground so I cancelled that leg of the trip . . . I told my men not to open fire on the off chance you showed up. I knew you still had it in you to be a good detective. You really are smarter than you look, though that isn't a particularly difficult achievement. How did you know I was aboard?"

"Maiden voyage, guy like you, with this many strings needing to be pulled, isn't going to be thousands of miles from the action. I had a hunch."

"I sailed on the *Titanic's* tenth anniversary cruise. Did you know it hit an iceberg and nearly sank on its maiden voyage? What a loss that would have been. Fate is amusing that way. I wasn't about to build something nicer and miss my chance." The skinny psychologist flopped into his chair on the other side of the desk. He gestured at the grandfather clock. "I even made sure that was set to Shanghai time for you."

"That was a nice touch," Sullivan agreed. He didn't tell Wells that Buckminster Fuller had come up with a way for the Grimnoir to play back the sounds of a communication spell. It turned out that the glass *remembered*. It was a nifty trick. Sullivan had listened to their conversation three times before he'd been certain that he could make out the faint noise of engines and propellers in the background. "Why'd you lie to me?"

"That's sort of my thing."

True enough. "The bomb is real, though. First thing I did was watch your crew. They're nervous, and most of them aren't good at hiding it. So I'm assuming you don't have some convoluted scheme—"

Wells chuckled. "I can assure you. As much as I like to see how far I can push people for my own amusement, I did not bring that bomb onto my own very expensive airship. Even I have limits. I've been conducting my own investigation since we discovered the device over France, but I've been stymied. When I heard you were near our next stop, I realized most of my suspects would know of your reputation, and I recalled fondly how you have a way of shaking things up."

"Like a rockslide," Sullivan agreed.

"I was thinking more like an earthquake. Now that the legendary Jake Sullivan, Knight of the Grimnoir, Public Enemy Number One, the man who singlehandedly stood up to the whole US government, told off Roosevelt, fought the biggest demon ever, and nearly ruined the Imperium, all while saving the whole world from an outer space monster—"

"That's laying it on a bit thick. Faye did all the hard stuff."

"I know that and you know that, but our saboteur probably doesn't. Now that you're here punching out Iron Guard, they'll have no choice but to make a move, and then I'll have them."

"I figured as much. So that's why you didn't want me to know you were onboard."

"If you knew I was here, you'd have been tempted to let me handle it myself." Wells grinned. For once his expression seemed completely genuine. "More importantly, I simply wanted to see if I could get away with it. I've missed you, Sullivan. You know how bored I get without a challenge."

It was a sad commentary on Sullivan's life that he'd worked with enough lunatics that he understood exactly what made them tick. "You want a challenge? I got five whole dollars says I figure out who the bad guy is before you do. Terms are that you have to tell me what you really know."

"It wouldn't be very sporting otherwise. I accept your wager, Mr. Sullivan."

"Was that your demon following me around?"

"Intriguing." Wells stroked his chin thoughtfully. "If I had a Finder aboard able to spy on everyone, I wouldn't need you now, would I?"

That was interesting. So now all he needed to do to save five hundred lives was win a five spot. Sullivan folded his arms and leaned back in his chair. "So let's talk about your passengers . . ."

As was expected, the steak was excellent. They also offered lobster for the New Yorkers and trendy Europeans, but Sullivan still thought of the big water bugs as cheap canned prison food, no matter how much butter you put on them. Despite his wife trying to get him to eat all sorts of weird seafood with eyeballs and tentacles, Sullivan would always stick with a good piece of cow.

He'd not been sure if the man with the demon would show up or not, but just as they'd taken his plate away and Sullivan was enjoying a smoke, a visitor arrived. He was a big fellow, about the same height as Sullivan, probably about ten years younger, and had the look of a tough guy. Sullivan tested his Power. The man had magic, and lots of it, but Sullivan couldn't tell what kind, though whatever it was left him feeling . . . *uneasy*. Not even offering to shake hands, the man pulled out a chair and sat at the table without any ceremony.

"You told the demon that you wished to speak with me."

He sounded German. Since their country had been a wreck since the end of the Great War, that meant he could be working for damned near anybody. "I told the Summoner I wanted to talk. You're not the Summoner."

"How do you know that?"

"Summoners are always squirrely. You look like you'd not be completely useless in a bar fight."

"Why? Are there more Imperium around that you wish to backhand?"

"So you caught that?"

The big German smiled. "I'm the man who sees everything, Herr Sullivan. I rather enjoyed you putting that Imperium swine in his place. You have quite the reputation for killing Imperium."

He wanted to see if he could provoke the guy. "If we were to compare the score, I still probably killed more Germans than anybody else, but it was easy to lose count at Second Somme."

Rather than get angry, the German chuckled. "I missed out on the Great War. When the Peace Ray obliterated Berlin, I was only a boy."

Me too, Sullivan thought bitterly, only he'd spent his late teenage years in the trenches of France. "You didn't miss much."

"The Summoner is one of my men." The threat was implied, he was not alone and Sullivan was. "He delivered your message. I am Otto Skorzeny. What can I do for you?"

Sullivan had never heard of him, if that was his real name at all. "What brings you to the *Oriental Elite*, Mr. Skorzeny?"

"Gambling, pretty ladies, good music, the usual," he answered as he stroked his mustache.

Oh, you really are good. "I swear it's like the walls have ears in this place . . . So you're the guy who sees everything, you happen to see that little fella in the glasses tailing you?" Sullivan nodded toward the front of the restaurant.

Skorzeny used the reflective surface of a framed photograph on the wall to watch the small man at the bar. "He is good, but he is not that good," he answered. "I believe he is a Russian."

Wells had known exactly who that passenger was, since it wasn't every day that some of Stalin's secret police were riding around on your airship. "He's NKVD. Last name of Beria. First name something I can't pronounce. He's a real piece of work. He's only been on the ship since Prague and word is all the serving girls are already scared to death of him, and none of them will be alone in a room with him."

"A classy sort." Skorzeny nodded. "Thank you for that information. I was not aware of his name."

"Were you aware somebody tried to smuggle a bomb on board?" Sullivan asked as he stubbed out his cigarette in the ashtray, carefully watching the German's reaction. "It's big enough to knock this ship out of the sky."

The German was either a really good liar, or he hadn't known. "Perhaps I am not the man who sees *everything* after all."

"This sure is an interesting party. Imperium Iron Guards, Russian spies, little old me . . . So who is it you work for?"

"No one who is of concern to your Grimnoir Society. I doubt we share friends but I know we have mutual enemies." Skorzeny stood up. "Our goals are not in conflict unless you choose to make them so. I like you, Sullivan. I respect your body of work. You are an inspiration to any man who is a student of unconventional warfare. It would be a shame to have to kill you."

He watched the German go. So did the Russian spy. Another Russian he hadn't made before followed the German. That meant the shifty little fellow in glasses was going to stick around to tail Sullivan.

Sure enough, when Sullivan returned to his room, Beria shadowed him. He pretended not to notice, but once he got back to his cabin he locked the door, moved the dresser in front of it, and slept with his .45 under his pillow.

According to the manifest, Skorzeny had boarded at the previous stop in Paris, Beria at the one before that in Prague, and Nishimura had been on this trip since the beginning, getting on in the free city of Shanghai. So, other than the deadly representatives of two of the most dangerous and malicious nations in the world—the Soviets and the Imperium—he also had the mysterious German operative up to something, and that wasn't even getting into the host of criminals and their triggermen on board who Wells had been sucking up to.

There were a lot of very dangerous men congregating on this ship.

Wells was confident that the saboteur wasn't one of the crew. He'd vetted them, and most of the lower skilled employees came from his home turf, which meant that if they did anything stupid their families would be in danger. Sullivan didn't care for it, but that was simply how business was done in Shanghai. The masters of infiltration were the Imperium Shadow Guard, but he couldn't see a reason for them to kill one of their own Cogs. He actually believed the German hadn't known about the bomb, so that left the Russians.

Since the *Oriental Elite* was slower than dirt and taking its sweet time, it would take another nine days of leisurely sailing to reach Buenos Aires. The crew had a Weatherman capable of magically altering the weather, but his instructions were to keep the winds comfy, not fast. With that much time over nothing but ocean, that meant there were basically two possibilities. If the saboteur was sane, they had nine days to catch him, before he set his bomb's timer and then disembarked; if he was suicidal, then he could strike at any time.

Unless there was another way off this tub . . .

On the second day out of Casablanca, Sullivan ditched his tail and snuck down to the cargo hold. Despite Wells' confidence in his staff, it was fairly easy to get by the guards on the door, and Sullivan wasn't exactly Shadow Guard material. He simply used his Power to make his body light as a feather, climbed into the superstructure, then dropped through the top of the cargo hold.

The crew had given the hold a thorough search after finding the first bomb, but there was probably a second one stashed somewhere aboard, and if there wasn't, there were plenty of chemicals aboard that could be used to cook up another, only Sullivan wasn't looking for bombs or components. He was looking for escape routes. Not for himself, since he'd already proven he could jump off of airships easy as pie, but for the bomber.

There weren't any windows in the hold, but enough light seeped through the gas bag overhead that he didn't need to use his hand torch to see. There was a single airplane tethered in the hold above a large drop door. It was a small Dornier Duck flying boat. A quick look through the window confirmed that it was a four seater. Sullivan was no pilot, but he'd flown enough to know that this little thing couldn't have that much range, but it could make an amphibious landing.

A regular cruise ship had lifeboats. Passenger airships had parachutes, though that was mostly wishful thinking since anything bad enough to make an airship crash was probably going to happen so fast that parachutes wouldn't really be an option. Plus, who were they kidding? It wasn't like any of these socialites would know how to use a parachute without breaking their necks anyway. There were chutes stored at the emergency exits, but they were locked up tight, and only the crew had keys. You didn't want just anybody being able to mess with an airship's parachutes. There were also life vests and inflatable rafts. If the saboteur was really desperate, he could set a bomb anywhere between here and South America, jump, and then swim for it. If he had accomplices, there could even be a boat waiting nearby for a pickup.

If the bomber didn't have to wait for landfall, then time was of the essence. Sullivan never cared for rush jobs, but he had a way of getting things done. If Wells wanted an earthquake, he was about to get one.

It was time to shake things up.

The angle of the sunlight was shifting through the dome.

"Why are we changing course?" asked one of the passengers.

"I am sorry, sir. I'm afraid I do not know," answered the nervous serving girl as she hurried past.

Sullivan sat at a small table at the edge of the casino floor, enjoying a fine scotch on Doctor Wells' dime, and channeling just enough of his gravity-altering Power to make a real mess of things.

The ship's nose was angled down. They were losing altitude. Gamblers began complaining as the spinning roulette wheels became unbalanced. They were far more worried about where that little ball would land, never realizing the real problem might be where *they* were about to land.

He had to admit, Wells' crew was solid. They didn't alarm the passengers as news of their impending demise spread through the ship. Very few of the rich folks noticed a few nervous crewmen in engineer's coveralls bolt up the stairs in an awful hurry, but a few of the toughs and security types did, and they alerted their charges. Word began to spread.

Sullivan watched the jitters set in as their nose-down profile kept getting steeper until the streamers and flags on the walls were hanging at an obvious angle. Then the *Oriental Elite* began turning hard. The captain was trying to get them back toward land before they lost too much altitude and hit the waves. The ship began to rattle. Compared to the lazy motion of the entire trip, things had suddenly gotten very rough. Ever since Shanghai, the ship's Weatherman had kept everything nice and easy, but now the winds weren't about comfort, they were about getting a strong push so they could move fast.

A red light began to flash and a warning klaxon sounded.

Now the passengers knew something was very wrong and their case of the jitters turned to fear. The band stopped playing when the angle got bad enough that the tuba player lost his balance and fell off the edge of the stage. Passengers began looking for safety, not that there was any place actually safe aboard an airship that was suddenly going down. Heels weren't the best type of shoe for a now steeply-angled dance floor, and some of the ladies took a spill on the hardwood. A few of their *gentlemen* abandoned them to save their own necks.

A bead of sweat was rolling down Sullivan's forehead. This wasn't burning that much of his magic, but it did require a lot of concentration. Not so much concentration that he'd spill his drink though, and as his glass began to slide across the table, Sullivan caught it. He only needed to keep this up long enough to spook the players he had eyes on. They had to really believe that the *Oriental Elite* was going down.

Professor Nishimura, Japanese robot designer extraordinaire, was not the easily riled type. One of his Iron Guard whispered something in his ear, but he brushed the soldier off. Even though the professor was having to hold onto the table felt to keep from falling off of his bolted-down stool, he kept on trying to play cards, and seemed a bit put off when his stack of chips toppled over and rolled onto the floor. He barked a command, and the junior Iron Guard whom Sullivan had slugged in the nose, got on his hands and knees and began picking up the chips. When the card dealer couldn't take it anymore and began sliding across the floor, even Nishimura had to call it a day. He threw down his cards in disgust. He'd probably had a very good hand.

The Iron Guard would have an escape planned for their VIP. The senior Imperium elite must have had enough, because he took

Nishimura by the elbow and gently hoisted him off the stool. Sullivan was too far away to hear the words, but it had to be some variation of *it's time to go.* The three Imperium men began making their way through the fearful gamblers. They were headed for the back stairs, which would take them to the cargo hold.

It all came down to this: If Sullivan was wrong, he'd just sabotaged a cruise ship for no good reason. A ship's officer had begun shouting orders, and because he had a fancy uniform and a cap with gold braids on it, most of the passengers were listening to him, so it was easy to pick out those who were paying attention to something else. There were three men sitting in a shadowed alcove by the bar, and they, too, were watching Nishimura. They all got up at the same time and began following the Japanese contingent across the gambling hall. Sure enough, one of them was the skinny Russian with the glasses, and he didn't look happy.

Now normally, if the two most evil countries in the whole world wanted to go and kill each other that would be their business, but his main concern was keeping the regular folks safe.

On that note, it was probably time to quit crashing the ship and scaring the hell out of everybody. Sullivan let up on his Power. The gravity-altering spell he'd carved onto the main bag's compressor system wouldn't have much strength on its own. Though enough magic was probably still lingering there, messing things up, to unnerve the engineers so they'd keep running for land. He'd hoped that would force everyone's hands, and it looked like he'd guessed right.

He'd forced the saboteurs to make their move early or abort their mission. No wonder Beria looked so angry, and Sullivan figured anything that upset a commie that much was a good thing.

Sullivan got up and rudely pushed his way through the socialites. There was just enough angle to the floor to make it hard not to knock anybody down. The Russians were moving about as fast as they could without drawing too much attention to themselves. Beria broke off and went to the right while the other two took the same path as the Japanese. Sullivan kept on Beria. If there was another bomb, he'd be setting the timer now while his boys jumped the Iron Guards. He didn't know what the NKVD's magical capabilities were, but if they were prepared to have an even fight with Imperium elite, they were either very capable, or extremely stupid.

The halls were crowded with passengers rushing from their rooms in various states of undress. Alarms and flashing lights had that effect on folks. Beria kept his head down and walked fast, bumping between the frightened. Sullivan plowed along after him, as far back as possible without losing sight. If Beria made him, he'd flee, and that would complicate things.

He didn't mean to step on that lady's foot, but she let up enough of an unholy screech that Beria turned to see who'd kicked a cat, and Sullivan was made. The Russian snarled, then ducked through the next doorway and disappeared. Sullivan shoved passengers out of the way and ran to catch up. When he reached the corner, Beria was gone. The hall was a dead end but he'd vanished. He'd not had grey eyes, so he wasn't a Traveler. He must have walked through the wall . . .

The Russian spy was a Fade.

"Aw, hell." It was a good thing he'd worked enough with Heinrich over the years to have a good grasp on how to track someone who could diffuse their matter enough to pass through solid objects. Sullivan's eyes couldn't see through walls, but his Power could, so he called on a little of it to feel all the gravitational forces around him. The view wasn't perfectly clear, but it would do. There was a lot of movement and shifts in weight distribution . . . But one figure of about the correct mass and density was hurrying up a ladder into the superstructure. That one passed clean through an access hatch, and was climbing up the *outside* of the gas bag. No wonder the crew hadn't found another bomb aboard the ship. Most folks wouldn't go wandering around the top of a moving airship, but it was easy to stash something when you could pass through solid objects and you weren't afraid of heights.

Sullivan didn't have time to double back and find access to that ladder. He needed to catch Beria fast. He needed a short cut. So he ran back into the hall, picked the nearest window, drew the big Browning automatic from inside his fancy new coat, and helpfully warned the fleeing passengers, "Cover your ears" before shooting a couple of holes in the glass. A lady screamed and a man cursed him, but Sullivan didn't have time to apologize for the impoliteness of sudden gunfire because he had a dirigible to save. When he kicked the glass out, there was a terrible rush of cold air. The passengers ran for their lives as Sullivan began to climb into the wind.

He caught a jagged edge. *Damn it . . . Ripped my new suit.*
Oh, well. It had been too flashy for him anyway.

Because all Gravity Spikers were big burly types, people tended to think of them as ponderous, but the smart ones learned how to cheat. It was easy to scale your way up the side of a moving blimp when you could magically make yourself nearly weightless. The *Oriental Elite* was only doing thirty knots, so scaling the side wasn't even a challenge for Sullivan. It beat the heck out of riding around on the wing of a biplane or leaping off the *Traveler* in a Heavy Suit.

Sullivan made it over the edge, let his weight return to normal to conserve his Power, and began stumbling along the top of the gas bag. The rubberized material squeaked and bounced as he moved across it. Beria was at the intersection of the gas bags, doing something to a big canvas sack that had been tied to the supports. Sullivan carefully noted the position. It was a good choice. The gas bags were broken into cells that could be sealed off, but even a small blast right there would take out at least four simultaneously. As heavy as this pig was, she couldn't afford to lose that much lift and they'd be taking a swim within minutes.

Beria saw him coming and stepped in front of the bomb.

"Give up," Sullivan ordered as he aimed his .45 at the Russian's heart. He had to raise his voice to be heard over the wind.

"Come no closer!" the Russian shouted.

"I don't need to get closer, dummy. I've got a gun." So did the Russian, but his pistol was in his pocket. Problem was, if the Fade was quick enough on his Power, he'd go grey when Sullivan pulled the trigger and the bullet would pass through him and hit the bomb. Depending on what it was made of, that could have very disastrous consequences. Beria gave him an odd little smile, indicating he was thinking the same thing.

"It seems we have an impasse. Perhaps we can come to an arrangement?"

"I'm listening." That was only half true. Mostly he was looking for an angle that would kill the commie bastard without blowing the top off the ship. He figured he had one, but Jake Sullivan by nature was a curious man, and he wanted to see if his theory had been right. Sullivan took a few steps closer so they could hear each other better.

"No part of any deal lets you lay another finger on that bomb. I only care about the safety of the ship."

"Very well."

Beria had one hand close to his pocket. Sullivan was pretty sure he knew what the Fade was going to try, because he'd seen Heinrich perform a similar trick when somebody had the drop on him. Beria would call on his Fade magic as he pulled his piece, Sullivan's reaction shot would pass through nothing, and then Beria would re-form and plug him. It was a neat trick when it worked.

"I can agree to that."

"Except Stalin needs you to blow up this ship so that the Imperium won't ever know you kidnapped their robot expert."

Beria frowned. "I do not know what you're talking about."

"It's a good plan. I'll give you that. The Imperium and the Soviets have a ceasefire. You get caught kidnapping one of their best Cogs, they're likely to get all sorts of upset, and we both know how Toru gets when he's angry. Only if the Imperium thought their professor died in a freak airship crash and his body was lost at sea, there's no questions, and no angry Iron Guard declaring war, just a tragic accident. They'd never know that you boys took that little airplane in the cargo hold and flew off into the sunset right before the *Oriental Elite* blew up."

"How did you know?" the Russian asked.

"I didn't. It was just a hunch. So I sabotaged the ship to see if anyone took the bait."

Beria seemed to appreciate that. "A clever ploy . . . It seems that completing half of our mission will have to do."

That was a complete lie. Sullivan could tell that Beria was gathering up his Power, getting reading to go grey.

"My men will already have taken Nishimura. We got the Cog before you could. I knew that I should have had you both killed the minute I was aware there were Grimnoir knights aboard."

"Nope . . . Just me."

He cocked his head to the side. "You are alone? What about the German?"

"He's not one of mine. And the Grimnoir don't know Nishimura from Adam."

Beria was surprised. "The Grimnoir are not attempting to kidnap the Cog too?"

"Why? Should I be?"

"Then you do not know about the Imperium plans for their super *gakutensoku* . . ."

"There's a—"

It all happened fast. Beria used Sullivan's momentary confusion to make his move. His body went grey and wispy as smoke as he grabbed for his pistol. Instead of pulling the trigger as expected, Sullivan surged his own Power, dropping several extra Earth's worth of gravity on the Russian. The Fade's body might have had less consistency than steam, but he was now heavier than a train, so he fell partially through the rubberized fabric of the gas bag before Sullivan cut his Power and let gravity return to normal.

Not realizing what had happened, Beria let his body solidify as his hidden pistol came up . . . Only he found himself a few feet lower than expected, with the pistol pointed at Sullivan's feet instead of his chest.

"Neat trick. Too bad I've seen it before."

The Russian looked down in shock. It wasn't even so much as it had cut him in half, as you couldn't tell when his body stopped and the thick bag started. An inch-thick slice of heart, lungs, and spine was now being shared with a whole lot of rubber and fabric. His legs would be dangling into the hydrogen-filled space below. Beria looked back at Sullivan in shock, but he couldn't even form words. The pistol dropped from nerveless fingers and bounced off the bag. Beria's head flopped forward and he was out.

"Good riddance to bad Russians," Sullivan said as he stepped over the dying man and went to the bomb. From what he heard, the serving girls aboard the ship would be a whole lot happier for the return trip with this joker gone. Assuming they got to have a return trip at all, but luckily the timer hadn't been set. Things were looking up.

And then there was an explosion at the bottom of the ship.

The cargo hold was a mess. They'd opened the bay doors to vent the smoke out. The remains of the Dornier Duck flying boat were still smoldering, but the ship's Torch and damage control team had gotten the fire under control.

The ship's captain had posted guards at the entrance to keep out the curious, but before Sullivan had to bull his way past them, he ran into Doctor Wells. The ship's owner had gone incognito, and was wearing an engineer's coveralls so he could come down and see the spectacle without drawing attention to himself.

"Hello, Sullivan. When I heard there were bodies down here, I must admit that I expected one of them to be yours."

"Sorry to disappoint, Doc."

"Judging from your filthy and disheveled appearance, I'm taking it that you've been busy."

Sullivan nodded. "I found your saboteur and tossed his bomb over the side. You'll need to send your damage control team up top to do some patching."

"Did you put a hole in my bag?"

"Something like that . . . Whoever you send, make sure they've got a strong stomach."

"I'm assuming this was all your fault. Was it really necessary for you to carve a spell into my engine room to frighten my passengers?"

"If an idea's stupid, but it works, then it wasn't stupid. You said your passengers were looking for adventure, well, there you go."

Wells sighed. "It appears your theory was correct. I haven't had time to reconstruct the scene, but it seems the Imperium and the NKVD had quite a fight, culminating in the destruction of my runabout. From what I've ascertained so far, the Imperium were boarding the aircraft when they were attacked. Judging by the bits of metal stuck in the hull and in the Iron Guard's corpses, I'd say one of the NKVD was a talented Mover. But as we both know, Iron Guard do not die easily, so they got out and went about murdering the Russians before they were brought down. The last Russian had his neck snapped right over there. In addition to my very angry clientele, I now have four corpses to deal with."

"Four? Where's the professor?"

Wells shrugged. "No sign of him."

The last piece of the puzzle clicked into place. "Where's the safest place to parachute off this thing?"

The parachutes and emergency exit hatches were kept locked up until there *was* an emergency. Unfortunately, Sullivan had given them more than enough emergency. In luring out one faction, he'd made the other one's job easier.

This area had been cleared of passengers after the captain had called off their crisis, so it was quiet as Sullivan ran down the passage. The stern was normally off limits, so it was all sheet metal and rivets. He found that the stern escape hatch was open, revealing a bright stretch of blue ocean below. Sullivan caught Skorzeny and Nishimura there, just as the German was about to cut the Cog's head off.

Sullivan hadn't seen *that* coming.

"Hold on now," Sullivan ordered as he aimed his .45. "Put the knife down."

"Easy there, Sullivan." Skorzeny was standing over the professor with a butcher's blade in one hand. Nishimura was lying on the grate, unconscious but breathing. "Why would the likes of you care about one more dead Jap?"

"Buddy, what I'm concerned about is none of your business."

"I must tell you, I've always looked at you as something of an inspiration. For how many stories there are about the ruthless Jake Sullivan and the insane objectives you've accomplished, the reality has left me sorely disappointed. You've grown soft."

"You're not the first man who thought that today." The German was already wearing a parachute and had a big leather satchel tethered around his body. Sullivan gestured with the muzzle of his pistol. "I'm guessing his head is supposed to go in the bag?"

Skorzeny was calm as could be. "My operation has a Lazarus. We don't need his whole body to find out what he knows. Once brought back from the dead, a severed head can talk well enough."

As a student of magic, Sullivan was fascinated by every type of Active, but on a deep, personal level Sullivan *hated* Lazarus magic. "What is it this guy knows that makes it worth blowing up five hundred people?"

"Something about Japanese giant super robots. He recently completed a project the Imperium have been working on since they saw what the god of demons did to Washington, D.C. I don't know the details. I'm only following orders."

"Can't say I'm too fond of the idea of the Imperium getting any new toys."

"Then look the other way for thirty seconds and you won't have to worry about it."

"Tempting . . . But that don't mean I want your bosses to have them either. Whoever they are, they're connected enough to know what

Stalin's secret police are up to, smart enough to let the NKVD do their thing and then steal the prize for themselves."

"I must admit I'm proud of my work. That last Russian never even saw me coming."

"Imperium gets robbed, you rob the robbers, and nobody's the wiser. Normally I wouldn't care, but the fact you were still gonna let the NKVD blow up the ship means you're no friend of mine."

"My superiors will deal with the Grimnoir Society in time." Skorzeny had a very cold smile. "I'll deal with you now."

Sullivan shot him in the chest, and when he didn't go down, Sullivan shot him again, and then again. He was a little surprised to see the man was still standing.

Skorzeny looked down at the red holes in his white shirt. "That really hurt." Then he hurled the big knife at Sullivan.

Sullivan flared his Power, hard and sloppy, but it worked, and the knife, now with the weight of a boulder hit the floor and left a dent in the metal. He put the front sight right between Skorzeny's eyes and pulled the trigger.

That round hit him square in the forehead, but it *bounced* off.

That should have bowled over even a Brute, but the German twisted his head back around, snarled, "You should have walked away when you had the chance," stepped over the unconscious professor and started toward Sullivan.

He'd fought far too much in his life to be easily excitable, and asked with more curiosity than nervousness, "What are you?"

"The future."

Skorzeny hurled himself down the corridor. Power flaring, Sullivan increased his density and took the hit. The fist hit him in the chest, and even with physics on his side, the impact was so hard that it bent the grate beneath his feet. Sullivan hit him back, magic and muscle, and damn near broke his knuckles on the German's jaw. He swung again, but missed.

Because Sullivan was suddenly blind.

He was too analytical to panic. His eyes were still working. It was just pitch black, like all the light had been sucked out of the world. Then something hit him in the ribs like a hammer, hard enough to lift him off the floor. The air flew out of his lungs.

Sullivan twisted gravity to the side, dropping both of them against the wall. Then he changed its direction again, bouncing them across the ceiling. They collided in the dark, and he kicked out, heel connecting with something solid. He would have tweaked gravity so that *down* was pointed at the escape hatch, but he didn't particularly want to drop the unconscious professor to his doom.

He hit the floor, got up, and ended up with a handful of what was probably the leather satchel. He yanked back on it, slamming Skorzeny hard into the wall. He still couldn't see a damned thing, but he could feel exactly where Skorzeny's body was affecting gravity, and from there he could extrapolate where to slug him in the mouth.

The artificial blackness instantly cleared. Skorzeny was right in front of him, smiling through bloody teeth.

There was a bright flash and a loud crack. Electricity leapt between them, blasting Sullivan across the space.

It took a second for Sullivan's muscles to unclench enough to move. His hands were tingling and his shirt had caught fire. If it hadn't been for his Healing spells, that shock probably would have stopped his heart.

"You like that, Sullivan? You Grimnoir aren't the only ones pushing the boundaries of magic." As the German spoke, he was doing something with his fingers, almost like he was drawing a design in the air. It might have been the electrical shock, but Sullivan could have sworn that there was a lingering glow in the air. *That's impossible. You can't draw spells on air.* But, fascinating as that was, Sullivan had an ass to kick.

Sullivan got up, but now Skorzeny was moving as fast as a Brute, hands flashing back and forth, and he hit Sullivan a dozen more times. The next thing Sullivan knew he was spinning head over heels down the hall to bounce off the ceiling and skid across the floor.

He'd landed next to the unconscious Cog. It took Sullivan a moment to collect himself. It was like being run over by a truck. The multiple Healing spells carved on his body were burning hot, gobbling up Power to fuel his life.

"You want to know about whom I answer to?"

The German was following him, again doing the trick with his fingers, and this time Sullivan was sure he saw the glow, and could almost trace the pattern.

"As much as you think you know about magic, somebody knows more."

Skorzeny extended one hand behind him, palm open. His discarded butcher knife leapt from the floor, streaked across the distance, and Skorzeny caught it by the handle. He brought the blade around.

"You've not seen anything yet."

"I was cocky at your age too, kid." Sullivan grunted as he stood up.

His opponent had just demonstrated Brute strength, Crackler lightning, the density manipulation of a Massive, the telekinesis of a Mover, and something unknown relating to light. There were only a handful of Actives in the world capable of accessing more than one area of the Power, and the only ones he knew of who'd ever used such a range so effortlessly were the Chairman and Faye back when she was the Spellbound. It was too bad he was in a fight for his life, because he really would have liked to learn more, but even Sullivan's curiosity had its limits.

"Before I kill you, Sullivan, I want you to know I wasn't lying when I said you've been an inspiration to me. It takes a big man to do the impossible. Do you have any last words?"

"Not for you." Sullivan looked back down the hall as he put his hands over his ears. "Now would be a good time to help, Doc."

The enormous elephant gun was incredibly loud in the enclosed space. Skorzeny was hit, swept clean off his feet, and flung down the passage. The 80-caliber bullet was overkill for elephants, so it didn't matter what kind of density altering magic Skorzeny had going on, he'd certainly felt that.

Doctor Wells walked in, rifle as big as he was still shouldered. "That was for upsetting my passengers."

The thick cloud of black powder smoke cleared. Remarkably, the German hadn't exploded on impact, but he was hurt. Skorzeny got up, shaking and grimacing. Whatever spell he had carved on his body was drawing so much energy that Sullivan could feel the Power being sucked in like a vortex. The huge lead bullet was lying on the floor, deformed and smashed flat against Skorzeny's skin. *Impressive.*

"Hold on," Sullivan warned Wells as he grabbed hold of Nishimura's belt.

Skorzeny realized what was happening, but he was too injured and had burned too much Power to do anything about it. "We'll meet again," he gasped.

"Bet on it." Then Sullivan broke gravity, hard and fast, changing the pull so that down led directly out the open escape hatch. Skorzeny fell down the hall and out the side of the dirigible.

Sullivan kept burning Power for a moment, holding on while Nishimura dangled in the air, just to make sure it wasn't a trick. When he was sure the German had been tossed, he let go and gravity returned to normal. The Cog hit the floor hard, but considering he was Imperium, he was really lucky Sullivan had bothered to hold onto him at all.

He limped to the escape hatch and looked outside. A white parachute had opened far below them and was drifting toward the ocean. Whatever organization this man belonged to, Sullivan had a feeling they were going to be trouble in the future.

Wells joined him at the hatch, rubbing his shoulder. Apparently even a Massive could feel recoil. He watched the shrinking parachute but didn't say anything.

Then Wells reached into his coveralls, removed a five dollar bill, and handed it over.

I have another Grimnoir trilogy planned which is set in the 1950s, a generation after *Warbound*. *Murder on the Orient Elite* sets up a few things and gives a couple of hints about events which will occur in the next trilogy, but the main reason I wrote this particular story is that I just enjoy writing Jake Sullivan and it was nice to revisit him a few years after his life has—relatively speaking—calmed down.

FATHER'S DAY

This story was originally published in the Shared Nightmares *anthology in 2014, edited by Steve Diamond and Nathan Shumate. The theme of the anthology is the same as the title, so I got to thinking about the worst nightmares I've ever had. For most parents our biggest fears aren't about harm coming to us, but rather to our family, and our inability to do anything about it. So I set out to write a gut punch for dads.*

"I WON'T LET YOU KILL my daughter."

The Program woman gave me a patronizing smile. She was used to dealing with parents like me by now. "Now, Mr. Brody, I can understand your concerns, but it isn't like that at all. She will be perfectly safe. In fact, she'll be well cared for in one of our finest medical establishments."

"Uh huh . . ." I pretended to study the paperwork she expected me to sign, and then I glanced around the tidy government office. There were posters on the walls about doing our civic duty to help defeat the Dreaker menace, warnings about sleeping only during the mandated times, and even cartoons for the kids about the importance of taking their mandated sleeping pills. The Program woman watched me with her cloying fake sympathy the whole time. A robotic security guard was standing directly behind my chair. That made sense. Some parents were bound to react violently when given the news that their child was being drafted to fight in the Dream War.

She must have gotten tired of waiting for me to sign, so she tried again. "We instituted mandatory blood testing for specifically this

155

reason. There are so few people who can do what she can. She has a wonderful but rare gift. Maximizing that gift will benefit the entire community. She's a very lucky girl."

I didn't like how this know-it-all bitch kept referring to my daughter. "*She* has a name."

"Of course!" But then the Program woman froze when she couldn't immediately recall what it was. My child was just another asset to these people to use up and throw away. Trying to play it cool, she glanced down at her data pad. "Wendy . . . And Wendy will be very happy living in the Safe Zone."

"You're going to make her into a vegetable."

"Somastasis is nothing like that." She lied right to my face. No compunction, no hesitation, just the party line.

"What is it then?"

"When the invasion began, Dreamers were the only reason mankind survived at all. Less than one percent of the surviving human population has the genetic capability to fight off a Dreaker attack during REM sleep. On their own, a Dreamer can only protect a small area, and only for short periods of time. The Public Safety Program developed somastasis so that special individuals like your daughter could share their gift with the whole community."

"You didn't answer my question. I know damn good and well what somastasis does. It's a medically induced coma."

She frowned. "I don't know about—"

"It's a medically induced coma, because sleeping all night isn't enough for you. Oh no, once you figured out how the Dreamers worked, first you put them on drugs and mandated that they had to sleep ten, fifteen, even twenty hours a day. For the public good you said, but that still wasn't enough for you parasites. You need them to fight twenty four seven, and you don't give a shit about what it does to them."

From the look on her face, I was beginning to get on her nerves. "It's a sacrifice for the good of mankind."

"The Dreamers already go to battle for the rest of us every single night. Every time that sweet little girl lays down her head, for her whole entire life, a thousand monsters have lined up to take a shot at her. Horrors you can't even imagine, but she fights the Dreakers so we don't have to. You don't know what that's like, doing that every single night, and you think that's still not fucking good enough?"

There was a vibration of an electric motor and one hard metal hand was placed on my shoulder.

"Stand down, Ajax," she told the robot before it ground my bones into powder. "There's no reason for profanity, Mr. Brody. If you become upset, I'll have security escort you from the premises."

Of course I was *upset*. Only a soulless bureaucrat could expect a father to respect bullshit protocols more than their own child.

"I understand your anxiety, I truly do, and I empathize with it." She'd probably been told to say that to angry parents during some sensitivity training. "Perhaps I failed mention that the families of our volunteers are extremely well compensated. Your loved ones will be provided housing in the Safe Zone and given a generous living stipend."

Like a bribe could replace a kid. "Fuck your money," I snarled. The robot squeezed my shoulder to remind me that it was illegal to be impolite to government employees. "You're condemning Wendy to hell."

The Program woman tapped her fingers on her desk, probably flagging me as a subversive in their system. "This is a public safety issue, Mr. Brody. If you don't sign those papers, we will be forced to take legal action."

I would have stood up and stormed out, but I was being held down by a robot.

"It will take a week or two for the orders to be processed through Public Safety. I suggest you reconsider during that time." The Program woman leaned forward conspiratorially, as if our entire conversation wasn't being recorded. "Look, you seem like a loving father, Mr. Brody, so I'm going to level with you. This is a national crisis. Frankly, the Dreakers are winning. A third of the country is lost, and we're doing better than the rest of the world. We *need* your daughter, and one way or the other, she's going in the Program. The Dreamers are our only hope."

Wendy had just turned six.

I had nightmares that night, but so did everyone else in the world.

The Dreakers were masters at understanding whatever was troubling you, and then they'd dredge up every ugly bit in your subconscious and use those to chip little bits off your sanity. It was like having a loose tooth that you just kept poking at with your tongue, wiggling it until it popped out.

So when the aliens invaded my mind that night, it was all confused images of Wendy being ripped away, of her brothers and sisters crying, of the lab coated Program officers sawing open her skull and shoving electrodes into her brain.

The Dreakers were persistent alien bastards. We didn't know where they came from. I couldn't understand the science of it, but they didn't exist in the same dimension as we did, so we couldn't see them, and no one could figure out how to communicate with them. We didn't even know what they wanted or what had brought them to Earth to begin with. One day the nightmares began and the world had begun falling apart. All we knew about the Dreakers were that they'd invaded the dreams of everyone on Earth, and so far, they'd managed to kill about half of us.

"I miss Mommy," Wendy said out of nowhere.

"Me too." I was tired and cooking our breakfast of powdered eggs and SPAM. There'd been no food shipments into our zone this week, so we were living off of what we'd managed to store. The electricity was out again, but at least the gas lines still worked.

"I'm sorry I couldn't save her."

"It's not your fault, honey."

Wendy didn't sound sad, just matter-of-fact. "I didn't sleep good that night so I couldn't keep the monsters away. They got in Mommy's head and broke everything. They made her too scared to live. That's why she took all the pills."

My eyes had gotten watery. "Don't talk about it. You're good."

"No. I'm not."

"Don't say that." I brought her the plate of eggy mush. She was wearing her favorite *princess* dress. I'd traded for it years ago, and it was falling apart, and she'd outgrown it, but Wendy wouldn't part with. She said it made her feel pretty. "Mommy always said you were a superhero."

"Kinda, but I'm not all the way."

Her older brother had found a box of crayons in the street when he'd been scavenging yesterday, and Wendy was drawing a picture. She set the old piece of scrap paper aside to eat. Her drawing was a bunch of green and black squiggles. "What's that?"

"One of the monsters. His name is . . . Well, it's a funny name, with a lot of s sounds in it," she said proudly. "*Sissassack*. But I can't say it right. He's the one that was inside Mr. Nelson's head when he shot everybody."

They hadn't bothered to reopen the school since the massacre. I picked up the paper and tried to decipher the picture. It was either too alien, or she was just that bad of an artist. "Why don't you draw something happy?"

"This is happy, Daddy." She looked up and beamed at me with her gap-toothed grin. "I found Sissassack last night and made sure he'll never hurt anybody again."

I sat down across from her. "How'd you do that?"

Wendy took the red crayon in her fist and violently scribbled all over the picture.

The bastards cut off our food rations. It was a warning that the government that had the power to give everything also had the power to take it all away . . . But I still wouldn't sign their damned papers.

"What're we going to do, Dad?" my oldest son asked when he relieved me from guard duty. The two of us were on the roof, watching the barricades. The further you got from the Safe Zones, the more the city turned to shit. To conserve the Dreamers we were all ordered to sleep at the same time. That was easy for the government to declare, since they weren't out here dealing with gangs, looters, or people the Dreakers had possessed.

"I'll trade for food."

"What've we got to trade?"

"I don't know." He was too young to know what a father was willing to do to provide for his children. "I'll think of something."

"We could go west. They couldn't take Wendy from us there. There's no government at all on the west side."

I shook my head. That side of Baltimore was controlled by warlords. Once they figured out that Wendy was a Dreamer, they'd kidnap her just as fast as the Program. "That's not a good idea."

He was scared and trying not to show it. When I was his age, I was playing video games and trying to get up the courage to talk to girls, not trying to make sense of the apocalypse. "Then what're we going to do?"

"I'll think of something," I said again. "I promise."

❖ ❖ ❖

The Program sent a team to retrieve her, but it was more like an army. Their armored vehicles crashed through our barricades. Helicopters hovered over the block, searchlights playing back and forth across the mostly abandoned buildings. The neighbors had sold us out. Even though Wendy had been protecting their dreams all these years, they were scared and hungry, so they told the Program right where to find us.

My oldest daughter tried to talk to them. They shot her down in the street. I was too stunned to move. Then my boy reacted, running to his sister, and they gunned him down too.

Wendy was hiding behind my legs, screaming and crying. *Don't let them take me away, Daddy! Don't let them take me away!* I tried to fight. It was like my hands were too clumsy to work. Though I'd tested it, the pistol I'd traded for wouldn't work. The trigger weighed a million pounds and when I did get it to shoot, I couldn't hit anything. The Program soldiers just laughed as they dragged me away from Wendy and beat me mercilessly with their batons.

I couldn't do anything, and the clubs just kept falling, breaking bones and splitting skin. Wendy was begging for them to stop. I reached out for her, but a Public Safety Officer, faceless behind his riot helmet, had grabbed her by the hair and was dragging her away. She was kicking and screaming, but he picked her up and hurled her into the open back of the armored car, where she bounced off the walls and lay crumpled on the floor.

The faceless man slammed the hatch shut.

"Daddy?"

I woke up, covered in sweat and shaking. I could still see my other kids lying dead in the street. I could still feel the clubs, but I was lying in my own bed. Somebody had turned the lights on.

"Wake up, Daddy." Wendy was standing next to the bed. She put one tiny hand on my arm. "You were dreaming."

"I know. I'm okay now." I hugged her tight. What good was a father who couldn't protect his own family? "I won't let anything happen to you." That had been too real. It had been a long time since Wendy had let something that awful slip into our house. "Damned Dreakers," I muttered.

"It wasn't the monsters this time. That dream was just you."

I started to cry.

❖ ❖ ❖

In the olden days before the invasion, they could have called on the phone, or sent an email, or even had a letter delivered. I remember when I was young, everybody, even poor folks, had a cell phone. But now there was no phone service, no internet, hell—we didn't even have reliable electricity, and it had been five years since they'd disbanded the postal service, so when the Program wanted something, they had to come in person.

They hadn't attempted to cross the barricade. It had been the Washington family who had been guarding the block last night, and they'd seen a Program car stop at the entrance and toss the package over the gate. The fat envelope had my name on it, but there had been plenty of warnings written on the package, so by the time I found out, the whole compound knew.

A judge had signed the papers for me. I had twenty-four hours to turn Wendy over to the Program, or we would be in violation. Anyone who harbored us would be criminals.

They'd burn the entire block if they had to.

"I hate to say this, but we got no choice, Brody. You know what they'll do if we don't turn your girl over." Douglas was the nominal leader of our block and my best friend. I could tell that the others had already talked it over before they'd fetched me. I already knew what they were going to say. "You helped build this place, and we're thankful for everything Wendy's done, but we voted . . ."

"After all that she's done for you, after all these years she's kept us safe, you'd just turn her out like that?" I had to ask, though I already knew the answer. Of course they would.

"You're the reason we ain't got no food deliveries," Colvin said. "Sorry, brother. They ain't leaving us no choice. My kids got to eat."

"So that's it? You survive one more shitty day, so you can cower through one more horrible night? What're you going to do without Wendy to keep away the Dreakers?"

"I don't know," Douglas said, spreading his hands apologetically. "I just don't know. We might get along without her, we might not, but we can't stand up against the Program. Aliens might screw with our heads later, but the Program boys will just shoot us now. We already took a vote. You and your kids can stay if you want, but Wendy's got to go. I don't know why you'd want to stay though, if the Program offered my family a spot in the Safe Zone, I'd take it."

"No possessed in there, that's for sure," Colvin agreed.

"You think it's so damned easy, you'd let them hurt one of your kids to save the rest? You chicken shits have no idea what that's like."

Douglas just shook his head sadly. "Naw, man, I figure I know a lot what that decision feels like." Then he walked away. Most of the other adults followed him.

"He stuck up for you, but votes a vote." Colvin poked me in the chest. "You got twenty-four hours, Brody. Pack your shit, because you've got to go."

For the first time in six years, there were no nightmares at all.

I dreamed about my wife before the Dreakers had broken her mind and spirit, back when she was kind hearted and full of love. I dreamed about the world as it used to be, with hope and promise. I dreamed about friends and family, dead or missing, but in my dream they were all alive, and I dreamed of my children growing up in that idealized old world instead of the real one.

It was wonderful.

When I woke up, Wendy was waiting for me. She was wearing her princess dress and a backpack with cartoon characters on it. The pack was stuffed with clothing and her favorite toys. It was like a child's interpretation of what you'd need on an epic quest.

"I didn't have nightmares last night. Did you do that?"

"That was my present to you. I tried extra hard to chase off the monsters 'cause today's Father's Day."

I hadn't looked at a calendar in a long time. "Thank you."

Wendy shrugged in that adorable way that only the truly innocent can. "I had to try hard to help just our house, so I let the monsters scare everybody else more than usual. Serves them right for being mean to you."

"What's with the backpack?"

"It's a long walk to the Safe Zone."

"We can't go there, silly. They're going to—"

"Shush!" Wendy held up one finger and poked me in the lip. Her mother used to do the same thing. "I know what they'll do. I see their dreams like I seen yours, and they're going to put me to sleep forever."

I gently took her hand and moved it aside. "Which is why we can't go there." I didn't know where we were going to go yet, but we had to go somewhere.

"You don't understand, Daddy. I don't mind. I see the dreams of the kids who are asleep all the time too. They were lonely, but they found each other. So they've made up their own world. On the light side are where all the people have gone. On the dark side are where the monsters come from." Wendy pointed around my bedroom. "This is in the middle part. I'm going to the light so I can save the middle. It's very nice there. That's why I tried so hard so you could see it for yourself."

My dream?

"Yes, Daddy. I didn't want you to feel sad for me. Mommy says it's time for you to let me go. I need to go be a superhero."

TOLD YOU it was a gut punch.

Years after this story was written I was approached by a fan at Salt Lake City ComicCon. She had just read "Father's Day" and loved it, and commented about how brilliant I must be to tie a post-apocalyptic, alien invasion, sci-fi story in with Peter Pan.

I got a really confused look on my face and said, "I did what now?" Don't get me wrong, authors love being called brilliant, but I had no idea what she was talking about. She explained that I had a magical Neverland populated by heroic lost boys and I even named the girl Wendy.

Wow . . . That actually would have been really clever, but honestly, I hadn't even thought of it that way. For future reference, whenever a fan thinks I'm smarter than I actually am, I'm just going to run with it.

DESTINY OF A BULLET

This story was originally published in Called to Battle: Volume One *published by Privateer Press, edited by Aeryn Rudel, Darla Kennerud, and Doug Seacat.*

*I've written a couple of novels (*Into the Storm, Into the Wild*) and several shorter pieces for Privateer Press set in their Iron Kingdoms universe. I really enjoy their setting, play their games, and paint their miniatures, but how I wound up writing for them is kind of funny.*

I registered on their web forum to put up pictures of my miniature painting and to get feedback from better painters. I never mentioned what I did for a living. Then one day somebody started talking about how super easy it would be for Privateer Press to compile fan fiction and sell it. I had to put my professional writer hat on, step in, introduce myself, explain how creating media tie in fiction works, and how it is a fairly complicated and challenging process requiring good fiction writers who either already know the world, or who are willing to learn it.

About fifteen minutes later I got an email from the company basically saying "Whoa? You play our game?" And I was all like "You read my stuff?" And the next thing I knew I'd written a bunch of stories for them. I can neither confirm nor deny that I was partially paid in miniatures.

Whenever I tell my fans that I'm writing a piece of fiction which ties into an existing world, whether it is for a game or some other shared universe, they always ask if they need to be familiar with that world before reading it. The answer is, no, not if I do my job correctly.

Volgorod, Kos Volozk, Khador, 607 AR

HE HAD ONCE HIDDEN in a pile of garbage for three days in order to kill a man. That job had been completed during a summer in Imer. It had been miserably hot, and insects had feasted on him continuously. Stinking of filth, badly dehydrated, sunburned, and sick, he had still made the two-hundred–yard shot on demand the instant his target had shown his head. One round. Nice and clean.

That job had been preferable to this one. For two days and two nights now he had hidden, watching the blank white of a high mountain pass. He was chilled to the bone but couldn't light a fire for risk of being seen. It must have been because of the unrelenting cold that he found himself thinking wistfully about the desert. The northern woods of Khador had never been intended for man. Fools lived here simply because they were too stupid to leave and too stubborn to die.

He had come all this way to put a bullet into a particular one of those stubborn fools.

Some folks called him a mercenary, others a hired gun. Most would argue he was nothing more than an assassin. Regardless of their opinion of how he earned his coin, everyone knew Kell Bailoch was the finest rifleman in western Immoren. Give him a clean shot and the gods themselves couldn't save you.

The hard part was the waiting. The sniper let his mind wander.

He had spotted them coming long before they saw him. Picking his potential employer out from the crowd had been easy. The hooded woman walked between two men in long cloaks. The common folk were deferential and moved quickly out of the woman's path. The two men were trained killers, and they couldn't help but act like it, with wary eyes constantly shifting as they scanned the busy market. Their predatory nature made them stand out among the shoppers.

Kell Bailoch preferred to blend in. It made his job easier. He kept his wide-brimmed hat low over his eyes and covered the lower half of his face with a scarf, masking his Cygnaran features.

He stepped from the shadows and followed the three discreetly for a time. The gently falling snow barely stifled the merchants' enthusiasm as they loudly hawked their wares. Fall in northern Khador was like winter in any other kingdom. Once he was certain this wasn't an elaborate trap, and they were isolated from potential eavesdroppers, Bailoch walked up behind the kayazy's guards and waited to be noticed.

It didn't take long. The first bodyguard turned, his hand inside his cloak and surely resting on a long dagger. The second moved immediately in front of the woman. They were quick, but he noted that neither looked toward the rooftops. *Sloppy.*

"What do you want?" the first guard demanded.

"I wish to speak with Mistress Padorin about a job," Bailoch answered. His Khadoran was unaccented, as bland as his appearance. "I was informed she's looking for me."

The woman turned, giving him a glimpse inside the hood of pale skin and blue eyes. She was rather young for the leader of a ruthless trade organization. "You are the one I was told about?" she asked.

Bailoch tipped his hat. The survivors of Talon Company could always be counted on for referrals.

"You're shorter than I expected." She appraised him. "Are you as good as they say?"

"Are you as rich as they say?"

She nodded.

"Then I'm good enough."

It was just another job, though colder than most. There had been so many jobs over the years they had begun to run together. Half up front, find a way to reach the target, take the shot, collect the remainder. Sometimes that meant investigation, preparation, disguises, infiltration, and cover identities, other times it meant good field craft or an elevated position and some patience. In the end it was all the same: get a line of sight and let Silence work.

When he had been a sixteen-year-old long gunner recruit, a marksmanship instructor had given him the most important bit of advice of his entire life. The bullet *wanted* to hit the target. That was its destiny. It was the shooter's weakness that stood in its way.

Shifting to keep the circulation flowing to his extremities, he checked the pass again. The target would have to come through it eventually. He was certain that approaching the isolated and fortified cabin of a paranoid master rifleman would have been a stupid move. Staking out this position was the surer, but far more uncomfortable, method to get a shot. In most of western Immoren this would already be considered a harsh winter, but to the rugged Kossites of the Scarsfell, the real snows hadn't begun falling yet. The target was a hunter who would be looking for game as long as possible in anticipation of the long winter, and when he did, he would pass through here, ready for the hunt.

Bailoch knew the feeling well.

Sivasha Padorin stood next to the roaring fireplace, staring into the flames. Bailoch's earlier assumption had been correct. She was young, twenty at the most, and more than likely too inexperienced for this line of work. He'd been informed that her father and older brothers had recently been murdered, casualties in the constant struggle between the factions of the Khadoran underworld. The political nuances were difficult for a foreigner to grasp, but it was a constant source of work. Surely it had been a surprise when the family business had fallen on her.

Bailoch doubted she would survive long in the cutthroat butchery that passed for kayazy business, but until then, her gold would spend as well as any other's.

They were alone inside one of the dozens of anonymous properties she owned around the city. Her bodyguards waited outside. That told Bailoch this was something she wished dealt with as discreetly as possible.

"Your target is a horrible man. He used to work for my father. We were very close once, but I want him dead for what he did to my family. He is a beast, a killer." She was slight, but he heard steel in her voice. "A year ago he betrayed my family. My father trusted this man, treated him like a brother. Yet he turned on us and gave our most vital secrets to competitors. My brother was murdered because of him. For such treachery there can be no—"

Bailoch held up one hand. "You don't need to explain yourself to me."

She looked up from the fire, surprised. "You do not care what evil he has done?"

"The bullet doesn't care. Why should I?"

Sivasha stopped. He had put her off balance. It was apparent she had already thought through what she was going to say to her hired assassin, as if she needed to justify her decision. "Very well. His name is Malko Varnke."

"You've got local hires. Why do you need me?"

"You are not the first I have hired for this work; he has killed all I've sent before. Varnke is a Kossite, winter-born in the deepest wilds of Vardenska, where the tribes still live by the old ways. He is one with the woods, as alert as the wolves he used to hunt for a living. Since he has wronged my family he has been living in the forest, where no one can catch him unawares. And he is one of the finest shots in the Motherland."

"It won't be a problem."

She paused for a long time. "He is Gifted. I do not know the particulars, as they were a guarded secret, but my father said he once served with the Greylords Covenant."

An arcanist? Magic had a way of making jobs complicated. "My fee just went up."

"Whatever is necessary. I cannot rest until I know Malko Varnke is dead."

For some reason he found himself taking pity on the girl, a rare thing indeed. "A word of advice: I've been doing this a long time. People die. Sometimes you're the one to kill them. Sometimes you need somebody else to do it for you. No shame in that. You don't need to share your reasons. Giving the order is the same as pulling the trigger. It just takes will."

"I have the will!" she snapped.

Perhaps she'd last longer than he'd first thought. "Good. That and ten thousand gold koltinas will put this man in the ground."

The thick furs he'd bought kept his body heat trapped. He'd also purchased a compact device from an alchemist in Korsk that produced a small measure of warmth for a few hours each time its capacitor was wound. It kept his extremities from freezing off during the nights. The device had cost quite a bit, but it was worth it: Frostbite in his trigger finger could ruin everything.

He allowed himself sleep in short naps. It was a risk he had to take, as there was no one to share a watch and no way of knowing when the target would try to cross the pass. The wolves and bears of the Scarsfell would more than likely avoid the smell of man waste and gun oil. There were other, far more dangerous and unnatural predators in these woods, but they were rare, and he was a light sleeper.

In his dreams, Bailoch saw ballistic calculations, wind speed, and trajectories, but never the faces of the hundreds he'd killed.

The cold grew deepest a few hours before dawn. When he raised his head and the bear skin lifted, icy air shocked him fully awake. Bailoch immediately scanned the snow below, looking for any fresh disturbances in the perfect white expanse. The snow was so reflective that even a bit of moonlight enabled him to see that there was nothing larger than a few animal tracks. It was exactly as he remembered it, and he had memorized every detail of this terrain.

He shook a fresh inch of snow from atop the furs. The shivering came next. It would pass. Bailoch wasn't worried about uncontrollable shaking causing him to miss. Only rookies tried to hold perfectly still when shooting. Everyone shook to some degree anyway; breathing, muscle tremors, even a heartbeat could cause the sights to move. Making a difficult shot was all about knowing your body's rhythms and firing at the correct time. An experienced rifleman didn't try and hold his breath—that only increased the tremors. The key was to shoot on the respiratory pause. *Inhale. Exhale. Squeeze. Bang.*

Only there was no *bang* with Silence. There was no click of the hammer being cocked, no snap of the firing pin, and certainly no alchemical roar as the blasting powder components met. His rifle was cloaked in magic that rendered it totally silent. The only noise was the buzz of the passing bullet, which anyone who had been shot at could tell you sounded like angry bees, and the impact, which sounded rather like hitting a melon with a club.

After scanning the pass, Bailoch checked his rifle. Moisture tended to condense on the blued steel during the night, and he carefully wiped it down with an oiled cloth. Dexar Sirac himself had enchanted Silence years ago, and to this day Bailoch had no clue if that enchantment would keep his rifle from rusting. He'd never taken the chance to find out. A rifleman took good care of his body and even better care of his rifle.

Bailoch moved slowly as he worked the cloth into every metallic nook. Big movements would attract the eye of anyone who was hunting him. He opened Silence's action, then removed the heavy, paper-cased round from the chamber, took out his cleaning rod, and gave the barrel a quick pass to make sure no moisture had condensed and frozen in the rifling during the night. You always clean from the breach, never the muzzle. Cleaning from the muzzle could scratch the crown, and that could affect accuracy. He'd earned a reputation for being deadly, and he knew that wasn't just because he was talented; it was because he was methodical. The world held lots of talented snipers, but few lived as long as he had.

The oilcloth rubbed over the magical runes engraved on the barrel and Bailoch paused. Once, long ago, a name had been carved there. The woman it had belonged to was a woman he had . . . known. But she was gone, scrubbed from his mind just as her name had been scrubbed from the steel. The sniper dismissed the thought and returned to his weapon maintenance. The scope rings were secure. The screws were tight. He rechecked the chamber—*Clear*—and pulled the trigger to dry fire. On a normal rifle he'd be able to listen for the metallic ring of the firing pin, but that was impossible with Silence. Bailoch was so familiar with this rifle that he operated entirely by feel, and everything felt just as it should. When the job was through, he would reward himself with a proper detail strip and deep cleaning of Silence's action.

He checked the round of ammunition before reloading. Bailoch used only the best components. The special paper casing was free of blemish or tarnish. The soft lead bullet was jacketed with a thin coat of copper, which kept his rifling from fouling nearly as quickly. Less fouling meant more accurate shooting should he find himself in a protracted engagement.

Bailoch couldn't see it, and he was certainly no Golden Crucible alchemist, but he knew that the casing held two sealed bags, each filled with an alchemical solution. When these bags were pierced by the firing pin and the solutions intermingled, they would ignite instantly and burn fast. That would create a growing gas pressure. It was the miracle of blasting powder, the wonder of the modern age.

Seeking the path of least resistance, the expanding gases would shove the bullet down the barrel at great speed, and if he was doing what he was supposed to, right into his target. The still-burning blasting powder entering the atmosphere was the cause of muzzle blast, only that wasn't an issue with Silence's enchantments. That made getting away, or making another shot without getting killed, much easier for him.

Bailoch may not have understood the magic behind alchemy, but putting bullets into things was what he'd been born to do.

There was a limit to how much pressure blasting powder could create inside a firearm and how fast it could hurl a projectile. The day alchemists figured out how to make it push a bullet faster was the day Kell Bailoch became far more dangerous. Gravity was a jealous constant that limited his range. Wind could push his speeding projectiles off course. In a mountain valley like this, it could be gusting in two different directions across that distance. When the time came, he would have only seconds to judge the distance and the wind, adjust his hold, and take the shot.

Silence checked, cleaned, and reloaded, Bailoch finally tended to his own physical needs. After relieving himself, taking a swig from his canteen, and gnawing on some ulk jerky, the sniper went back to his frozen vigil as the sun came up.

In the distance, a lone figure appeared, trudging through the snow. It was time.

Sivasha Padorin poured him a drink and then poured one for herself. "To a successful hunt."

Bailoch ignored the glass she set in front of him and reached out for the other one. A clever assassin would poison the glass rather than the drink. He took up the tumbler and eyed the clear liquid suspiciously.

"You are a paranoid man, Bailoch." Sivasha smiled, took the glass originally intended for him, and pounded down the drink in one gulp. She grimaced, then wiped her mouth with the back of her hand. "Some of my father's finest *vyatka*. It is older than I am."

He gave her an appreciative nod. "To a successful hunt." The favored drink of the Khadorans, made from fermented potatoes, could be used to strip the paint from a warjack. It burned going down and then sat like a fiery lump in his stomach, making him sweat. He could see why the people of the frozen north liked the stuff.

She took the bottle and poured them both another few fingers of the potent liquor. He'd already gotten the first half of his fee up front and felt fairly certain he wasn't being set up, so the sniper took the glass, though he would pace himself in these unfamiliar surroundings. Despite her size and age, Sivasha seemed capable of keeping her wits despite strong drink, but that was expected of a Khadoran. She gulped down the second and poured herself a third.

"I must tell you, Bailoch, I've dreamed of that one-eyed bastard's death. Since his betrayal I've feared he may someday decide to return and meddle in my family's business again. This worry has gnawed at me."

"What's more important, the revenge or protecting your business?"

"In Khador, revenge *is* business. I want Varnke to suffer."

Bailoch took another sip. "If all goes well, he won't."

She eyed him frankly. "There are many stories about you . . . ."

"I'd wager most of them aren't true."

"If even a fraction of them are, though, I must ask . . ." Sivasha paused. "Why?"

Bailoch leaned back in his chair and took another sip. "Why what?"

"Why do you still do *this*? You have been doing it for a long time, no? How long has it been?"

"That I've been shooting people for money?" He'd enlisted in the Cygnaran Army as a long gunner at sixteen. Then he'd joined the Talon Company, and that had been fun while it had lasted—until they'd been branded war criminals. He'd been freelance ever since, drifting from war to war and taking on various jobs. "I don't know. Coming up on thirty years, I guess."

"You must be wealthy by now." Sivasha nodded at the sack of gold coins sitting on the table between them. "You command a hefty fee."

He reached over and hefted the bag, as if he could tell the value of the coins just by the weight. Bailoch had made fortunes and lost them. Gold was necessary to live, but he was prepared to leave it behind without hesitation in order to get out of a situation alive. He dropped the sack back on the table. "Man's got to work. I'll earn what I can, until I run into somebody better than me and I die."

Sivasha chuckled. "Why, you're an amoral, pragmatic fatalist. Are you sure you've not got Khadoran blood?" She shook her head, already more serious. "I understand. I am kayazy. My family rose from peasants to businessmen with the power of nobles because of our hard work and cunning. And now the business is mine to protect. I did not ask for this life, but when my family were butchered like pigs, this became my life. I had no choice." She finished her third drink. "'Earn what you can, until you lose to someone better.' I like that."

Bailoch shrugged. It wasn't often that he pondered philosophy with an employer.

The approaching figure was humanoid, dressed in furs, and approximately five hundred yards away. The drifts weren't deep enough yet to call for snowshoes, but the footing along the narrow, rocky pass still had to be slippery. Regardless, the figure was moving quickly and confidently along the tall rock wall.

Lying prone in his insulated furs and water-resistant leather armor, Bailoch slowly removed the canvas lens covers from his telescopic sight and moved into his shooting position. Silence's handguard rested gently on top of a fallen log. He never let the barrel rest against anything, as extra pressure from hand or rest could change the tension on the barrel and affect accuracy. The steel butt plate he set firmly against his shoulder. His cheek rested on the stock. The cold glass of the telescopic sight had been coated with a special alchemical mixture to keep it from fogging up once it was only an inch from the warmth of his face.

The magnifying scope seemed to enlarge everything a dramatic seven times, but it offered an extremely narrow field of view. It was like trying to look down a long, dark pipe to find a pinhole of light at the end. An inexperienced shooter with an inconsistent cheek position would have to fumble about to find what he was looking for. Bailoch found his potential target instantly.

The figure turned out to be a human male with a thick black beard. Long dark hair hung out from beneath his fur hat. Sadly, that description could fit much of Khador's northern population, and Bailoch wasn't being paid ten thousand koltinas to murder some random hunter. The optical quality wasn't sufficient to allow him to pick out any of Malko Varnke's distinguishing features at this range. He settled in to wait for the man to get closer. His finger would remain indexed outside the trigger guard until he was ready to fire, but the simple wire crosshairs continued bouncing back and forth across his view of the Khadoran's chest.

Four hundred yards.

The man was making good time. Fit and strong, the sure-footed woodsman moved quickly from rock to rock, avoiding the wide white spots that could be concealing crevices. He looked to be somewhere in his forties; they were about the same age. The man was dressed like a Kossite, in grey and black furs, and carried a long rifle slung over one shoulder.

Three hundred yards.

The Kossite paused on top of a jutting stone lip to survey the rest of the pass. He was wary. As he turned his head side to side, Bailoch confirmed that he wore a black patch over his left eye. That matched Sivasha's description of the target. If there was another Kossite hermit in the area with one eye, he was about to have a very bad day.

Satisfied that the pass was clear, Malko Varnke hopped down from the rock and continued on at his swift pace.

Bailoch could easily take the shot now. The sun had peeked over the mountainside, and with the light-amplifying properties of his telescopic sight, he could see clearly enough. The wind was strong, though. He glanced at the pine trees around him, watching how the branches rippled. Then he looked back across the pass, watching the patterns and eddies on the surface of the snow. Five miles an hour eastward at his position, with gusts ten miles an hour across the clearing to the west. Nothing he couldn't compensate for.

Two hundred and fifty yards.

Silence was one of the most accurate firearms in Western Immoren and Bailoch was one of the best shots. He was deadly with the most cumbersome of blunderbusses; a precision instrument like this simply increased his potential. His rifle was a magical marvel, capable of shooting a two-inch group at one hundred yards. He could take Varnke from here but held on, having memorized the layout of every rock, bit of plant life, and patch of ice in the pass. The Kossite was moving between some tall rocks, which would provide him easy cover in case of a miss. Bailoch picked another spot: mostly open snow atop grass, with no real cover for ten yards in either direction and a two-hundred-foot-tall, icicle-covered rock wall as a backstop. If he missed, he'd still have time to get off a follow-up shot.

Ever so slowly, Bailoch moved his right hand to his mouth and pulled off his leather glove with his teeth. Then he returned his hand to the firing position on Silence's stock. It was ice-cold to the touch. The sniper shifted his body slightly, so as to not put as much pressure on his chest. His breathing was slow and easy.

Two hundred . . .

Malko Varnke walked into the chosen clearing.

Bailoch placed the pad of his finger on the trigger. Half a pound of pressure was all it would take.

The crosshairs were no longer on the man but above and ahead of him. It took time for a bullet to travel through the air, so you had to lead the target, allowing the bullet to intersect with it. Bailoch automatically and instinctually adjusted for the wind and elevation as Silence's muzzle tracked just ahead of Varnke's path.

One ninety . . .

Malko Varnke froze in place.

Bailoch did the same.

At this range, the Kossite's frown was clearly visible through the seven-power magnification. Somehow he knew something was wrong. A sound, a smell—it didn't matter. Something was off, and that meant danger. Varnke turned, lips moving, and there was a shimmer in the glass of the scope as glowing runes formed around the arcanist's hand.

Bailoch pulled the trigger. All the snow in the clearing exploded upward.

Silence made no sound, but the recoil still thumped his shoulder, and the scope lifted. A wall of icy wind crashed down the canyon, blowing snow and dirt everywhere and obscuring his target. *Cursed magic!* Bailoch calmly broke open the action and began extracting the ashen paper debris. He shoved another round into the chamber and closed the breach. *Now, where are you?*

The wind died off and most of the snow fell back to the ground. There was no sign of Varnke.

Now came the tricky part. If he'd run, Bailoch would have a shot, which meant Varnke wouldn't run—he'd take cover. If he'd taken cover, he'd have his own rifle out, and he'd be searching for his attacker. The first one to bolt would be seen and would die.

Careful to move only his eyes, Bailoch searched the pass. If he were a Kossite with ice magic, where would he go?

The shimmering of magic runes drew his attention. Not in the open—Varnke was far too clever for that—but Bailoch caught the reflection in a sheet of ice hanging from the cliff above. He tracked it back and found the rocks Varnke was hiding behind. *Damn.* He didn't have a shot, and the Kossite was casting a spell.

Energy crackled in the air. Suddenly the world turned white, and an unbelievable cold struck his flesh. It was as if he'd been plunged into the heart of a blizzard that was trying to rip the life right out of his body. He needed a new angle to get a shot around those rocks. There was no time for hesitation. His body didn't want to respond, but Bailoch leapt up and staggered through the hammering wind. Despite the magical attack, he felt calm. He would either die or he would win. Fretting about it seemed pointless. His hiding place was elevated, but a good sniper always had an escape route, and he forced himself toward the side of the bluff.

It was a ten-foot drop, and he hit hard and rolled through the snow, careful not to let his precious Silence strike the ground.

The compact blizzard above him tore his hiding spot to bits. Gasping for breath, he realized it was clear here, and that meant Varnke had a shot. Bailoch scrambled for cover. The Kossite's rifle bullet tore bark from a nearby tree and pelted him with splinters, but then Bailoch was running through the trees.

The lingering magical cold made thinking difficult, but he knew Varnke would have moved too, and now he'd be looking for another shot, because that's what Bailoch would do in his situation. He went low, hugging the ground, crawling through the dead underbrush. Bailoch pulled up alongside a thick tree and scanned, but Varnke was already hiding as well.

He'd left his glove in the blizzard. His right hand was bright pink and quivering uncontrollably. Dealing with frostbite could wait, though. He had a sorcerer to kill. When Varnke didn't get a shot, he'd use more magic to flush out his quarry. That meant time was on Varnke's side.

Bailoch had to push him, get the Kossite to reveal himself . . . and he had to do it fast.

He sank back down, deeper behind cover, and shrugged out of the heavy bearskin. Now the cold *really* hit, but if this worked, he'd be able to put it back on in a moment, and if it didn't—well, either way he wouldn't be cold for long.

He found a sturdy stick, placed the fur over it, and then shoved it past the side of the tree. A second later the Kossite spotted the movement of the fur and fired. The bullet pierced the skin. Bailoch spotted the flash and the smoke before he heard the gunshot. He moved the stick, letting the coat sway, and then hurled it out of the trees and down the cliff side.

Varnke reloaded as he came around a boulder at the base of the cliff, runes of magical power swirling about his body, ready to finish his wounded attacker, unaware he was chasing an empty fur.

He realized his mistake as Silence's muzzle poked past the tree.

He'd prepared a defensive spell, and snow and wind exploded outward again, strong enough to deflect a bullet. He wasn't about to fall for the same trick twice.

The crosshairs danced across the icy sheets at the top of the cliff, far above Varnke's head. Over two days Bailoch had memorized every nuance of the surface. The sniper picked out an icicle, big enough to cause a shower of debris but thin enough to be broken by a single heavy round. His heart hammered, but he felt only cold so deep it burned. His breath shot out in painful clouds of steam. He was in an awkward improvised position.

It would have been an extremely difficult shot on a nice day in the sun.

The bullet wants to hit the target. That is its destiny. It's the shooter's weakness that stands in its way.

Kell Bailoch was a consummate professional, and he wasn't about to thwart the destiny of a bullet.

Adjust for distance. Compensate for wind. The crosshairs shook across the surface of the icicle. Hold over. *Exhale. Squeeze.*

Silence made no noise as the recoil thumped his shoulder.

CRACK.

The icicle broke free and spun downward into a suspended sheet of ice. It shattered, taking snow and rocks with it, and that all fell in an ever-growing cascade of destruction.

Malko Varnke's ice storm died off, just in time for him to look up into the rushing thunder.

The young, reluctant leader of a kayazy faction poured him one last drink.

He'd had too much, but the fire was nice, the room was warm, the chair was comfortable, and it had been a long time since he'd enjoyed the company of a beautiful young woman.

"Is that all there is to it then, Bailoch? Survival? Money? Power? Is that all there is in life?" Sivasha was a little drunk herself. "We do a job that makes us important and vital, and maybe we're good enough at it that we get to live longer. Is that it? You kill people, over and over and over. You've assassinated generals, and politicians, and priests—so many, for so long . . ."

"It's what I do."

"But *why*? I'm stuck. You're not. One job, that much gold, you could walk away, be a farmer or a gunsmith or something. You could choose another path. Why this one?"

That was a good question.

Malko Varnke had been struck by the rockslide. His legs were crushed. He was bleeding from a gash in his head that had opened clear to his skull. His beard was soaked red and he was coughing blood.

The sniper limped up to the fallen man. He'd retrieved his coat and had Silence cradled in his arms. This job was almost done.

The Kossite looked up, confused when he didn't recognize the man who had ended his life. "Why you?"

Kell Bailoch brought up Silence to finish the job. "Because I'm the best."

BUBBA SHACKLEFORD'S PROFESSIONAL MONSTER KILLERS

This story originally appeared in the weird west anthology, Straight out of Tombstone, *edited by David Boop, published by Baen Books. It is set in my Monster Hunter International universe, and is the first full story I've written about the legendary founder of Monster Hunter International, Bubba Shackleford. The character Mohtahe Okohke was originally created by George Hill. The character of Hannah Stone was created by Hinkley Correia.*

BUBBA SHACKLEFORD got off the train in Wyoming, eager to find some cannibals to shoot. He loved his job.

The town was bigger than he'd expected. With the hardscrabble frontier behind them, Cheyenne had turned into another bustling center of American commerce. The platform was crowded with folks coming and going, giving the place an industrious feel. It took a hardy people, tough as nails, to civilize this rugged a land, but they'd still be scared to death if they knew what manner of evil was breathing down their necks.

Then Bubba noticed the signs. Weary eyes from staying up all night keeping watch. Nervous glances sent in the direction of every stranger. No children running about. And an unusual number of cheap wooden coffins stacked in front of the undertaker's. Yes, sir, Cheyenne had itself a monster problem.

This was his company's first monster killing contract in the West, and the furthest he'd ever been from home. He was a Southern man, born and bred, so he didn't care for the way the air here was dry and sharp enough to make his nose bleed, or the way everything as far as the eye could see was so unrelentingly *brown*. It was March, and there was still dirty snow piled in the shade. Wyoming struck him as a harsh and unforgiving land, nothing like his blessed green home in Alabama. For the life of him, he couldn't figure out why anyone would want to live in such a godforsaken waste.

"Wyoming sure is pretty!" Mortimer McKillington exclaimed as he lumbered down the train's metal steps.

"You say so, Skirmish." He'd hired the big Irish strongman because he'd figured anyone tough enough to be a New York bare-knuckle-fighting champ *might* be hard enough to be a good monster hunter. He was, and then some. Over the last year, Skirmish—as his friends called the freckled giant—had proven not only to be good with monster killing, but also an obnoxiously optimistic traveling companion.

"I do." Skirmish took a deep breath, expanding his barrel chest. "Ah, smell that fresh air."

It smelled like horseshit and coal smoke to Bubba. "Have the boys unload the animals and wagons. I'll look for our client."

"Cheer up, boss. This is an adventure."

"I'll be cheery once we put these man-eating bastards in the ground."

"And we get paid."

"*And* we get paid." Because battling the forces of evil was rewarding and all, but on its own paid for shit. Now, having a big company like the Union Pacific give them a sack full of gold coin to kill the monsters damaging their tracks? That was much nicer.

He didn't have to search for long, because his new clients immediately sought him out. They'd known which train he was on, and Bubba Shackleford did tend to stand out in a crowd. They must have been given his description, which was usually some variation of tall, broad shoulders, narrow waist, long mustache, probably looks like he's ready to shoot somebody. The words short-tempered and pragmatic often made it in there too, but Bubba didn't mind. Establishing a proper reputation went a long way in the monster killing business.

Two men were pushing through the crowd, heading his way, one fat, one thin, both in tailored suits remarkably free of grime. The round fellow in the bowler hat had the look of a businessman. He pegged the one that looked like a tubercular rat as a government man. They all tended to have that same disapproving air about them.

"Excuse me, sir. Are you the monster killer, Bubba Shackleford?" the plump one asked. Before Bubba could so much as nod, he was already getting his hand vigorously shaken. The businessman's hand was very soft. "I can't believe an actual monster killer, here!"

"Keep it down about the *monster* business, Reginald," the thin one hissed as he glanced around.

"I'm Reginald Landon of the Union Pacific. Welcome to Wyoming, Mr. Shackleford. We're so glad you made it on time! This is Mr. Percival from the governor's office."

Whenever a hunter got this warm of a welcome in civilized society, it meant things had gotten desperate. "From your harried demeanor, gentlemen, I assume there's been another event since our last telegram?"

The company man gave him a grave nod. "People have been disappearing after dark. They hit one of our depots west of town last night. Four men dead, ripped limb from limb, and their flesh consumed by the ice-hearted beasts."

"Perhaps we should retire to someplace more private to discuss the matter," Mr. Percival stated, as he watched Bubba's men unloading crates of ammunition from the train. "Washington was very specific that this needs to be dealt with *discreetly.*"

"Discretion is the general rule for this sort of affair," Bubba agreed.

The McKinley administration was adamant that monster problems be kept from the general public's knowledge. Good thing too, because otherwise the quiet handlers of said problems, such as himself, would be out of business.

"The Army sent a patrol from Fort Russell in reprisal, but the soldiers never returned." Landon looked around at the crowd, then leaned in conspiratorially, presumably so as to not cause a panic. "The Indians are saying the poison woman has come back from the dead to curse us. This is the handiwork of *Plague of Crows.*"

He'd heard that name. A legendary evil back from the grave? Bubba pondered on that new fact for a moment. "Gentlemen, we may need to revisit the amount of my fee."

❖ ❖ ❖

Whenever some foul abomination started eating folks, the common response was to gather up a bunch of brave men to track the beast down. That often worked, but killing monsters was dangerous work and too many of those brave men didn't come home. A vigilante mob could usually get the job done, but often at a terrible cost. That was how Bubba Shackleford had first been exposed to the supernatural, and it was only through luck and pluck that it hadn't culminated in a massacre.

The more civilized a place was, the more likely monsters became the law's problem to deal with. Only there was a heap of difference between dispensing justice to some run-of-the-mill murdering outlaw and something like a foul nosferatus, or a flying murderer bat, or a tentacle bear. There were a handful of sheriffs and marshals of his acquaintance who were worth a damn against the hell-spawn forces of evil, but most were sadly lacking.

The Army? They had the bravery and the guns, but they were the most hidebound and hamstrung bunch of all. Every monster was different, and if you wanted to beat them, you needed to learn fast and adapt faster. Soldiers were always useful, but best when led by an officer with the wit to grasp the inconceivable, and the freedom to get the job done. Good luck with that!

The first time Bubba had killed a monster, he'd made a bit of a name for himself and, strangely enough, job offers had begun to arrive. It turned out there was always some critter causing trouble somewhere. The work suited him, not to mention it was *far* better money than farming. It was a fine job, provided you didn't mind extreme violence, physical discomfort, and the constant looming threat of death. Those early years had been more miss than hit, but he'd survived while the things he was chasing usually didn't.

In time he had joined forces with other men uniquely suited to the monster killing arts. Bubba had never aspired to leadership, but they all looked to him for guidance. Until one day he'd found himself the official boss and owner of a real company.

It was purely by accident that Bubba Shackleford's Professional Monster Killers had become the most successful—albeit possibly only—company of its kind. His operation was above the rest because of knowledge, dedication, and preparation, but above all else, it was because they possessed an adaptability of the mind. The supernatural could neither surprise nor confound them. They could not be shaken.

Their attention was undivided.

Killing was their business.

Rooms had been provided at a hotel near the station, but most of his men were at the local saloons, and would probably drag themselves in sometime before dawn. There would be drinking, gambling, whoring, and possibly some fighting, but hopefully no hanging offenses committed because he couldn't spare the manpower.

Bubba Shackleford sat alone at the hotel bar, in front of the same glass of whiskey that had been sitting untouched for the last hour. In his hands were the telegrams that had been waiting for him at the Western Union office. They were all from his secret weapon, the Scholar.

He still didn't know the Scholar's identity, just where to send messages to reach him. Hell, the name Scholar had come about because the only signature on the letters he had received had been the letter S, and the name fit. The notes had arrived shortly after Bubba's reputation as a monster killer had spread among those in the know. Whoever S was, he wanted to keep his identity secret, and he seemed to know damn near everything there was to know about certain kinds of monsters. Bubba figured that S was probably an employee of the government who would be jailed if word got out he was telling secrets. One of McKinley's agents had confided in him that the reason they kept monsters secret was something about how the more folks believed, the stronger monsters got. Bubba didn't know about that. It sounded like horseshit to him, but as long as the government contracts paid on time, he didn't care.

Repeatedly he had tried to pay for the information provided, but Scholar would have none of it. His reasons for helping remained his own. Regardless of his mysterious motivations, Scholar was right more often than not, and some of his clues had proven vitally helpful in the past.

The first telegram had been sent a couple of days into their train ride.

DESCRIPTION MATCHES INDIAN LEGEND OF CHENOO ONCE HUMAN CURSED HEART SLOWLY

*TURNS TO ICE CAUSING MADNESS CANNIBALISM
AND MUTATION WILL RESEARCH AND REPORT -S*

Chenoo was a new term for him, but Bubba wasn't familiar with the legends of this region. He'd need to remedy that. There was nothing quite as unpleasant as coming across a new beastie and having it suddenly squirt flaming blood out its eyes at you, or discover that bullets just bounced off its hide. Though Scholar seemed to know a lot, many critters still remained complete unknowns.

The most recent telegram had arrived yesterday.

*HAVE RETAINED SERVICES EXPERT REGIONAL
FOLKLORE WILL CONTACT IN CHEYENNE CHENOO
EXTREMELY DANGEROUS USE UTMOST CAUTION
RAYMOND -S*

Strangely enough, Scholar was about the only person around who still used Bubba's birth name. Even his sainted mother had given up on Raymond years ago. Bubba paused to drink his whiskey, which wasn't half bad since it had been imported all the way from Tennessee. The Union Pacific rep had made no mention of any knowledgeable types in town, so he could only assume the man hadn't arrived yet. Sometimes the "so called" experts were right about monster vulnerabilities, and sometimes they were wrong, but it usually beat flipping a coin.

He heard boots on wood, and turned to see that one of his men had returned to the hotel. Balthazar Abrams had been one of the first of the professional killers, hired because he'd been quick enough with a knife to leave a ghoul in pieces in a New Orleans alley, and proven indispensable ever since.

"Telegrams? You heard from the Scholar, boss?"

Bubba motioned for him to take the stool next to him. "Things we're hunting are called Chenoo. Used to be men, but their hearts turn to ice. I doubt that's a metaphor."

"Things used to be men, they're the worst. So these Chenoo alive, dead, or atwixt the two?"

"I don't rightly know, but Scholar's sending us an expert." The proprietor had heard the conversation and had come wandering back in from the kitchen. "Bartender, another whiskey, and one for my friend here."

The bartender paused when he saw Abrams, and a look of surprise came over his face. "This is an upscale establishment, Mr. Shackleford. We don't cater to his kind here."

Abrams had been born a slave, but he'd been a free man for over three decades, and was as good at killing monsters as his best white man—who happened to be Irish—and, frankly, Bubba didn't care what some pencil dick thought about any of his crew.

"Pour or I'll come over that bar and pistol-whip you to within an inch of your life." He used the coldly casual tone he normally reserved for contract negotiations or ordering executions.

"What? I'll get the sheriff!"

"Tell him he'd best bring friends."

The way Bubba stated that must have made it abundantly clear that he meant every word. The bartender swallowed hard, fetched a bottle and another glass, poured them both a—very shaky—shot, and then fled to the back room.

Bubba took another drink. "I cannot abide a man lacking in hospitality."

"I swear, you're going to pick a fight that gets us killed one of these days," Abrams muttered.

"More than likely." He passed the telegrams over so that Abrams could read them. Every man in his crew was literate, and if they weren't when he hired them, they were expected to learn fast. Abrams was a sharp one, and since he was good at ciphering, even trusted to balance the company books. For the rest, he didn't care if they could read the Bible, but they'd at least be able to decipher the instruction manual for an unfamiliar explosive device and retain their fingers.

"When the Scholar is warning you to be careful, you know it's bad."

"The fat man from the railroad told me some stories about what happened to their workers. Something's been prying up track to derail trains. A work crew went out, got attacked. Only a few made it back alive, but the town doc never seen the like of what happened to those. The curse starts with a chill they just can't shake, then it crawled in them, deeper and deeper. Settles in the heart, they say. The afflicted act like they're freezing to death, always shivering, like they needed to get something warm in their belly. They tried hot soup, whiskey, but they only got crazier and meaner, insisting that the only thing would make them warm again was drinking hot blood, and then most couldn't talk at all. They became nothing but animals."

"Unfortunate," Abrams said as he unconsciously shifted his stool a little closer toward the fire.

"By the time they get the look of a man froze to death, they'd turned pure evil. Most of them lost their minds, killed some folks, and fled. They're still out there. One barely kept his mind, saw what he'd done, got down on his knees and begged for death. They put nearly forty bullets in him 'fore he expired."

"And that one asked for it. Imagine what the ones who don't want to die are like."

"From the way that whole Army patrol disappeared, I'd say they're stridently opposed to the idea. Locals think this is Plague of Crows' doing."

Abrams gave a low whistle at that name. Everybody in their field had heard of her. She'd raised unholy terror in this region when the railroad had first come through. It had taken a lot of blood and treasure to stop her the last time. "You renegotiated our pay, right?"

"Damn right, I did."

A young lady walked into the room. It was a bit odd to see a girl of such an age, probably not even twenty, out at this late hour of the night, unescorted. However, from the way she was openly and brazenly wearing a gun belt and matching Colts over her skirts, she didn't seem the type inclined to be chaperoned.

She spotted Bubba, took a moment to compose herself, and walked toward them wearing a look of intense concentration. She was a dark-haired, big-boned, solid country girl. Bubba nodded politely. "Ma'am."

"Mr. Shackleford, sir." Apparently she had done her research. She stopped before them, cleared her throat and spoke loudly, as if she was giving a prepared presentation. "I'm Hannah Stone."

"Are you our regional folklore expert?" Abrams asked.

"Huh? No." That question seemed to throw her off of her prepared remarks. "What?" The poor girl looked rather nervous. "I don't know what that is."

"Drink?" Bubba offered, because that seemed the gentlemanly thing to say, and southerners had a reputation to keep up.

"No thanks. Makes the hands shake, can't shoot as good." She took a deep breath before blurting out, "I'm applying to join your gang."

Bubba shared a look with his perplexed associate. "Gang makes it sound like we're here to rob the bank."

"I know what you do! I've seen monsters. I know they're real."

He had entertained variations of this conversation a hundred times. Would-be monster hunters were constantly knocking on his door looking for work—he turned most of them away, probably doing them a favor—but he always kept an eye out for talent. Only this was his first ever employment petition from a lady.

It was inconceivable. It was one thing having a man's death on his conscience, but he couldn't imagine sending a girl to her doom. "I'm sorry. We ain't hiring now."

But she was a determined sort. "Word is that you're always looking for sharpshooters. I'm the best shot you'll find in this state and I need the work. I figure a man who'll hire Negroes, Mexicans, and Irish might hire a woman." She looked at Abrams. "No offense."

"None taken." Abrams seemed rather amused by the whole thing. "Our Irishman's not so bad."

"I've done men's work before. I used to work for Buffalo Bill Cody. Mr. Cody said if a woman could do the same work as a man, no reason she couldn't, and get paid for it too."

"Buffalo Bill? Wait . . . Hannah Stone. I've heard of you!" Abrams clapped his hands with glee. "We're in the presence of a celebrity, boss. Annie Oakley taught her to shoot."

"Mr. Cody made that up for the show. I already knew how to shoot when I got there and I was a much better shot than *her*." It was obvious Hannah was not fond of her supposed mentor. "But she was more famous and popular because she was better at the talking part . . . and show business . . . and generally liking people."

Well, she certainly wasn't a cup of sunshine. Bubba remembered her story now. It had been in the papers all over the place.

"Way I heard it told is you got fired from Buffalo Bill's Wild West Show because there was an accident and your partner got hurt."

Hannah thought about how to phrase her response for a long moment. "The events which occurred could be described in such a manner."

"You were supposed to quick draw, shoot from the hip, and knock a cigarette from out of this fella's mouth at ten paces."

"Twenty. The crowd always loved that trick. We did it plenty of times. Last show there was some . . . extenuating complications."

"That's some mighty big words to say you blew his lips off."

"Well, in my defense, Mr. Shackleford, Bob was being awful shaky that day. I'd warned him not to skip breakfast."

Bubba didn't know what to say. Hannah remained standing there awkwardly. She tried to smile. It looked painful. He felt bad for her. But not bad enough to give her a job that would just get her killed. "It was a pleasure to meet you, Miss Stone, but truly, you've been misinformed as to my company's intentions. Good luck in your endeavors and good night."

Hannah's eyes narrowed to a determined squint. "Well, fine then." She stomped away.

Abrams waited until the surly young woman was gone before he picked up his whiskey and chuckled. "Women hunting monsters? Imagine that. Next thing you know they'll want to vote!"

When Bubba finally retired to his hotel room, he nearly shot the Scholar's expert on regional folklore.

He'd used a key to open the door, walked into the darkened room, paused . . . and immediately drew his Colt and leveled it at the shadows in the corner. He thumbed back the hammer. He couldn't see her, but it was a woman's voice that came out of the darkness.

"How'd you sense I was here?"

Bubba never knew. It was just instinct, but it seldom led him astray. And right now his instinct was telling him whatever was in the shadows of his room was *very* dangerous. "Come out where I can see you."

"I don't belong in the light. You pull that trigger and you won't live long enough to regret it."

"Lady, if you think I'm the one who'll be regretting matters, you must be unfamiliar with how bullets operate."

"Do not test my patience, Raymond Shackleford. I have been asked to help guide you. I am not your enemy. The one you call Scholar and I have made a deal."

"Well, ain't that something?" Any monster hunter worth his salt learned not to make deals with voices in the dark. His eyes were adjusting, and now he could barely make out a narrow female shape, but his gut was telling him this wasn't no normal woman. Only Scholar hadn't let him down yet, so he held his fire. "Who are you?"

"Mohtahe Okohke. The white man calls me by a different name."

"Plague of Crows," Bubba muttered. Witch. Necromancer. She'd sacrificed the living, raised the dead, scourged the plains, and terrorized settlers and Indians both. "Plague of Crows died."

"Briefly. Only do not fear. My war is over. I've made peace with your kind for now. The death that's upon this people is not my doing. Not too far from Granite Springs there is a new mine dug. Inside, a Stonecoat slept, until they blasted into his home. He made the ice hearts, and their curse will spread until his anger is spent."

He kept the Colt on her. "What's a Stonecoat?"

"A spirit of deep earth and cold streams, with skin like rock and slush for blood. Bad medicine, Raymond Shackleford."

"How do I kill him?"

"Even if you make it through his Chenoo, you can't kill a spirit. And you will probably die in the attempt."

"If it was easy, they wouldn't need someone like me."

"There have always been warriors like you, Raymond. The Stonecoat may no longer recognize this world, but he will recognize you, *if* you are brave enough. If he sees there is still worthy strength in this world, the spirit can return to his rest." Two glowing white orbs appeared in the shadows. Her eyes were too unblinking and round.

"That's all?"

"It is enough. Now my part of the bargain is done. I go to collect what is mine."

Suddenly there weren't just two lights, but dozens of glowing eyes from head to toe. A terrible screech filled his ears, a rush of air, and then he was surrounded in beating wings. Talons scratched him as the stream of thrashing birds poured past, through the open door, into the hall, and down the stairs. Bubba heard the proprietor scream incoherently as the flock of crows burst out the front door and into the night.

Damn it, Scholar. What have you gotten me into?

Bubba Shackleford lowered the hammer, holstered his gun, brushed the black feathers off his bed, and went to sleep.

The professional monster killers set out early the following morning.

It wasn't until Bubba got dressed that he realized Plague of Crows had scratched two words into the hotel room's wall for him. The proprietor was going to love that. The witch had also left him a present. It was a stick. It had been colorfully painted and had some beads and feathers on it, but it was still just a stick. He pondered on the short message for a bit, took up his fancy new stick, and went downstairs to get some coffee.

Outside, the men prepared. Despite the governor's admonition to keep things quiet, their two armored war wagons always attracted some attention. The odd-looking combinations of wood and sheet metal were far lighter than they looked, mostly because—to the contrary of what most bystanders assumed—they weren't designed for stopping bullets, but rather were to provide emergency shelter from tooth and claw. He had built a war wagon heavy enough to stop rifle bullets once, but it had been such a pain in his ass on the one hunt they'd tried it on—they'd spent so much time getting it stuck in the mud and exhausting horses—Bubba had abandoned it in a Mississippi field to rust.

Each wagon was pulled by a full hitch of sturdy Clydesdales. It appeared that they'd made the long trip just fine and were eager to get to work. Bubba always used his own horses and never counted on local stock. Most horses weren't worth spit when monsters started howling and blood started flying, so he stuck to animals of a proven calm nature. The rest of the men were on horseback, of various breeds, but all of sound temperament. Bubba hated losing animals almost as much as he hated losing men.

In addition to the small crowd who had gathered around to poke at the war wagons and ask questions his men weren't likely to answer truthfully, he spied the young sharpshooter, Hannah Stone. She was down the street, sitting on a horse and watching them. She was wearing a big hat, a duster, men's trousers—no awkward sidesaddle for her—and appeared outfitted for a long journey, which immediately gave Bubba a bad feeling. So he wandered over.

"Good morning, Miss Stone."

"Mr. Shackleford."

She was wearing at least two revolvers he could see, there appeared to be a whippet gun hung from a rope beneath her coat, a Winchester repeater in a scabbard on one side, and a longer buffalo rifle in a scabbard on the other. There were shells poking out of every pocket. On the balance, it was enough lead and steel that he felt bad for her horse.

"That's an awful lot of firearms upon your person this morning, Miss Stone."

"Well, I wasn't sure which ones I'd be requiring today, Mr. Shackleford, so I brought an assortment. I'm going for a ride."

"To where?"

"Wherever the wind carries me."

More like wherever the Chenoo carried her off to eat her. The obstinate little girl intended to follow them looking for monsters. "There's dangerous things out there right now, Miss Stone. I wouldn't advise such a course."

"I've killed a monster before."

"I don't doubt that, but did you go looking for it?"

"Well . . ." That gave her pause. "No. It was self-defense. But I'm still going out today."

"I ought to make you stay."

"And how do you think you're going to do that, Johnny Reb? I'm sure the good folks of Cheyenne would love to watch some stranger try and carry off a local girl on his back like some manner of barbarian. Or are you going to have me arrested for riding my horse on a public street? "

She had him there. "You are remarkably stubborn."

"I prefer the term steadfast. Like a rock."

Like a pain in my ass. "Suit yourself." He went back to the wagons, wondering how guilty he was going to feel when she got herself eaten by Chenoo.

Garlick was driving the lead wagon, and Pangle was manning its potato digger. Hagberg and Abrams were on the second wagon and its gun respectively. Bubba, Skirmish McKillington, Hub Bryan, and Mexican George were on horseback. Two always ahead of the wagons, and two behind, taking turns eating trail dust. Four trained hunting dogs ranged about, chasing rabbits, happy to not be on a train. One sharp whistle would bring the dogs back and put them to work. They had spare horses, spare guns, enough ammunition to hold a small war, and every totem, trinket, and supposedly magical whatsit you could think of, from half a dozen faiths, some of which might even be helpful.

As the wagons rumbled along the dirt road, Bubba pondered on using his growing wealth to purchase one of those newfangled "automobiles" with a gasoline engine that he'd been reading about, just to see what kind of weapons and armor he could mount on one to see if it was any good for monster hunting. He was an innovative sort like that.

He had a map, the directions were clear, and there was easy road the whole way. Even with the lumbering war wagons, Granite Springs was a leisurely day's ride. They would arrive a few hours before sundown. Taking their time would ensure the horses were recovered from the train ride, and his men from their hangovers.

So they rode until the afternoon, found an abandoned homestead that made for a good defensible position, and parked the wagons in front of it. From the dried blood and scraps of clothing inside the cabin, the Chenoo had already taken the previous residents.

They mounted the potato diggers on the war wagons' roofs, rolled out their cannon, and made camp. Bubba set watches, then ordered the construction of a bonfire sufficient to be seen for miles. It would drive off the lingering chill and also hopefully attract some Chenoo. Plague of Crows had made the Stonecoat sound territorial, so maybe it would show itself. If that didn't work, they'd hit the mine early in the morning.

While his men worked, Bubba climbed atop a war wagon and scanned the horizon with his telescope. There was one rider in the tall grass behind them. Hannah Stone really had followed them. "Aw, damn it."

"What is it, boss?" Skirmish shouted at him. "We got Chenoo?"

"Worse. Job applicant." He'd been hoping she would get a little bit out of civilization and get cold feet, because it took guts to ride through the wilderness quiet and alone while you knew monsters were lurking about, but no: She was too hard-headed for that. It would be dark soon. It was one thing to brave Chenoo in his fortified encampment, but one girl alone on the plains would be easy pickings.

"You want that I should scare her off?" Skirmish offered helpfully.

"She's likely to shoot you. I've got this." Bubba climbed off the wagon, whistled for a dog, and walked to where he'd tied his horse. "I leave her out there alone and she's gonna die."

"Well, that would certainly learn her," Skirmish shouted after him.

As he rode, there was an awful screech on the wind, a sound so angry and hungry that it caused all the hair on his arms to stand up. His hunting dog, Beaux, began to whimper. There were Chenoo near and hunting. If he sent Stone away, she'd never make it back to town before dark, and some of the nearer homesteads might not be much safer abodes. He reached her a few minutes later. Stone was riding, wary, with her repeating rifle in her hand. She'd heard the scream too.

As Bubba drew near, he loudly hailed her, so as to avoid ending up like poor lipless Bob. "Damn your obstinate hide, girl. I can't believe you're going through with this."

"Yep." She was scared—probably regretting her choice now that the Chenoo were making a bunch of racket nearby—but on the balance, mostly smug. "You want another gunhand yet?"

"Well, you ain't hired, that's for damn sure, but come on. You're at least staying close for safety."

Bubba Shackleford really couldn't abide a failure of hospitality.

The shrieks had increased in intensity, and they were much closer now. The sounds were blood curdling. Abrams and McKillington already had everyone in position and the bonfire was raging as Bubba and Hannah came tearing in at a full gallop.

Bubba pointed out the men for Hannah. "You've met Balthazar Abrams already. The big one with the freckles is Skirmish McKillington. The real ugly fella with one eye is Sid Hagberg, loves himself some dynamite. The scarecrow-looking one is Orson K. Pangle, Esquire, solid with a gun. Harvey Garlick is the little one that used to be a preacher; pay him no mind if he gets spun up. Hub Bryan was a good cowboy but better monster killer. And Mexican George is over there on look out, but he's our best rider and a crack shot."

"Why do you call him Mexican George?"

"Because nobody in Alabama would call him Whore Hay. We had two Georges at first, though White George got his hand bit off and quit, so I suppose it could be just George now, but it stuck."

Hannah took in the roaring bonfire, and the position of the wagons. "You want the monsters to see you. You're trying to draw them in."

Perceptive. "More I can draw off tonight, less I have to fight tomorrow inside a mineshaft. The dogs will warn us if they get close, and then we turn their ambush back on them."

"The doc told me they had to shoot that one cursed ice heart forty times," Hannah pointed out.

One of Scholar's telegrams told of an Indian legend where you had to shoot a Chenoo in the heart with seven arrows for it to die, but he was a man of the modern industrial age. Bubba gestured at the machinegun mounted atop the nearest war wagon. "That's what those are for."

Hanna looked at the Colt-Browning M1895 suspiciously. "Heard of these things. Seems wasteful, spraying all those bullets over the countryside."

Of course a sharpshooter would feel threatened by the idea of being replaced by volume. "Bullets are cheaper than men and I'd rather spend brass than blood. They'll probably attack in the middle of the night. We let the Chenoo come to us through a wall of hot lead, and then you can do your thing. Try to listen for once, and you might live 'til morning." He began to walk away.

It appeared that it was beginning to sink in that she'd gotten herself into some dire circumstances. He had to admit he was enjoying her discomfort. It was one thing to talk about hunting monsters, but it was entirely different when you could actually *hear* them.

"Wait, Mr. Shackleford, where are you going?"

"To eat supper and get some sleep before my watch."

A Chenoo screeched. She jumped. This one had to be less than a quarter mile away. The hunting dogs began barking in response. "You can sleep through that?"

"Well, they ain't going to get this over with any faster if I'm tired with a growling stomach. Sleep well, Miss Stone."

The Chenoo struck in the darkest hour.

The shrieking had stopped after midnight. Since the monster killers knew they were still out there watching, the quiet was worse than the noise. Only, their dogs were well-trained, so when the monsters tried to sneak up, rather than barking, they pointed. Hub Bryan and Orson Pangle were on watch, and they'd immediately gone to waking everyone else up.

The men got out of their bedrolls without a sound, guns already in hand. Bubba had slept in his boots and the thick leather coat that served as armor against claws and teeth. He signaled everyone to move into position. Low and slow, his killers got ready. The last person he woke up was Hannah because he didn't want her startled and making enough noise to warn the Chenoo. Only by the time he crawled over, she was already sitting up, next to a wheel on a war wagon, eyes wide, watching the swaying underbrush and shadows cast by their huge fire.

"Couldn't sleep," she whispered.

Bubba was perfectly well-rested, but he'd done this sort of thing a lot.

He spotted something white and glistening moving through the brown grass. The Chenoo may have lost their human reason, but they still had animal cunning. They were moving toward the homestead's corral, probably to slaughter their horses, so there could be no escape. But he'd been ready for such a move, and one of the machineguns was already pointed in that direction.

It was his first look at the monsters. Some were still shaped like men, only with skin so white they near glowed, and their flesh pulled tight over pointed bones, lips drawn back to show their naked teeth, red eyes bulging from their sockets. Some of those were still wearing scraps of their army uniforms. The ones who'd been cursed longer, they weren't men at all anymore, but all twisted up, hands like claws, stooped like apes, speckled with spurs of bone and blue pustules, and giving off so much cold that the dew had frozen to them in shimmering sheets of ice that cracked and left sparkling dust as they stalked forward.

Shivering despite the bonfire, Bubba knocked on the side of the wagon. "You got company, Balt. Far end of the corral. Get to threshing." Then, using hand signals, he told the others to keep watching their appointed fields of fire. "Now!"

Abrams popped his head and shoulders out the hatch on the top of the wagon and took up the potato digger's grip. The gun's nickname came from the reciprocating lever under the barrel, which would dig a hole in the dirt if you were shooting it prone. He'd had to repeatedly assure Skirmish that potato digger wasn't some Yankee insult toward the Irish. Fire blossomed out the end of the potato digger in a continuous roar. Pangle must have seen something on the other side of the homestead, because he opened up with his machinegun too, and now both of them were burning money into noise. Bullet after bullet slammed into Chenoo, ripping off chunks and flinging them down, jerking and twitching. Their blood flowed like slush.

"Goodness gracious! That was magnificent!" Hannah shouted as both guns ran through their belts. Sharpshooter snobbery only went so far in the face of such magnificent destruction. "I need one of those!"

If only the Chenoo were so easily impressed, but the rest of the monsters sprang up from their hiding places and rushed the homestead. Bubba realized that this wasn't a raid. This *horde* was every missing person in the region. Their unearthly screams pierced the night as the spirit-haunted husks rushed across the fields. All of the monster hunters started shooting, working levers and bolts as fast as they could.

The monsters were tough to kill, and for each one dropped, others gained ground. Most of his men were shooting new Krag-Jorgenson rifles, which were fast to load, but they couldn't keep up with this onslaught. Surprisingly, Hannah was as good as her show biz reputation suggested, and she was working her Winchester's lever as quick as a sewing machine's needle, methodically putting slugs through hearts and heads. Pangle and Abrams got their potato diggers reloaded, and their volume of fire increased dramatically again.

He saw where several Chenoo had bunched up to climb the fence, and shouted for Skirmish to fire the cannon. It was loaded with grapeshot. The big man yanked the cord. There was a deafening boom and when the boiling cloud of smoke cleared out, there was nothing but a pile of splinters and frozen meat where they'd been standing.

Skirmish moved to reload the cannon, but before he could do so, a *boulder* fell out of the sky and smashed it flat. His man sprang back to his feet, astonished but in one piece. However, their cannon was a goner. Did these damned things have a *catapult* or something?

No. It was worse. Bubba spotted where the big rock had come from. And it hadn't been launched. It had been *thrown*. The being was a hundred yards away, vaguely shaped like a man, only ten feet tall and wide as a wagon.

"What is that?" Hannah Stone shouted.

"Stonecoat," he answered. And there was no path through the mass of rushing Chenoo to do what Plague of Crows' message had told him to. "It's an earth spirit who—"

Only Hannah Stone hadn't waited long enough to hear the answer, and had instead picked up her buffalo rifle and promptly dropped one heavy round, smack dab into the middle of the Stonecoat's forehead. Gravel chips flew off, but it didn't so much as flinch. Instead, it began ponderously moving their way.

Bubba was watching and calculating all of this with a mind as cold as a Chenoo's heart, and he saw exactly how the battle was going to unfold. The monsters weren't dying easily, they were too numerous, and the swarm was nearly on top of them. "Into the wagons," Bubba ordered. He didn't like abandoning valuable horses, but didn't see much choice.

It was four men per wagon. They clambered through the doors and pulled them shut behind. The inside of his wagon was extra tight, because they had an extra body. It wasn't exactly ladylike, but Stone crawled over Bubba's legs so she could stick her sawed-off shotgun through the firing slit in the wall and promptly blew a hole through an old Chenoo's head. His killers stuck their rifles through the other firing slits and kept up the onslaught. The interior quickly filled with choking fumes. The wagon rocked as the Chenoo crashed against it, like a boat in heavy waves. They began to scratch and tear at the seams.

"Boss, the big one is coming this way!" Abrams shouted down through the hatch.

"Good," Bubba stated as he pulled the colorful, supposedly magic stick from out of his coat. Then he wouldn't have to run as far to reach it. He began climbing up. "Move aside, Balthazar, I'm coming up."

He squeezed past and onto the roof. It was worse than he'd thought. Chenoo were strong, and they were sticking their claws through the slick sides and pulling themselves up. He turned just in time to witness the Stonecoat reach the other war wagon. The spirit stuck one great hand beneath, and effortlessly *flipped* the wagon on its side. It crushed a bunch of Chenoo in the process, but the Stonecoat didn't seem to mind.

It turned its attention toward their wagon and approached, rumbling and flowing across the ground. Its body was made of millions of moving pieces, it was like watching a rockslide . . . *up*. The Chenoo on that side of the wagon were smart enough to get out of the way, leaving Bubba a clear path to follow some very questionable advice.

That witch had better be telling the truth.

Bubba stood atop the war wagon and shouted at the Stonecoat. "I'm Bubba Shackleford, professional monster killer!" He pointed Plague of Crow's stick at the spirit. He shook it and the beads rattled. "Go back to sleep, you old spirit! I protect this land now!"

"What the hell are you doing, boss?" Abrams shouted as he struggled to clear a jam from the potato digger.

"Establishing dominance." Bubba replied.

"It's big as a locomotive!"

"It's a warrior thing. *Yeeeeeee haaaaaaaaaaaa!*" Then Bubba leapt over the side.

The message Plague of Crows had scratched on his hotel room wall had been simple.

Count coup.

His boots hit the ground hard, and he rolled onto his shoulder, but nothing broke, and there wasn't time to dither with tons of living gravel coming to crush him. Bubba sprang to his feet. The plains warriors counted coup by touching their foe and getting away, only as it loomed over him, he realized just how suicidal that was. Every sensible man in the world would have turned and run for his life, but sensible men did not become monster hunters. Bubba charged the behemoth.

The Stonecoat ponderously lifted one huge arm overhead. Dirt and bits of rock rained down. It was prepared to deliver a blow that would smash an ox into paste, but Bubba ran right under that fist, still bellowing his war cry.

Reaching up, he whacked the gigantic monster square in the face with a decorative stick.

The spirit paused for just a moment. If it had eyes, it probably would have blinked.

He'd touched his enemy in the middle of battle. Which was good, but the second part of counting coup was getting away alive.

Bubba dived to the side as the fist came down. The impact shook Wyoming. It missed him by a cat's whisker, but the ground beneath erupted upward in protest, flinging him through the air. He crashed back down to earth, flat on his face, then scrambled on his hands and knees as the monster lifted one epic foot to stomp him like a mouse. But by the time that impact came, he was already sprinting away.

He ran toward the bonfire until he realized it wasn't following him, so he turned around. *Did it work?* The Stonecoat was just standing there. It probably didn't speak English, but Bubba taunted it anyway. "That's right, Stonecoat. You got touched. So quit your bellyaching and take your ragged ass back to your hole."

Then he realized that his breath had come out as steam. Despite being twenty feet from a roaring blaze, it was freezing cold. Bubba looked around and realized he was now completely surrounded by ice hearted Chenoo. They hissed at him through their exposed teeth. The circle was slowly closing in.

Maybe it was time to be diplomatic. Miners had blown up its house after all. He pointed the stick at the Stonecoat. "You leave us alone, and we'll leave you alone. Nobody will trouble your rest again."

It stood there for a glacially long time. It was obvious that the Chenoo were beholden to its will, because there was absolutely nothing stopping them from rending Bubba limb from limb. The hunters in his wagon had stopped shooting to watch, and the only noise was the crackling of flames and the shouting coming from the hunters in the rolled-over wagon who were now stuck.

There was a rumbling, like an earthquake. Bubba knew that was the spirit talking. There were no words, but pictures formed in his head. Courage was sufficient. It was going back to the depths. Cover it in water and sand, and trouble it no more. The pact is done.

"I'll inform the governor." This looked like a good spot to make a reservoir.

The Stonecoat slowly lifted one hand. When it dropped it, every Chenoo soundlessly collapsed, like puppets with their strings cut. Then the Stonecoat itself was gone, the spirit whisked back to its hole. The body remained, but it was no longer animated, and the rocks parted in a shuddering cloud. When the dust cleared, all that remained was a tall pile of gravel.

Bubba tossed Plague of Crows' stick into the bonfire. He didn't know if it was actually magic or not, but it was best not to trifle with such things. They always came with an unexpected cost . . . Besides, he had a sneaky suspicion he would run into her again one of these days.

Other than some bumps and bruises, and Hub Bryan breaking an arm when the wagon flipped, they were unscathed. While they rode back towards Cheyenne, Abrams figured that even once they ate the cost of the ruined wagon and cannon, this was going to be by far their most lucrative job yet. Monster killers loved getting paid.

"Split eight ways, it's still the most gold any of us have ever seen," Abrams shouted. The men cheered.

Bubba was riding alongside Hannah Stone. The young woman hadn't said much since the battle. She'd conducted herself admirably in the fight, and a flexibility of mind need not be limited to the supernatural.

"Make that nine ways, Balthazar." She looked over at him and grinned. This time the smile was real.

BLOOD ON WATER

By Hinkley Correia and Larry Correia

"Blood on the Water" was coauthored with my sixteen year old daughter, Hinkley, and this is the first time it has appeared in print.

The Diary of Hannah Stone

   As the first female member of Bubba Shackleford's Professional Monster Killers, I believe it expedient that I begin a journal to document my experiences.

   I first joined the company approximately a month ago. I had left Buffalo Bill Cody's Wild West Show due to creative differences, and was temporarily searching for work in Cheyenne, Wyoming, when the good Mr. Shackleford and company happened to pass through. Mr. Shackleford was leading a small hunting party to track down and exterminate a pack of Chenoo cannibals. When we happened to cross paths, I was invited to join their quest because Mr. Shackleford knew my illustrious reputation as the finest sharpshooter in the region.

   After a long and arduous battle we managed to eliminate the foul creatures. Once the smoke had cleared the good Mr. Shackleford officially offered me a job with his company. I have been traveling with the Professional Monster Killers ever since. I will endeavor to record our adventures with the utmost accuracy.

   We are currently journeying by rail to the recently added state of Utah. A few days ago we received a letter from a Mr. Wilford Woodruff of the Mormons, seeking to hire our services. Apparently some foul creature has made its home in one of Utah's northernmost lakes. It is unknown how long it has dwelled there, perhaps subsisting off of fish and wildlife, but recently it had taken to devouring people, which was most unacceptable. We have been commissioned to deal with this nefarious beast.

As Mr. Shackleford gathered the company, he pontificated upon the idea of someday having teams of professional monster killers scattered about the continent, ready to respond quickly to monster threats without the necessity of us riding from town to town first. Someday perhaps Mr. Shackleford—being a man of great industry—will build such an empire, but now is not that day, which is why I'm writing this in a train car chugging relentlessly westward.

Due to our small and efficient company of eight men, one woman, four dogs, twenty-two horses—riding and pack—and one war wagon (the second had not yet been fully repaired from our encounter with the Chenoo) we were able to mobilize quickly. We loaded thousands of rounds of ammunition, many pounds of dynamite, and our two Colt-Browning machineguns upon the train. Because our new client informed us the monster was aquatic in nature and exceedingly large of stature, Balthazar Abrams—who serves as our quartermaster—sent a telegram to San Francisco arranging the purchase of several whaling harpoons, and requesting expedited shipping to our new location.

That is the thing about hunting monsters. We must be prepared for everything, and if we are not, then we must adapt quickly. Everything can be killed. We just so happen to be very good at killing the big things. I am most eager for the opportunity to harpoon something.

If Hannah Stone had to choose the one thing about Utah she hated the most, it had to be the weather.

While she had lived in the West for much of her life, Hannah had never cared for the climate. So naturally, they just had to go to Utah in the "spring" after one of the harshest winters in years. In the mornings it was freezing cold to the point that she needed her thickest coat, then the afternoons would be so hot and dry that she'd empty a good-sized canteen in under an hour. Rain would flood in, even when just a few hours prior, the only clouds in the sky were wispy and small. The worst part, though, had to be the snowstorms. Just when it looked like the weather was finally going to regulate itself, clouds would roll in and drop inches of snow. There was just something not right about a snowstorm in May.

Ten minutes ago she'd sat by the little hotel window to enjoy the sun while she ate her lunch. Now she was watching snow flurries. Utah could go straight to hell.

But Hannah didn't so much as mutter about that. Garlick and Abrams were also present. The other Professional Monster Killers laughed and poked fun at her whenever she complained. Sure, the men complained just as much, if not more—the weather, the pay, the food, the distance traveled, the hours in the saddle, the aching bones, so on and so forth—but they only seemed to notice when she did it. It was natural, Hannah supposed. She was not only the newest member of the group, but also the youngest and the only woman. She knew Bubba hadn't wanted to hire her for those exact reasons, thinking monster killing was too difficult for womenfolk or some such nonsense. Except she'd been too stubborn to leave and Bubba had been too much the Southern Gentleman to let her die.

Despite her annoyance at being treated like a child at times, for the most part she got along well with her compatriots. The Professional Monster Killers were a rowdy band that said what they meant and meant what they said. They didn't care for the opinions of most normal folk. Nor did they care that she wore men's trousers, or that she would much rather beat the other hunters at poker than do needlework, or whatever boring thing it was that more traditional ladies were supposed to do to keep themselves entertained. The group was outspoken and Hannah respected that.

However, that nature was probably the reason why Bubba always met the clients alone. A few hours after going to meet with their client's representatives, he returned to the hotel, looking stern and glum as usual.

"Balthazar, Harvey, Miss Stone," he said by way of greeting. "Where's the rest?"

"I believe, for most of them, sleeping off a drunk, boss," Balthazar explained. This may have been Mormon country, but Ogden was a town born to cater to the railroad, so the religious types ignored the little Sodom and Gomorrah of the mountains. "The boys were excited for the change in scenery. They were up late."

Balthazar was too old for that nonsense, and Garlick fancied himself something of a preacher, but the rest did enjoy their saloon tours, loud piano music, and women of ill repute. Despite that, all of them had remained respectable gentlemen and treated Hannah as a lady at all times; though she liked to think that was because they respected her, she was perpetually armed, and would shoot anybody who looked at her cross-eyed, she'd also found out that Bubba had warned them the first one who acted the ass toward her, he'd castrate like an unruly bull calf.

"Shall I summon them, Mr. Shackleford?" Hannah asked.

"Slumbering past noon like bums . . . Please do."

She put her fingers to her lips and let out an unholy high-pitched whistle. It was the next best thing to firing her revolver into the air.

"While those roustabouts stir, I'll tell you three the bad news. They've tried to kill the monster themselves several times, but the thing never appears when armed men are waiting in ambush. It's too clever for that and remains hiding in the depths. Yet it continues to pick off victims, sometimes even slithering up into the shallows and plucking travelers from the shore. Witnesses describe a creature of incredible size."

Abrams chuckled. "They always do."

"Yet these weren't the types prone to exaggeration. Several confirmed that it was seen effortlessly dragging a full grown horse and rider into the water. This is nothing natural. It's got a neck like a serpent, with the head of an alligator upon the end, but a bulbous body with tentacles like a squid."

Garlick pounded the table. "It's the Leviathan of Revelations! I knew it!"

"No. It ain't. Calm yourself, Harvey. Not every miscellaneous critter we come across is opening the seventh seal and bringing about the apocalypse."

"That's not how—" Garlick started to correct him, but Bubba held up his hand.

"And even if some critter was ushering in the end times I wouldn't particularly care, but I would ask for an increase in our fees."

"Then let's mount up and go shoot us a lake monster." Hannah was extremely excited, having never shot a lake monster before.

"Don't be hasty, Stone."

She bit her tongue. Hannah was aware of her reputation for being infamously obstinate and aggressively quarrelsome, but contrary to popular belief she did listen to her boss most of the time. Partly because he was the one who paid her, but mostly because she had started to look up to him as a mentor. Bubba was the one who issued the smart orders that kept them alive in a fight, and she'd rather not die before she got a chance to live the rest of her life.

"There's something not right about these stories. I'm no natural philosopher but a hybrid of distant ocean and swamp creatures ending up in a fresh water lake in the middle of the continent don't make a lick of sense. If this is the product of foul sorcery or some form of spirit, we need to know, because there ain't nothing more annoying that having bullets pass through something like it's made of smoke. So we'll take our time, figure out the nature of the thing, then make our move."

Bear Lake is several days' ride to the north of the train station, through high, rugged mountain passes. Currently we are traveling by horse and wagon toward Cache Valley.

One thing that Mr. Shackleford always stresses is the value of good research. If all anyone needed to do to make a career of monster eradication was a shotgun and some grit, we would be out of a job. When embarking on the hunt for a trophy animal, an accomplished hunter will spend just as much, if not more, time preparing, than in the pursuit itself. We are much the same.

However, information pertaining to the supernatural is often lacking in accuracy. We hunt creatures of legend and fairy tale, so the natural place to look would be those old stories. On occasion, they will have some good information, but often over the decades the stories have broken away from the actual facts and gone down divergent paths. Unfortunately, blatantly asking a normal person off the street if they had seen a monster was simply not going to go well. President McKinley has on two prior occasions sent Mr. Shackleford strongly worded letters admonishing him upon the necessity of keeping the existence of monsters secret.

So a professional killer of monsters must tread cautiously, relying only on the best sources of information.

Hannah never understood why Bubba trusted the Scholar.

She had been winning the current hand of poker against some of the other Professional Killers when Skirmish McKillington—their massive-yet-friendly Irish boxer—burst into the parlor, telegrams in hand. "Boss! Words back from the Scholar!"

"Thank you, Skirmish." Bubba took the telegrams and began to read. "Well, I'll be damned."

Bubba was usually a cautious man when it came to trust. Since she had begun working under him, he had warned her of the dangers of cavorting with shadier characters far more than she could bother to count. Thus, naturally, Hannah found it mighty hypocritical of him to trust the advice of a mysterious and unnamed outsider. There was something mighty shifty about somebody who signed his correspondence only with the letter S.

Despite his suspicious nature and unknown intentions, the information the Scholar sent was usually fairly accurate, and when he couldn't be sure of his own research, he pointed them toward a "regional folklore expert." This was generally someone who had actually seen the monster firsthand, or at least had a vague understanding as to what it was. Hannah was curious as to what manner of man he must have been to know all of these strange people, considering the last "expert" dispatched was a powerful witchdoctor poison woman who could turn into a murder of angry crows.

"The telegraph operator confirmed the same thing we already heard," Skirmish told the rest of them as Bubba read. "There's an eerie howl that goes out over the lake, echos for miles, heralding the coming of the beast. When they hear that sound, the locals go inside and hide their children. "

The small boarding house they were renting in the tiny town of Pickleville was empty except for their company, and the sharpshooter could tell why. Blue-green wallpaper was peeling off in the corners and edges of the room, and the whole thing smelled like mold and mildew. The proprietor was a scruffy-looking sort that liked to glare at the group whenever they raised their voices, as if they were going to scare off the rest of his nonexistent patrons. They probably would have gone somewhere else, but the rooms and the booze were cheap, not that Hannah would be having any of the latter. Drink made her hands too shaky to shoot straight, and it made it harder for her to successfully cheat at poker.

"I knew there was something unnatural about this creature," Bubba said as he put down the telegrams.

"Well, sure, boss," Skirmish replied. "I figured that was implied by all them tentacles."

"Not that. The Shoshone had legends of a lake spirit. Jim Bridger even saw it when he came through here back in the twenties, but our target don't match his description at all. Poking around town, though this area has been settled by white men since the sixties, this squid beast was only first spotted a few years ago, and has only in the last two seasons taken to eating people. I think our monster is a relative newcomer, and now I know from where . . . Stone, get your gear and saddle up. We got some investigating to do."

Hannah was a little surprised. Bubba had never called upon her to aid in any witness interviews before. She tended to do rather poorly in the speaking-to-people part of the job. It was probably something to do with her aggressively oppositional nature, and the fact that most folks were stupid and annoying. "Why me?"

"A traveling circus is similar to a Wild West Show, right?"

"I suppose."

"Good. Then you should feel right at home. I believe we're dealing with an escaped circus freak."

It is quite common for those of us in this profession to run into difficulties. Sometimes the monster we're hunting turns out to be quite a bit stronger than we thought it would be, or an entirely different creature altogether. Death is not an uncommon occurrence. Other times, the fault lies with the clients, who will occasionally try to swindle their way out of paying, though they usually back down after realizing what manner of professionals they are dealing with. Often we have difficulty with the local population either meddling, chasing off our prey, or getting themselves eaten.

Sometimes the problem with the locals is even more challenging in nature. In the case of the Bear Lake Monster, there was an individual who actually wished to protect the creature and shelter it from harm.

Some supernatural creatures, such as nosferatus or other beings of such dark persuasion, have the ability to manipulate people's minds. This charm is usually broken when the source of the manipulation is exterminated. It is far more difficult when the person in question is genuinely emotionally attached to the beast we're trying to eliminate.

Then it gets complicated.

❖ ❖ ❖

Everywhere was lush and green, and wildflowers of all sorts of colors popped up in clumps all around the trail they were riding. Hannah probably would have thought it was very pretty, if she bothered enough to care. The grumpy young woman was instead focusing on the task ahead of them. Shooting was easy. Talking was hard. So get through this, shoot the monster, then go onto another job in another place and kill whatever problem they had there. Repeat.

Hannah liked to think she had "a roaming spirit," though when she'd attempted to describe her general feeling of discontent to Bubba, he'd called it 'being young and stupid.' She couldn't help that she couldn't stay in one place for long. That's why she joined Buffalo Bill's Wild West Show to begin with. All she had to do was travel around with the group and perform a few tricks for an adoring crowd. The only downside had been when she actually had to interact with that crowd. She couldn't help that she had an angry looking face, even when she wasn't angry at all. It tended to put folks off.

A small cabin came into view through the trees. There was no smoke coming out of the chimney or movement coming from within, but the tidiness and overall condition of the place meant it was lived in. They were a long ways out from town.

"Somebody was searching for privacy," she mused.

"Keeps to herself something fierce, they say. Avoids nearly everyone. The locals figure she's a witch."

"Oh." Hannah had actually been thinking this kind of seclusion would be nice.

Bubba loudly hailed the cabin as they approached. When nobody shouted back or shot at them, they dismounted and hitched their horses to sturdy branches. As Bubba knocked on the door, Hannah could hear shuffling and the occasional falling object through the log walls.

"Hello. I'm Bubba Shackleford. I mean you no inconvenience but there's an important matter to discuss."

After a few moments the door opened a crack and a face popped out.

Now, Hannah had seen plenty of ugly people in her comparatively short lifespan, but this woman took the cake, pug dog ugly. Hannah was a tall girl, but the lady that answered the door was abnormally short, probably only reaching the sharpshooter's stomach. Only the lady was so wide and thick that they probably weighed about the same. Her face was square, well, it was probably square, it was hard to tell with the matted beard which stretched from below her large, bulbous nose to her waist.

"What'chu want?"

Hannah looked over to her boss, to the strange woman, and back again. If Bubba was surprised at all by her appearance, he certainly didn't show it. Then again, he's probably seen weirder.

"I'm assuming you're Mildred Jemfinder. I believe you have some information on the Bear Lake Monster."

The lady swung her head back and forth, as if checking for something, before opening the door the rest of the way. The two hunters took that as their cue to enter.

The inside of the log cabin was nowhere near as clean as the outside was. Piles of junk were illuminated by whatever light had managed to sneak in around the furs covering the windows and the now open door. She had accumulated everything: old newspapers, Sears and Roebuck catalogs, empty sacks, old bottles, scraps of cloth, and various metal trinkets. Through all the mess, Hannah saw the faint glimmer of reflected light on top of the mantle. It was some kind of large seashell, with shimmering colors of all shades. She'd only noticed it due to all the contrast from the otherwise dismal room. Its frequent use was obvious, due to the lack of dust. A brief moment of eye contact indicated that Bubba had seen the shell too.

The extremely short woman picked her way through the clutter before shoving more trash off of what turned out to be a chair. With some difficulty, she managed to firmly plant herself in said chair before crossing her arms and looking at the two.

"What'chu want with Bubbles?"

Hannah could only look at Mildred with incredulity. If you had a horrific monster in the lake not too far from her home, would you name it Bubbles? It seemed a mighty innocuous name for something that kept eating folks.

"I wish to know what he really is."

"Why'd ya think I'd know?"

Bubba reached into his coat and removed a tattered and yellowed piece of newsprint. "A few years back, Dr. Swan's Magical Menagerie of

Mystery got off the train and set up shop. It says here the freak show included such oddities as a snake man, a boy with two heads, and a *bearded lady.*"

"Paid good 'nuf." Mildred spit on her own floor. "Didn't like 'em pullin' on me beard to see if'n it was real. Humans is stupid."

Hannah had no idea what was going on. "What are you?"

"Smarter'n you, missy."

"I figure the old Germans named your kind a dweorg or a twerg. Dwarf, I suppose we'd call it now. Not that I care what you are or why you're aboveground, because according to this, the biggest draw of Dr. Swan's show weren't no bearded dwarf, but a baby sea monster, captured off distant Indonesia, and kept inside a big tank in a dark tent. It cost a whopping fifty cents to get inside to see it, but it was so impressive, folks still paid up."

"That they did, hunter. Bubbles was a star."

"I never told you I was a hunter."

"Didn't have to. Got the look 'bout ya. Some things never change."

"I should have said most folks paid to get in. Some kids snuck under the back of the tent, except one got plucked up by a tentacle, plopped into the tank, and promptly eaten."

"Little brat should'a heeded the warnin' sign."

"According to this article, the public devouring of a youngster, coupled with other strange goings on around the circus, including a few missing persons, caused the sheriff to run the good Dr. Swan and his troop out of town."

"Ain't nothing good 'bout that doctor. T'was an evil company, his. Swan's a collector of dark an' vile things. Some o' the things in his show ain't o' this world, an' he pays 'em in souls."

Bubba nodded thoughtfully. "I'll be sure to pay him a visit . . . After it ate that kid, they were going to destroy the sea monster, only someone smuggled it away first."

"Bubbles meant no harm. He's a good boy. Didn't deserve no killin'. Loaded him on a wagon and we ran away. I put Bubbles in this lake. Sure, t'wernt salt water, but Bubbles' kind is made from old magic, an' tough. Minded our own business from then on, we did."

"He's been eating people!" Hannah exclaimed.

"Well . . ." It was hard to tell with the beard, but Mildred might have been a little ashamed. "I was keepin' 'em fed. He knew to come when

I called. Chickens first. But out o' his little tank, he kep' on growin' bigger an' bigger. Then I fed 'em goats. Thought I was keepin' up, but he must'a got feelin' peckish. But no need for killin', hunter. I bought me a herd o' cows. Plenty o' cows to go 'round. He'll be a good boy from now on, I promise."

"Ma'am, I know you're fond of him, but in my experience, once a creature gets a taste for human flesh, they'll continue to murder. He's a danger to every soul who comes near this lake. I can't let that stand."

"You'll never catch him! He's only a wee 'un, but he's too clever for the likes of ye! Bubbles' kind knows when to hide from hunters!"

"Yet you've got a way to call him to shore to feed."

"Nay! I said too much!" Mildred was outraged. "This be his lake now! Folks get ate, that's on them! Now get outta me house!"

"You want that I should shoot her?" Hannah whispered to her boss. "Out! Out!"

After a bit of negotiation, we managed to convince Miss Mildred to give us the magic conch shell in order to preserve the future of the beautiful lake and its inhabitants. She was sad to let her old friend go, but she agreed that it was for the greater good.

Hannah hadn't ended up shooting the bearded lady. Bubba Shackleford was far too gentlemanly for that sort of thing. So instead they'd gone back to their horses, found a good spot in the woods to conceal their location, and then waited for Mildred to leave her cabin in order to tend to her small herd of cattle.

"I don't know about this, Mr. Shackleford," Hannah whispered as they approached the cabin. "Thieving seems wrong."

"We can't let her pet monster's rampage continue. That echoing call the locals think is the monster probably ain't coming from the beast. It's Mildred blowing a horn calling Bubbles to supper. I'm betting that fancy shell came from the traveling circus too. Probably how the doctor captured it from the sea to begin with."

"Well, this still isn't very dignified!"

Bubba began climbing through one of the windows. "Just keep on lookout. Getting back shot by an angry dwarf while committing burglary would be an ignominious way for a Professional Monster Killer to expire."

Bubba made it through the window while Hannah kept watch. A moment later he came back with the mysterious conch shell. Then they ran for it.

The plan was fairly simple. Once by the shore, Mr. Shackleford would blow the horn, and we would wait in ambush. Hopefully, it would mistake our horses for a feast. Once we had a clear view of the creature, we would harpoon it snugly, and then drag it into the shallows with our Clydesdales. With the sturdy brown horses towing it to such an advantageous location, we could slay it easily without blindly firing and wasting precious ammunition.

Due to the preponderance of snow last season and the fresh runoff, the water level was high. So we picked an area of beach where it was shallow and level for about fifty feet, before dropping off into the abyss. Most of our company concealed ourselves in the trees and waited.

Bear Lake was very pretty this time of year. The waters were the same blue as the sky. Mountains rose majestically into the sky across the lake. I could easily see this being painted and hung up in a rich man's home.

It was such a shame that the clear blue water was going to be red by the end of this.

The water was seeping through the fabric of her pants and down into her boots, making her feet wet. It wasn't a pleasant feeling, but it wasn't like there was any alternative. The only spot of cover on this damnable beach were the scrub trees and brush near a stream, and everything was damp and cold. The Professional Killers were waiting, weapons in hand, waiting for their prey, waiting for the perfect moment to strike.

Waiting was awful. Hannah believed waiting to be the worst part.

Bubba was actually standing in the open, holding onto a rope which was in turn tied around the neck of a sacrificial cow. He'd blown the horn—a weird plaintive wail presented dinner—a scrawny used-up milk cow they'd gotten for cheap—and gone to waiting like the rest of them.

Rustling leaves broke the silence, and a small figure burst out of the surrounding woods and headed directly toward Bubba. The silence was even more ruined by the screeching obscenities of the dwarf woman, who must have heard the echoing sound of her stolen conch shell and come running. Most of the company remained focused on the water, searching for any kind of movement. The bearded lady made her way down the shore and into the water with surprising speed.

"Now, what do you think you're doing? Stealing a woman's personal belongings wit' intent to shed the blood o' an innocent creature?" If Mildred wasn't red in the face before, she certainly was now. In fact, she was turning slightly blue around her shirt collar.

"It would certainly seem as such." Bubba tore his eyes off the lake to look at the dwarf lady. Under normal circumstances, he might have been polite and offered some monetary compensation, or at least an apology. Thing is, a man can only deal with so much before he lost his patience, and that threshold was crossed a long time ago. "It ain't no innocent. You brought a damned sea monster here!"

"He's just a baby!"

"That eats people!"

"Stupid useless people! Now gimme that back!" Mildred wrestled the conch shell out of the larger man's hand, before clutching it close to her body. "How *dare* ye? I have half a mind to report ye for theft!"

Hannah noticed something slithering in the water and opened her mouth to call it out—just as the tentacle snapped out of the water and yanked Mildred under.

Their target was just a dark shape in the shallows. Sadly it became much easier to spot when it began chewing on poor dumb Mildred. The hunters reacted near instantaneously. Skirmish threw his harpoon, missing by inches. Mexican George was next, his aim a bit higher, and managed to nail it. The beast erupted from the water, shrieking, and started thrashing around.

It was the oddest critter she'd ever seen. Its body was a big fleshy globe, big around as a five-hundred-gallon water tank, but with a whole bunch of little "arms" that looked like hoses sticking out the side, each one wiggling like a headless snake; but sticking out of the body was one thick snake, only that really turned out to be a neck, complete with a head with big teeth and eyeballs and the works. Then—almost thankfully—it went back under and out of view.

Lesser men would've run, but this was all in a day's work for Bubba Shackleford's Professional Monster Killers.

Armed with her buffalo rifle, Hannah watched the splashing water carefully for an opening. If it slipped that harpoon, it would be gone in no time, so she had to be careful. Seeing a flash of grey flesh, she hoped for the best . . . and fired. Another shriek told her all she needed to know.

Pangle threw his harpoon. Though he wasn't near as strong as Skirmish or George, he'd bragged about how he'd thrown the javelin in competitions at his fancy, back east college. This one lodged itself deep into the body of the monster.

"Pull!" Bubba ordered.

Hub still had his arm in a sling from the Stonecoat incident, so he was stuck driving the team. When he saw the second harpoon strike, he put the horses to work. The ropes snapped taut.

Bubbles was apparently not pleased with this and tried to pull back.

Meanwhile, Bubba's captive Holstein had panicked and was making a break for it. He let it go, drew his pistols, and commenced firing. Shockingly enough, Bubbles was outpulling the team of horses, and they were some mighty big horses. "Don't let it get away!"

The monster had already gone back deep enough, the gunmen no longer had a shot, so Hannah slung her rifle over her shoulder and grabbed hold of the rope to try and help. Which looking back and considering the mass of the animals involved, was a rather futile gesture.

Rope ran over her fingers, trying to slip out of her grasp. She nearly lost it, but managed to tighten her grip to hold on. The sharpshooter had to dig the heels of her boots into the sand just to stay upright. That didn't last long, and she ended up getting yanked down clear into the cold water.

"Time is of the essence, killers," Bubba said as he waded back onto shore, calmly reloading his guns. There was no sign of Mildred. He holstered, then grabbed Hannah by the arm and pulled her up as she gasped and sputtered. "It's a matter of teamwork, Miss Stone. Stick to what you do best."

Chastened, she reloaded her Sharps.

Hagberg was ready to light their dynamite, but they couldn't risk an explosion freeing their harpoons yet. Their throwers, picked because they had the strongest arms, had retrieved their second harpoons, and hurled those as well. This time Pangle missed, but Mexican George and Skirmish struck true.

Now there were four ropes on the beast, and it began gradually losing the pull. Soon it would no longer be shielded by the water.

"It's losing blood and sure to tire," Bubba shouted. "As soon as it's in view, fire the machineguns."

All in all, it seemed to Hannah that things were going fairly well.

Until Bubbles gave up on trying to escape, and went on the offensive instead.

First, one tentacle rose, then a second. Both appendages slapped back down near the hunters, spraying water everywhere. It got in Hannah's eyes. When she could see again, the monster was slither-dragging itself up the shore. It was apparent that Bubbles had decided that it wasn't going to be bullied on its home turf. Purplish grey tentacles squirmed about behind a dark and pointy head, which culminated in two beady, black eyes and rows of shiny white teeth.

"Fire upon that ugly bastard!" Bubba commanded.

Tentacles flailed all around the hunters, trying to bat them to the side. One of the fleshy tendrils managed to hit Hannah, crashing her into Skirmish, and sending both of them into the water. She was getting mighty tired of winding up in this damnable cold lake. This time, she managed to keep her head above the water. Until a tentacle wrapped around her ankle—which hurt something fierce—and began dragging her lakeward.

Skirmish began hacking at the tentacle with his knife. She drew both her Colts and went to shooting. The majority of her bullets hit meat, and the tentacle released.

That was when Sid began to chuckle manically.

Now, Hannah might not have been part of the company for very long, but she had come to understand a few key things about each of the other members. Little things, like Pangle was an avid reader, or that Mexican George was very good with horses, or that when Sid Hagberg started giggling, you needed to get out of the immediate vicinity, because that man had a love of dynamite something fierce. Skirmish was even more aware of this and scrambled to his feet, yanking Hannah with him. The two splashed toward safety.

A large explosion rang throughout the air. It was a good blast, but a bad throw, and detonated a bit too far to the monster's side. It downright rattled Hannah's calm. Bubbles gave an almost mocking roar at the failed attempt to blow it up.

"Next time a warning would be appreciated!" Skirmish bellowed.

"I did!" Sid was indignant as he lit another stick of dynamite to toss at the creature. "Ain't my fault y'all were splashing around not paying attention!"

While that attempt to blow it up had failed, it did give Hannah some time to recover and get back to shooting. Skirmish, however, had lost his gun in the watery tussle, so excused himself to run back to the wagon for another weapon.

The monster's charge up the beach had taken the slack out of the ropes. Hub Bryan didn't know what to do about that, but Bubba began shouting at him. "Get to pulling! We'll drag this sumbitch clear to Salt Lake City if we have to."

Bubbles was now rolling about on the sand, but that didn't seem to make it much less deadly. It was riddled with bullet holes, but seemed so riled up it didn't show any inclination toward giving up. One of their machineguns had jammed—again—but the other was still making a lot of racket and poking a whole lot of holes.

Skirmish came running back armed with a pickaxe. Hannah thought he was being foolish for grabbing a short-range melee weapon instead of a gun, where he would have to walk up to a creature that had a considerable range advantage, a few thousand pounds on him, and mouth snapping shut like a triple-layered bear trap.

A tentacle wrapped around Sid Hagberg, yanking him and his bag of dynamite into the air. He screamed in a very unmanly fashion as he was held over that terrible snapping maw. Sid lost hold of his dynamite bag and red sticks bounced off Bubble's hideous face, but unfortunately none of those fuses were burning. This was an unfortunate development for Sid personally, but it also meant that their machinegun had to stop its indiscriminate spraying of bullets so as to not mulch their own man.

Which just demonstrated why skill would always be superior to technology. Hannah hurried and dropped another shell into her Buffalo gun. It was one hell of a shot, trying to hit the waving tentacle holding Sid, and not Sid, but it was a far bigger target than a dime tossed in the air, and she'd done that a dozen times a show.

CRACK!

The tentacle popped into fleshy bits, and Sid landed head-first in the shallows, which looked like it would hurt, but was a lot nicer than landing in those teeth.

Despite these unfortunate developments, Skirmish looked gleeful.

"I've got an idea!" The big man roared and charged the monster, pickaxe raised.

"Dear Lord, not this again," Bubba muttered. "Cover Skirmish!"

Hannah rolled her eyes at the man's stubbornness as she reloaded. She may have thought it was a stupid idea, but she knew she had to make sure to provide enough covering fire so that he could at least get close enough to do whatever madness he intended to do. Tentacles were still thrashing around, spraying cold water into the air. She cut a tentacle in half right before it would have smacked Skirmish in his noggin.

Somehow Skirmish made it through all that. The monster turned its pointy head his way, seemingly amazed at the depth of human stupidity. But whatever thoughts Hannah had about this being a poor idea slipped out of her mind when that pickaxe came *down*.

Skirmish hit it right in the nose so hard he drove the pick clean through the grey hide. The Irishman was strong as an ox. There was a crunch of bone and thick red blood squirted out. Bubbles' head hit the sand. The axe only stopped its descent because the handle was pressing into the top of the creature's snout.

Bubbles' black eyes widened, but when it tried to bite Skirmish, nothing happened. It turned out he'd embedded the pickaxe clear into its lower jaw, sticking the two halves together.

The sharpshooter could only watch in awe. She hadn't been expecting that to be effective at all, let alone end up being one of the most glorious moments she had ever witnessed. The sea monster seemed positively stunned.

She might have continued to marvel had Bubbles not suddenly gone all spastic, rolling about. Ropes snapped and screaming horses were pulled off their feet. One of its tentacles swept her legs out from under her and made her fall on the sand. If it wasn't angry before, it certainly was now. Bubbles gave as much of a roar as it could with its snout pinned shut, and ended up batting Skirmish away with one of its many slithering appendages.

From her vantage point on the ground, she noticed that one of Sid's lost sticks of dynamite had wound up wedged between Bubble's teeth . . .

It was up to her. Everyone else was pretty preoccupied with not getting smacked around. Bubba was dragging the unconscious Sid away from the flashing tentacles. With the ropes broke or harpoons knocked free, Bubbles was getting away, *and he was dragging Skirmish with him!*

Still sitting on the sand, Hannah crossed her legs, braced her elbows across her knees, took a deep breath, and steadied her heavy rifle.

Bubbles was rolling wildly. The red stick was a small target and it was getting farther away by the second. She'd made a lot of trick shots in her life. The last time she'd screwed one up had left a man disfigured and the spectators traumatized. Only Skirmish McKillington was about to get drowned or ate if she didn't do something about it, and she actually cared about her companions in the company, which was rare, because frankly, people annoyed her.

As nervous as she was though, she aimed—trying not think about how this was like Bob's lips all over again—and fired.

The slug detonated the stick of dynamite. The resulting blast tossed gallons of blood into the air.

Once all of the red droplets had gotten done falling out of the sky, and she had managed to blink the liquid out of her eyes, it was clear Bubbles wasn't moving, just a big lump lying in the shallows, with a big leaky hole through the side of its head. But Skirmish certainly was moving! In fact the man was swimming for his life. At first, she thought that she had managed to kill the monster, but it must have twitched or something, because Bubba yelled at everybody to lay fire into it until they were sure it was dead.

Half a minute of continuous gunfire later, Bubba Shackleford finally shouted for everyone to stop, because now they were just having fun and wasting money.

The injuries to our company were relatively minor, consisting mostly of contusions, concussions, and near drownings, and the sea monster had grown far too heavy to transport, so we removed its damaged head to present as evidence of a contract fulfilled. We left the body and tentacles for the buzzards. We were later informed that the head was taken to the nearby Agricultural College of Utah for study, but was later seized by deputy marshals.

With Bubbles' reign of terror lifted, the good folk in the surrounding towns threw a party in our honor. There was a night of dancing and celebration. I received a very distasteful proposal from a local boy, and was so taken by surprise and offense that I immediately broke his nose with the butt of my revolver.

However, even during the merriment I could tell that Mr. Shackleford was eager to move onto the next challenge, because there's always another town and another monster. And if no contract presented itself, I could tell that the idea a haunted traveling circus secretly up to no good somewhere within the borders of our nation gnawed at Mr. Shackleford.

Even before the party started he had already sent a telegram to our Scholar asking for directions to this nefarious Dr. Swan. For Mr. Shackleford is a man of action, not given to hesitation, so early the next morning our company set out on our next adventure.

And thus ended another contract for Bubba Shackleford's Professional Monster Killers.

IN THE INTRO to *Bubba Shackleford's Professional Monster Killers* I mentioned the character of Hannah Stone was created by Hinkley. That's because Hannah was her character during a Deadlands weird west role playing game. (On a related note, Mortimer "Skirmish" McKillington is my son's character, and you'll probably meet my other daughter's character in a future Bubba Shackleford story). Hannah, the antisocial trick shooter was a perfect fit when I was writing the first Bubba story so I borrowed her.

Afterwards, though, my daughter said she would enjoy trying to write a story from Hannah's perspective. It was really fun for me to team up with one of my kids. My daughter normally writes under a pen name that she has currently forbidden me from revealing. I can respect that.

THE LOSING SIDE

This story originally appeared in the Onward Drake anthology, in October 2015, edited by Mark L. Van Name, and published by Baen Books. It was a collection of stories inspired by David Drake.

When I was approached about this one, I had a geeky fan boy moment. I think Dave Drake is amazing, so I jumped at the chance to write something Drake inspired. However, my favorite thing of his is Hammer's Slammers, and he doesn't let just anybody play in that world. I figured it was worth a shot. I did my homework, reread a bunch of Hammer's Slammers stories, and pitched an idea from the perspective of the poor suckers who had to fight against those badasses. I was honored that he let me write this.

It was also a good excuse to play a whole bunch of World of Tanks for research. Yeah . . . Research. That's the ticket.

Despite the narrative to the contrary, my father was a good man. During the revolution the royalists called him the Butcher of Bangoran. General Vaerst was our spokesman, our inspiration, and their scapegoat. At the end of the war, the royalists dragged him out of the palace, stripped him naked, beat him, and then executed him with a ceremonial sword on the steps. They left his body to rot there for a week as an example.

I don't know who the royalists' god is, but my father was their devil.

In reality, he was just another husband and a father, no different than the tens of thousands of others who died during the revolution. He was a man who loved his planet, but who'd been pushed too far and took a

223

stand against tyranny. It turned out that he was really good at it. I don't think Dad ever thought his words would start a revolution.

The last time I saw him was the night before my company shipped out for West Moravia. At that point, we'd been fighting for two years. Dad was worn out, but the people were sick of those slaving royalist bastards and had risen up, so we were winning, and that kept him going. As we sat in his command bunker, listening to the shelling of Vakaga City above us, eating a last meal of ration bars, we talked about everything. About friends and family lost, but about how it would be worth it so that my children—his grandchildren—could grow up with freedom for the first time in our planet's history.

That was when he got the report that the royalists had somehow borrowed enough money to hire off-world mercenaries. At the time, I didn't understand why Dad looked so stricken.

"What's wrong?" I'd asked. "We're winning. We've got them on the ropes. Once we take the west, they'll fold."

He had gotten up and begun pacing. You have to understand, my father only paced when things were really bad. "I told the council we needed to lock them in, get them on contract, but those cheap do-nothings wouldn't listen to me. Now it's too late. We should have hired them when we had the chance."

"But what difference are some mercenaries going to make?"

"They're Hammer's Slammers, son. They'll make all the difference."

The explosion from the 20cm main tank gun obliterated half the apartment complex around us.

"Back up!" I shouted at the driver, but Cainho knew his shit, and we were already heading into the subterranean parking level before the Slammers' tank could get off another shot. The flash from the blast had momentarily fuzzed out our tank's scanners, but we'd gotten a peek, that's all that mattered. The spotted target's position would be relayed to everyone else, and hopefully something they threw at it wouldn't just bounce off that monster.

"Shogun Six, this is Phantom One. Heavy in the open," I called in as our Lynx sped through the empty garage. I brought up the map, and tapped out a path for Cainho to follow. "We're moving to Isen Street."

"Roger, Phantom. Engaging the heavy. Proceed to Isen."

Not that I wouldn't have kept going anyway. If my little scout tank waited long enough to get orders confirmed, we were dead. If one of our scout tanks was doing anything other than running or hiding, it was dead. We'd learned that the hard way.

As we bounced up the ramp and out into the street, the sensor package showed clear both ways, but half a second later I got a warning ping. Movement on the left, just a flash of iridium armor through holes punched in a concrete wall. *Combat car.* "Pig at nine." Its gunners hadn't seen us yet, or we'd be eating cyan bolts. I tagged a new path through the wreckage of what looked to have been a tractor dealership. The Lynx was the fastest armored vehicle on the battlefield, and in Cainho's skilled hands, it was a nimble little beast. He got us behind another wall and the flaming remains of some piece of industrial equipment and we hid.

"Shogun Six, this is Phantom One. Just spotted a pig at the end of Isen."

"Got it, Phantom. Tagged."

We waited. I could only pray that the nearby building fires were screwing up their thermal.

I could hear our gunner above me. Blanchard was breathing heavy as he tracked the combat car. Our 60mm autocannon hadn't had much luck penetrating even their smaller vehicles, especially not from the front. On the other hand, their tribarrels would rip right through any part of our Lynx like it was made out of paper. *Come on . . .*

It was hot. Beneath my armor, I was drenched with sweat. My sinuses were filled with the stink of carbon and blood. I was so tired it took a moment to remember where the rotting blood stink had come from. That's right. It was the same reason there was a hole in the driver's compartment I could see a beam of daylight through, and why we'd just picked up a replacement driver. In the heat of the moment, I'd already called Cainho by the wrong name a couple of times, but Haarde was dead . . . *What . . . Two days? Three?* They'd bled together. I couldn't remember.

"Keep moving, asshole," Cainho begged. "Nothing to see here."

Like their big tanks, the Slammers' combat cars were hover vehicles. I imagine they had to be really loud inside, floating on top of all those powerful fans. Our Lynx ran on rubberized tracks and had a small thorium reactor, so it was actually a pretty quiet ride. The combat cars had more human eyes manning guns all the way around, but their sensor suites didn't seem as good as the heavies, and not nearly as good as ours.

The one thing my home planet was good at was tech, much of it designed by my family's company. Moravia was great at designing sensor suites, which meant we got fantastic recordings of us getting our asses handed to us by the mercs with the heavier armor and bigger guns.

The combat car flashed past the holes and sped down the street in the opposite direction.

We could all hear the rumbling thunder of artillery through our thin armor. They were dropping shells on the tank. Red dots rained down my display, but one by one they flashed out of existence as the tank picked the shells out of the sky with its 20cm air defense system. Cyan bolts flew upward and explosions ripped across the air.

Something get through. Something . . .

The last red dot disappeared.

"Blood and martyrs," Blanchard snarled from the turret. The gunner's targeting displays had told him the same story. "Can't anything hurt these fuckers?"

"I heard a guy in the 6th rushed one with a satchel charge and tossed it under the fans," Cainho said as he maneuvered the Lynx around wrecked cars and rubble. "Blew it all to hell."

"Wishful thinking. They've got a point defense system for infantry too," I told my crew. "If that story's true, it's only because that tank was broken. A combat car, maybe."

The symbol of the tank disappeared from my map. The AI could no longer tell with certainty where it had gone. It could make logical predictions, but the mercenaries had figured that out first day, and were being annoyingly unpredictable. They were clever like that.

"Shit," Blanchard said. A missing tank meant they were going to make us go looking for it again.

"*Phantoms.*" They didn't bother with our full call sign, because Phantom Two through Six were gone, all lost over the last twenty furious hours. It turns out when a soft little scout got hit with a Hellbore there wasn't much left. "*This is Shogun Six. We need eyes on that tank.*"

"Keep your pants on, asshole." That wasn't for the command

channel. That frustrated muttering was for my personal gratification. Shogun Six was twenty klicks from this slaughter. The AI might not know where that tank had gone, but my gut knew. It was waiting to pop us. The sensors on their big tanks were ridiculously good. I needed to look at the terrain models of this disintegrating city and figure out how to approach without getting our asses vaporized.

"3rd Armored is approaching the east end of the park. They need to know where that heavy is."

The interior of the Lynx was tight. My compartment was worse. A lot of scout tank commanders liked to get their heads out of the cupola, thinking that made them more aware of their surroundings, and their visor would keep them up with the computer's feeds, but that was a trick. That was them lying to themselves. The sensor suite provided *too much* information, and most commanders found it overwhelming being bombarded by that much info for long. I'd been so plugged in and fried by the last few days of fighting, that I had the opposite problem. I was scared to unplug.

"There. You see the path, Cainho?"

"Got it, Vaerst." The new driver was excellent. He should be. Like me, he'd been fighting royalists since half the army had said enough with this tyrannical bullshit and the first shots were fired at Bangoran. He'd been an experienced tank commander himself up until a few days ago, when he'd had to bail out after his vehicle had been set ablaze by a tribarrel. The rest of his crew hadn't made it out. "You know, third is only running some cobbled-together surplus."

In other words, they were as doomed as everyone else they'd thrown against these merciless bastards.

"Third is driving Pumas. Our 60mm barely scratches the paint. We have to get real lucky to do any damage, but those have 120mm guns. A good shot might punch one of those land whales," Blanchard said hopefully.

"Yeah . . . Well, let's find them a target."

Who were we kidding? The Slammer tanks were 170-ton iridium wrecking balls with guns that could shoot down satellites. Dad hadn't been kidding. They were running the most advanced armored vehicles in history. Even their light combat cars weighed nearly twice what our Lynx did.

The kingdom's hardware was obsolete garbage in comparison. Our software was good. Our systems were good. Our soldiers were tough. But, hell, I might as well say we had truth and justice on our side too, since it turned out that all meant jack and shit when the bolts began to fly.

While Cainho moved us to the next hiding place, I expanded out the map until I could see the entire Moravian coast. That was one of the dangers of being too plugged in, too aware. *Curiosity.*

We were getting crushed.

"The Slammers are really that good?"

"They're the best," Dad said. "Alois Hammer has put together one of the most successful fighting outfits in human history. No bullshit, no politics, no ass-kissing. They don't play games, they don't have to make anybody happy. They agree to a mission, sign a contract, then they fill it. They're very good at that. Maybe the best there's ever been. And sadly for us, they've landed in the west."

"They can't be that good." Oh, how naïve I'd been back then. I'd seen some combat by that point, so I thought I knew a thing or two about war. My brothers were fighting for liberty, for our families, and for each other. I couldn't comprehend someone fighting just for money. "Only honorless scum would fight for anyone as evil as King Soboth!"

But Dad was wise, and he just shook his head sadly. "It isn't about good or evil to them. Hammer doesn't give a damn about Soboth beyond the fact the man is willing to mortgage a planet to save his crown. They only care about completing the mission and getting paid. Most of their trigger pullers won't even bother to read the briefings to learn what each side believes in, just which color uniform they're supposed to shoot. They've done it on plenty of other worlds, and they'll do it again somewhere else when they're done here."

"Not if we beat them."

Dad just laughed.

I watched the displays in horror as 3rd Armored was ripped to pieces.

The old Pumas crashed through the trees of Grand Park, big guns booming. The Slammers' tanks were moving across the grass, far too fast, and every time one of those 20cm Hellbores went off in a blinding flash, another one of our tanks turned into an expanding ball of plasma. The combat cars were darting about, using the terrain, popping over rises to rip off bursts from their tribarrels. They were concentrating on our infantry. Rockets and small arms fire were lancing out from the surrounding buildings' windows, but the tribarrels responded and ripped those facades into concrete dust.

"Shogun Six, this is Phantom. Targets are marked."

But there was no response, just dead air. I pulled back the screens. Shogun was gone, icon blinking red. The artillery battery was overrun. I didn't even know where those attackers had come from. No time to think about it. We were on our own.

A warning pinged, but Cainho's instincts had kicked in even before the AI had decided we were in danger and our Lynx was already scooting backward down the hill. A combat car was flying across the lake in a huge spray. Water exploded into steam as molten bolts lashed out and tore apart the rocks we'd been hiding behind. Flaming gravel clanged against our armor. That's about all it was good for.

There was nobody left to spot for. That fucking combat car had been chasing us all morning, and it was used to us running away. It would be expecting more of the same. As Cainho reversed us through the manicured flowerbeds, crushing carved topiary beneath our treads, I flagged a new course for him. "Come around the bottom of the hill." Using the terrain, we could stay low until the last second. "Blanchard, shoot that pig in the ass."

The Lynx hit the bottom and turned on a dime. The combat car would be climbing the hill. The AI told me that it was unlikely the pig would silhouette itself on that hill, even for a second, but I knew the AI was wrong. We'd been an annoyance. They wanted us dead, and they would figure if they risked climbing, they could get a few shots at us while we scurried for cover.

We swung around the bushes and every warning ping we had went off at once. Sure enough, the combat car was above us, tilting across the blasted rocks. By the time I shouted, "Fire!" Blanchard had already launched the first burst right into their fighting compartment. The rounds that hit the iridium armor left orange glowing dents, but the ones that entered fragmented inside and caused the vehicle to puke fire. Blanchard kept the triggers mashed, raking 60mm AP into that pig. A severed arm sailed through the air. An empty helmet bounced down the hill.

The combat car began to skew sideways. One of the tribarrels was cranking our way, but the edge of its skirts ground on the rocks, and the blast of air pressure suddenly drove one side of the pig into the dirt. The tribarrel fired wildly. Cyan flashes ripped burning holes into the grass towards us. "Pull back," I ordered. Cainho calmly reversed as Blanchard kept shooting. The helmet crunched beneath our treads. The gunner was so focused on killing that pig that his last few rounds hit nothing but the earthen berm we were now hiding behind.

We'd only been in the open for a moment, but already other things were vectoring in to kill us. The compartment was filled with powder smoke. Fans were blowing and the respirator in my helmet had kicked in. I tagged another route, keeping our head down, using the streambed and drainage culverts, and before I was even done, Cainho had us tearing across the park, quickly accelerating to sixty KPH. Considering the state of the ground, it was stupidly fast, but if we slowed down, we were dead.

There was an explosion from the top of the hill. Something had cooked off. We'd killed a Slammers' combat car. We'd actually done it. I had nobody to call that in to, and by the time I checked the screens, the twenty Puma tanks of 3rd Armored were all dead.

I had never seen my father like this. Even though we'd fought hard, built an army, hell, built a whole government, overthrown a king, and beat the wretched royalists, it was like he already knew we'd been defeated.

"Our only hope is to wear them down. Attrition. The people are on our side. The king will get what he paid for, but not a peso more. Hit and run, bleed them as they bleed us. To Alois Hammer this planet is just an entry on a profit and loss statement, but it is our fucking home."

He didn't sound convinced.

"I'm sorry, Captain Vaerst. Your father is dead."

I'd been plugged into the Lynx's systems continually for so many days that actual face-to-face human communication took a while to sink in. I stared at the major for a really long time, not understanding the words coming out of his mouth. There were no symbols, flashes, lines of movement and terrain paths, AI estimates, pings for threats, or stress load-outs. All I could communicate now were tanks, how to keep mine alive, and how to make theirs dead, fast. It was like I was stuck in high gear and couldn't downshift.

"He was murdered by royalists during peace talks at the palace." The major rested one gentle hand on my armored shoulder, taking my dimwitted exhaustion for shock. He patted me. "There, there." And it raised a cloud of dust. "We can take you off the line until we know what's going to happen in the capitol."

That was meant to be comforting, but I didn't . . . couldn't *get* comfort. For the last three weeks, I'd fought in my tank, slept in my tank, shit through a chute in the bottom of my tank, drank from a tube in my tank, and ate ration bars that were occasionally dropped through the open cupola of my tank whenever we stopped to resupply. So I just stared at the major, unblinking, until he took his hand away.

"Or not . . . That's fine, Captain. The battalion is falling back toward the river today. Carry on." He unconsciously wiped the dirt on his hand on his fatigue pants as he walked away.

I went back to my tank.

Cainho was asleep in the shade between the treads. Blanchard was painting another marking on the Lynx's battered turret. The sixteen red vehicles were royalists. The four black ones were Slammers. According to the screens—and the screens were my whole world now—nobody else had pulled off anything close to that. Sadly, *every* Slammers vehicle could paint a board like this . . . If they even bothered to count us.

But I didn't care. I just wanted to sleep.

"You know what they're saying about our little Lynx around camp? *Too cute to die, too deadly to live.* We're one tank, but they're calling us Task Force Phantom, all by ourselves . . . Good girl," Blanchard said, touching the turret with more actual love and kindness than the major had just shown me. "Word is they saw a heavy in the forest fifteen minutes ago, Cap."

I wasn't plugged in. I'd missed that ping. *Weird.*

"Before this is over, I really want to paint a heavy kill on here," Blanchard said wistfully as he put away the stencil and spray can. We'd replaced the 60mm autocannon with a 3cm power gun we'd looted off a Palace Guard wreck a week ago. It was a hell of a lot of gun for such a little tank. The main differences were that we killed things better now, but the compartment always smelled like melting plastic instead of burning carbon. I kind of missed the carbon smoke. "Did I tell you they blew up my town, Cap?"

Blanchard had taken that hard.

"Yeah, man. I know." He didn't need to tell me. I'd been there with him when it had happened.

"Whole damned town . . . Sniper fires from a window, they blow up the whole town. You don't need to blow up a whole town. That's overreaction. That's just plain rude. I really want to paint a black heavy on here."

"Let's go find one for you then." I thumped Cainho's leg with my boot.

He snorted and woke right up. "Any news?" our driver asked immediately.

"Something about the capitol . . . My dad . . ." Neither of those things was near this camp or this forest, so it was out of my hands. I popped a couple of Stay Awake pills. "I don't know . . . Let's go."

Once I got my helmet on the AI booted up, I could see clearly again. Fox company was in the north of Glad Wood, and they'd tagged a heavy. It only took a few seconds of running probabilities to see the mercs intended to seize the bridges at Constantine. I flagged it, but our chain of command had fallen apart, and our orders were a mismatched bunch of panicked gibberish. They sounded like squawking chickens over the net. They were sure upset about something.

It didn't matter. We'd just do what we always did. Harass the shit out of the other side, murder them when given the opportunity, and then run away to do it again later.

I checked the grids, the tank stats—the chameleon projector needed to be replaced soon—the tactical maps, expanding out further and further until I could see the whole war. It wasn't until I watched the news footage of the mob beating and kicking my father, and then clumsily hacking at him with a golden sword, that it finally registered.

This was what it felt like to lose a war.

My father knew that night why we wouldn't win.

I didn't understand until later. When my little tank was broken and full of holes, and I was bleeding, wading through the mud, dragging my burned gunner away, and that giant fucking monster tank came over the rise, riding on a dozen tornadoes, and it aimed that giant space gun right down at us, and blinded us with a spotlight, like some wrathful ancient war god . . . and as we stood there blind, battered by the wind, being weighed and measured and found wanting, then I knew too.

I spent the next few years in prison, mulling over the reasons we lost.

My father wasn't a real general. He was a businessman who got rich designing and exporting sensor packages for military vehicles, who could give a rousing speech, and who had the balls to stand up against a tyrannical lunatic. But he never wanted to make war.

Alois Hammer was born to make war.

I was a soldier. Everyone here knows my service record, but I was nobody. I knew heroes. Real heroes. I saw our best and brightest fight for what they believed in . . . and I watched them die.

Because Hammer's Slammers exist only to make war.

We were fathers and mothers, brothers and sisters, students, teachers, workers, merchants, and slaves . . . turned soldiers. And once the war was over, they all went back to being whatever we were before.

Hammer's Slammers were soldiers. Then, now, forever. Period.

So here we are, years later, and another Vaerst is standing before this council. You're beating the war drum again, calling for another rebellion, and you need yourselves a general, and who better to be your figurehead than a war hero?

I will heed your call. I will accept this commission, and I will help the people throw off the yoke of tyranny . . . on one condition.

We hire Hammer's Slammers.

This time I want to be on the winning side.

THE GREAT SEA BEAST

This story originally appeared in Kaiju Rising: Age of Monsters, *edited by Tim Marquitz and Nickolas Sharps, published by Ragnarok Publications.*

THE GREAT SEA BEAST revealed itself.

First, spines of bone, each one as big around as a tree, broke the ocean's surface. Next came the great bulbous head, its skin a deep red except for where it was covered in barnacles and black growths from the depths. Then the eyes appeared, two great white oozing blobs, and beneath those was a mass of writhing tentacles, longer than anything found on even the largest of the giant squid. There were still freshly drowned corpses of Minamoto clan sailors trapped in those tentacles.

As Munetaka watched, the tentacles moved the bodies into the vast wet hole that served as the creature's mouth, to be ground into a red paste between teeth like millstones. The head alone was larger than his ship, and when the shoulders broke the surface, it was larger than a castle. It was so large, so inconceivably vast, that it was like watching the sea birth a new island, only this island was heading straight for them at a seemingly impossible rate of speed.

It was incredible. It was a god made flesh.

The ocean crashed around the creature as if it were a rock cliff. Waves created by the monster lifted the *Friendly Traveler* and sent them hurtling back down. His tiny wooden ship was nothing before the Great Sea Beast. Several other Minamoto clan vessels had already been smashed into splinters by the thing's wrath. Their lord's warship was broken and sinking. They were on their own.

He spied the jagged cliffs. "Hold this course!" Nasu Munetaka bellowed at his panicking crew. He looked toward the opposite horizon. The sun was just beginning to rise. "Hold this exact course."

It would close with them in a matter of minutes. They would all die, crushed, drowned, or devoured. The brave sailors adjusted their sails and kept them on the wind. Lesser men leapt overboard or cowered in fear. The other samurai were struggling in vain to figure out the magical horn they'd taken from the gaijin, while their priest begged the water dragon to rise from his coral palace beneath the sea to protect them.

But Captain Nasu Munetaka did not ask the heavens for aid nor did he resort to foreign magic. He simply stood at the stern of the *Friendly Traveler*, calmly stringing his bow, watching the demon that had haunted his dreams come for them.

He had been waiting half his life for this moment.

His hands did not tremble.

Twelve years before, he had woken up screaming.

Someone was carrying him, cradled in their arms like he was a baby. They were trying to be gentle, but every touch was made of agony. The half of his body which had been out of the water had been burned crispy by the sun, and the half that had been submerged had been eaten away by salt water. His skin was peeling off in black or blue strips.

Munetaka was the son and grandson of warriors, so he tried not to scream. His throat was so dry it was more of a soundless hiss anyway and his body was so wrung out that there was no indignity of tears. And then he remembered through the haze of sun drenched pain how he'd come to be here. The village had to be warned. Frantic, Munetaka clutched at his rescuer's shirt and tried to tell him of the crimson demon rising from the sea, but he couldn't form the words.

"Bozu! Help us. The fishermen found this boy washed up on a reef."

With eyelids dried partially open, he could barely see, but Munetaka knew they were inside. He could feel absence of the angry sun. The rescuer laid him on a mat. Thousands of hot needles stabbed through Munetaka's back. He'd never before realized that his skin served the same purpose as his father's armor.

Someone knelt next to the mat. Cold hands touched the sides of his face and tilted his head for examination. "A shipwreck?"

"Yes. They said he still had a death grip on a broken board."

"He must have been in the water for several days . . . Ama! Get my medicine pouch. I'll need some water boiled. These wounds must be cleaned."

"We forced some drink down his throat when we found him. He didn't vomit most of it back up."

"Good, then he may still live . . . Can you hear me, boy?"

The crimson demon comes from the sea. Run. You have to run. You have to get away.

The memories came back, breaking through the walls of his mind. He was too young for a voyage up the coast, but he had tagged along on his father's patrol, sneaking in to hide amongst the piles of rope. By the time he was discovered, they would be too far from home to turn back. His father was a stern man, as was required of a Minamoto clan ship captain, but Munetaka knew that he secretly enjoyed having his son onboard his ship. Someday Munetaka would be a captain too, and he'd be the one to keep the seas around Kamakura free of pirates and Tairu clan scum, just like his father, and his father before him. Once found, he'd not even received too much of a beating. He suspected his father had been more than a little proud of his daring. The captain had even told his men that Munetaka was their good luck charm. It was the happiest day of young Munetaka's life, until the luck ran out and he had watched helplessly as the ocean turned red and the Great Sea Beast slaughtered everyone.

He snapped back to the world of sunburned pain. His flesh was so softened by days spent soaking in salt water that even the tatami mat was cutting through him and the monk was fretting as Munetaka bled all over the polished wooden floor of the monastery. The monk was asking him another question.

"What happened?"

Death had happened, only somehow it had forgotten to take him too.

Ten years before, his lord had condemned him.

"You waste my time with this?" Lord Minamoto Yorimasa raised his voice. "I should have you killed for your impudence, boy."

Munetaka kept his eyes on the floor. He could feel the angry gaze of the court on him.

"Your request is denied. There will be no expedition. The Great Sea Beast is a lie. You are the only witness. A child who drank too much salt water and cooked his brains in the sun imagined a demon to blame for his father's carelessness. Your father died in a storm like a fool. Knowing your family he was probably drunk and drove *my* ship onto the rocks. A stupid man, always wasteful and drunk."

The shame was unbearable. His father had been the best captain in the clan, but the truth was whatever the lord commanded it to be.

"My advisor said you display a constant tremor in your hands. You are too young to already be a drunk like your father. You are an embarrassment, and yet you dare to come before your lord and ask that I grant you an expedition to hunt for an imaginary monster? Especially now while the Tairu clan encroaches on our lands. What do you have to say for yourself, Munetaka?"

It was said that the exposure had stunted his growth. His voice was as small as his body. "Should it come again, we are all in danger. If we cannot hunt it down and kill it, we must be ready for when it returns."

The lord laughed. "Now you are telling jokes for my amusement. You must wish to be the new court fool. Even if such a thing was real, then it must be a spirit of the ocean. It could not be defeated with arrows or spears."

"No, my lord, I saw it clearly. It was no ghost or spirit. It was shaped like a man and walked upon the seabed. Its skin was like a whale and its face was like many squid, but it was still a creature of flesh and bone."

"And you alone are the only one who has ever seen such a magnificent sight."

"There are other witnesses," Munetaka said softly. "Only last year, three fishermen near the lighthouse at—"

"Peasants!" the lord snapped. "Their word means nothing. Their minds are soft, and your drunken tales have filled their hearts with fear. My fisherman are scared now because of you. Production suffers as they imagine a big red shadow beneath them, piss themselves, and flee back to shore. Even some of my samurai have been dumb enough to listen and believe your fanciful tales." He turned to glare at one of his retainers.

The young scribe Saburo lowered his head and backed out of the line, shamed by the attention.

"My lord. forgive me, but I remember clearly what I saw. The crimson demon was far bigger than your castle." He dared to raise his voice. The retainers began to mutter at his bold words. "It lifted my father's ship in one hand as it licked the sailors from the deck and then dropped us when it was done."

"Silence!" The whispering stopped. The lord would have no scandal in his court. "Listen to me very carefully, young Munetaka. Go back to your village. There will be no more mention of this sea monster. You will not speak of it again. It never happened. I have declared that it does not exist. Your father, despite his weakness, served me well, and that is the only reason I am being so lenient with you now. Return to your studies. I've been told that you show no talent with the sword and you are a disaster upon a horse, but the clan will find some use for your life eventually. Dismissed."

Eight years before, he had discovered his purpose.

"Nasu Munetaka, if rumor is to be believed, you are possibly the worst student who has ever been sent to me. You are small. You are weak. You shake like a leaf. Hold out your hands."

"Yes, sensei." Munetaka did as he was told and stuck his hands out, palms down.

"They expect me to teach the art of the bow to such as this?" The old man watched Munetaka's hands tremble. "Pathetic. They told me it is because you swallowed too much seawater, but I suspect that you are simply a wretched pig dog who lacks character. You have already demonstrated that you are a liar."

The other students snickered. Even though he'd been forbidden to speak of the Great Sea Beast for years now, their daimyo's condemnation had followed him everywhere. Nasu Munetaka was considered a liar for telling the truth. "Yes, sensei."

"Lower your hands. Your last sensei told me you have been squandering your inheritance on gambling and pleasure women, and that you often come to training reeking of alcohol. You're a disgusting mess, but if there is to be a war against the Tairu, we will need bodies. If you are late again to class, I will use you as a target."

The sensei continued down the line. "You will draw until the second thumb joint nestles upon your jaw." The other students had already prepared their bows and they stood eager at the edge of the grass of the practice field. Munetaka hurried to catch up. His father had been a superb archer and Munetaka would not fail him. "Each of you will release two hundred arrows today. First your arms will ache, then your fingers will bleed, and then you will experience pain like nothing you have ever imagined. You will pray for death long before that, but you will not stop until I tell you to. Ready! Draw!"

The targets were men made of straw. They seemed very far away. Munetaka raised the yumi. It was longer than he was tall, but because it was designed to be gripped on the lower third, he could still use it. His hands were shaking so badly that he had a hard time nocking the arrow.

"Release."

A dozen arrows flew downrange. Most of them fell short and stuck into the grass. Not a single target was struck. Munetaka's hands were shaking so badly that he wasn't ready in time.

"Hurry, idiot. You will draw back fully and then release the arrow in the same motion." A few of the other students laughed. "Shut up. Did I give you permission to find that amusing? Now, Munetaka."

It was incredibly difficult to pull it back and the yumi creaked as it bent.

"Imagine it is your sea monster," one of the other boys shouted.

And for just a moment, he did, and they were on a sea of red. His fingers slipped. The string slapped into his left wrist with a *snap*. The arrow flew wildly to the side, burying itself deep into the ground.

The sensei casually backhanded the loudmouth. "Multiple idiots. Wonderful. But if it really was bigger than our lord's castle, that would probably still have struck your monster. Try it again, fool, and no distractions this time. The rest of you wait."

His father had often told him that the arrow knew the way, so it had to be true. He could only trust that his father would guide the arrow's flight. Muscles strained as he struggled to pull back the string as he glared at the target, imagining that the straw man was his sensei, and as his fingers reached his cheek, he let go.

Red fletching appeared in the center of the dummy's chest.

The sensei nodded at Munetaka. "It is rare that a liar can shoot true. Again."

His wrist stung from the string. He took another arrow from the bundle and, since the yumi seemed to fight him less this time, had it nocked far more quickly than the first.

The second shot hit within a few inches of the first arrow.

"Again!"

The third was just above those.

"Hmmm . . ." The sensei stroked his long mustache thoughtfully. "Maybe the rest of you should arrive stinking of cheap booze too . . . Now imagine it is this sea monster of yours, Munetaka. Show us what you would do to it now."

He was a screaming child on a sea of red, holding onto a fragment of a boat, struggling to stay above the waves, as tentacles fed men into a wet hole filled with giant teeth.

Only he was no longer a little boy. *Father, guide my arrow.*

His hands did not tremble this time.

The fourth arrow streaked directly through the center of the straw man's face.

Four years before, the hunt had begun.

Munetaka was awakened by the grunting of pigs. A wet, pink snout was biting at his face to see if he was edible so the young samurai slugged the pig in the eye. It squealed indignantly and retreated. He found himself lying in a pile of straw, his back against a peasant's shack, and a sake jug in his lap. It sloshed when he moved it, so he choked down the remainder. It was the cheapest swill in Kamakura, but it got him drunk enough to sleep, and that's what counted.

"I figured you'd wake up if that pig started eating you." There was a man leaning on the fence. His kimono bore the mon of the Minamoto clan. "If not, then that was some strong drink."

"Who're you?" Munetaka asked as he scratched himself.

"The better question is, Who are you, Nasu Munetaka?"

"Who's that? I'm just some drunk ronin," he lied.

"No. I recognize you. You do not look so different now, like a shorter version of your father. They say you would have been a handsome one if the sea hadn't poisoned you, so that's why you are still nothing but skin and bones." The man gave him a sad smile. "They say you're the best archer in all the land. They say you killed a hundred Tairu soldiers at the battle of Uji."

"*They* say lots of stuff." He had no idea how many he'd killed, but he'd shot at least twenty. It was hard to keep track. Lord Yorimasa had still lost though, and after his suicide, they'd tossed his head in the river.

"Yet now you've been reduced to a life of crime, smuggling, and drinking. That's rather sad. It's to be expected though. You can't tell someone their entire life that they're a liar without honor, and not expect them to make it the truth."

"You're lucky I'm too hungover to string my bow to shoot you, friend." The man seemed kind of familiar, but Munetaka couldn't place him. "Do I know you?"

"I'm Saburo," he answered as he climbed over the fence.

"The scribe?"

"Scholar, diplomat, things like that. In fact I've just returned from a mission to the Song court all the way across the sea, but I still remember your tragic story."

"Yeah . . . Just a story . . ." Munetaka rubbed his bleary eyes. "Our dead lord saw to that."

"Most of all, I'm a collector of stories. The gaijin have stories too." Saburo removed a piece of paper from his kimono and handed it over. "Like this one, about a war between witches and a king, where foul sorcery was used to turn a leviathan of the deep into a giant monster to wreck the king's fleets. It comes all the way from a land called India."

Munetaka could not read the strange foreign writing, nor could he recognize the coastline shown on the map, but at the bottom was a drawing and it was . . . "No." The eyes, the tentacles, the spine, the blood red hide, It was *perfect.* His mouth was suddenly very dry. His hands began to shake so badly that they threatened to crumple the ancient paper. "It can't be."

"So it is the same then?"

Even though Saburo was of higher station, Munetaka leapt up and grabbed the scribe by the shoulders. "Can you take me to its lair?"

"It is very far away."

"I know a good ship."

"It is in a strange gaijin land. We'll need warriors."

"Then we will find them!"

Saburo grinned. "I've always wanted to be part of a story."

Six months ago, he had found the source.

The samurai had fought their way through the jungle temple, leaving a trail of dead and dying in their wake. One of the foreigners charged them with an oddly curved dagger. Munetaka drew an arrow and launched it in one smooth motion, piercing the throat and sending the gaijin to the stone. Two more cultists followed, screaming, but Munetaka released two more arrows in rapid succession and dropped them both. He stepped over the dying, and observed his crew. They were hacking the last of the cultists to bits. Worshippers of foreign devils were no match for Munetaka's experienced warriors.

In honor of their god of the depths, the cultists painted their skin red. Munetaka had painted their temple red with blood to defy it.

"That's all of them, Captain. We took no casualties."

"Good work." Munetaka gave the ronin an appreciative nod. "Spread out and search."

This land was always hot. The air was constantly moist. It made their equipment rust and their armor chafe. For years they had followed clues and consulted with wily foreigners. They had been caught up in battles and plagues. They'd crossed an ocean, a dozen kingdoms, and marched hundreds of miles, and every inch of it had been filled with discomfort and misery. It stood to reason that such an awful creature had been spawned in this cursed land. Despite all of those tribulations, the warriors he had gathered still followed him. He didn't really understand. Munetaka had no real station. There was no honor to be gained in following someone considered to be a delusional madman, yet they followed his orders and trusted him with their lives.

Perhaps, if the Great Sea Beast hadn't ruined his life, turned him into a drunk, and gotten him disgraced with his clan, Munetaka might have made a good captain after all . . .

They entered a great stone room, lit by flickering torches, covered in gaudy carvings and murals. In the center of a great basin was another statue of the Great Sea Beast, dyed red from the accumulated sludge of thousands of human sacrifices. Munetaka snarled, "Damned foreign devils."

"Remarkable. This is the home of the cult of the Great Sea Beast."

Saburo was examining the murals. He alone could read their gibberish. "This is the repository of all their knowledge." The scribe seemed giddy with excitement.

"All I need to know is where to find it and how to kill it."

Saburo traced his finger down the wall. They had struck enough of these temples that Munetaka recognized the story shown in the pictures: witches dragging a leviathan from the depths, cutting it apart, and torturing it with their gaijin sorcery until it had been twisted into the savage creature that had ruined his life. However, this series of pictures was different than the others.

"Interesting. They cut a bone from the leviathan. A horn . . . When the witches blew on the horn, it made sounds that could awaken and summon the Great Sea Beast." Saburo reached for a thick wooden lever on the wall and pulled it down.

There was a sudden grinding inside the wall. Munetaka had an arrow nocked within an instant. Rusty chains rattled through channels in the floor. The stone wall split, then slowly ground open. "What manner of gaijin trickery is this?" He pointed his yumi into the room, but there was only shadows. "Fetch a lantern."

Flickering light filled the newly revealed chamber. There was something odd hanging from chains attached to the ceiling. The mysterious device's surface was grey and porous of texture. It was an oddly curled bone, only it was as big as an ox, and standing next to it was one of the red-painted priests wearing only a tiger pelt. He began gibbering furiously in their strange language when he saw the samurai approaching.

"You'd best shoot him quickly. He says that if we come any closer he will unleash the monster and send it against our home island," Saburo whispered.

"Good." Munetaka made an exaggerated show of gradually drawing back his bow. "Let him."

The priest rushed and pressed his mouth to the bone. Air resonated through a maze of chambers. A deep, eerie rumble filled the temple. The sound seemed to grow and grow. The hair stood up on his neck. It was a long alien wail that shook all the warriors to their bones.

Munetaka could have killed the priest immediately, but let the monster come. That took care of finding it. The priest looked up, triumphant, but seemed a bit surprised when Munetaka showed absolutely no fear. Realization dawned that the samurai wanted the beast exposed. Only then did Munetaka drill him through the heart.

The assembled ronin stared at the body for a moment, unsure what their captain had just allowed to happen.

Munetaka took a flask from his pocket and took a long drink. *There was no turning back now.* "Take the horn back to the ship. Have the priest cleanse this gaijin filth from us." He began walking away. "It's time to go home."

Ten days ago, his clan had learned the truth.

The crew of the *Friendly Traveler* had seen the smoke rising over the horizon hours before they'd seen land. There were bloated corpses floating on the surface as they approached the harbor. After such a long journey, it had not been the joyous homecoming most of them had been hoping for.

There had been a town here once. Now it was nothing but a ruin. Buildings had been crushed. Fires had caught and spread out of control, consuming everything. There had only been a small castle here, but it had been smashed to pieces and spread across the rocky shore. There were bodies everywhere. Peasants were trying to pull survivors from the rubble.

Two men stood at the rail, watching the dead float by.

"Is this what you wanted, Captain?" Saburo asked.

"No . . ." There were children crying in the streets.

But now they understand.

His crew was shocked by the carnage. They were hard men, but it was hard to comprehend destruction on this scale. He'd warned them . . . "Take us in. I want to find out what direction it went."

The docks were gone. Several masts sticking out of the water explained the fate of most of the ships stationed here. One warship had been picked up and hurled three hundred paces inland, and half of it was sticking out the side of an inn. There were other warships still in one piece, but they had most likely arrived after the Great Sea Beast had left. They had been gone so long, and there had been a clan war going on when they'd left, so Munetaka wasn't sure who would be in charge when they got back, and he was too pragmatic to risk flying his clan's flag. When he saw that the other warships were Minamoto he ordered their own flag raised.

The crew of the Minamoto warships were so stunned that they barely noticed the arrival of the *Friendly Traveler*. Munetaka hailed them, answered several angry challenges, and was then allowed to come alongside a much larger, newer warship. Ropes were hurled back and forth, and the *Friendly Traveler* was hauled in close, partially so they could communicate more easily, but more likely because they looked like pirates and the clan was not about to let them escape.

There were shouts as they drew closer, warnings that the harbor was treacherous with sunken ships that could damage their hull and questions about if they too had seen the giant crimson demon, which was half the size of a mountain.

Munetaka was surprised to see the personal mon of the Minamoto daimyo on the guard's armor. Lord Minamoto Yoritomo himself—the successor of the man who shamed him—approached the rail. The entire crew bowed . . . except for Munetaka.

"What're you doing?" Saburo hissed. "Are you drunk?"

"Only a little," Munetaka answered.

The lord's eyes narrowed dangerously at this slight. Dozens of Minamoto soldiers nocked arrows, awaiting the order to execute the impudent captain. "Who are you?"

"I am Captain Nasu Munetaka, son of Captain Nasu Tadamichi. Twelve years ago, the Great Sea Beast killed my father and sank his ship. I alone survived. I saw this monster and I told the truth. I intended to hunt it down and send it back to Jigoku. Your predecessor called me a liar and a fool. He mocked me and dishonored my father. He declared this monster a myth." Munetaka pointed toward land. All eyes followed.

There was a giant footprint, shaped like that of a lizard, only as wide as the lord's warship and pressed deep enough into the sand to fit a house.

"Do you believe me now?"

His entire life had come down to this moment.

The sea outside Kamakura was red with blood and lit by burning wreckage. The air was choked with smoke and the screams of the injured. The Great Sea Beast's arms were humanoid, only its hands ended in three webbed fingers, and it was swatting boats from the ocean like a child in a bathtub. Hundreds of arrows were lodged in its hide. It had been struck by balls of flaming pitch from the warships and the whaling harpoons of desperate sailors, yet it showed no sign of slowing.

A Minamoto warship rammed straight into the monster's stomach. The flesh dimpled as the bow gave, but it did not pierce the ancient flesh. The Great Sea Beast let out an ear-splitting roar, scooped the warship up and hurled it inland. The tiny dots spinning off of it were sailors and samurai. The ship landed on the rocks and exploded into a million pieces.

"Saburo!"

The scribe ran to him. "Yes, Captain?"

"Sound the horn."

"But we don't understand how the gaijin magic works! It could just enrage it further."

"Excellent. Do it now."

The scribe knew not to question. "Yes, Captain!" He ran to do as he was told.

Munetaka picked one particular arrow from his quiver. Though the shaft had belonged to his father, he'd replaced the arrowhead with one he'd fashioned himself. It was slightly different in shape from his regular armor-piercing points but the balance was perfect. He'd carved a piece of bone from the gaijin horn. If it had really come from the body of the leviathan the Great Sea Beast had been fashioned from, he would send it home. He'd had the arrow blessed by priests of every faith he'd come across in his travels. Surely some god would be listening.

Saburo blew the horn. It was nothing like the strong, resounding bellow created by the tiger priest, rather it was a harsh note that trailed off into a painful warble.

Yet, it worked. The Great Sea Beast turned and roared a furious challenge. It started toward them. The waters were shallow, so it seemed to grow taller as it walked across the seabed, exposing even more of its corpulent self to the air. The waves became increasingly violent.

Taking out his flask, Munetaka enjoyed one last drink. It was the finest sake in Nippon, and he'd saved it for a very special occasion. Only the best would do for today. Putting the flask back in his kimono, Munetaka took another look at the horizon, then back at the creature, carefully estimating its speed. "Hold this course no matter what."

"There's rocks straight ahead, Captain!"

"No matter what!" he shouted.

Closer.

He readied the special arrow. There would be only one shot.

The other ships were forgotten. A warship clipped the beast's side and was sent spinning away. A single, crazed samurai leapt from that ship onto the beast's flesh, stabbing at it while trying to climb up its body as if it were a mountain. The monster did not seem to notice. It was entirely focused on the *Friendly Traveler.* The warrior lost his grip on the slick hide and disappeared into the churning waters.

Closer.

Munetaka took a deep breath, then slowly exhaled. His body moved in time with the violent rolling of the deck beneath his bare feet.

"We're almost on the rocks!"

"Steady . . ."

The Great Sea Beast loomed over them. The air stunk of rotting fish. A black rain began to fall upon them, and he realized it was demon blood weeping from a thousand shallow cuts.

His hands did not tremble.

The golden edge of the sun broke over them. Vast white eyes, accustomed to the darkness of the deep ocean, twitched and mighty lids slammed shut with an audible *slap.* He'd looked directly into those giant merciless eyes so long ago, and he'd wondered afterwards why it had spared him. At the time he'd thought it was because he was insignificant. He was a bug to the Great Sea Beast, not even worth crushing.

Now he understood that he had lived because it was his destiny to end this abomination.

While staring into those white orbs before, he'd seen that there was a tiny circle in the center, an off-white pupil, only visible when you were close enough to choke on its stench and its tentacles could taste your blood on the water. He intended to put an arrow through that pupil and straight into the creature's brain. Two hundred paces away, at an extreme angle, from a rocking ship against a rapidly moving creature the size of a castle, and his target was as big around as the bottom of a sake cup.

Only Munetaka had spent many long hours studying the bottoms of empty sake cups.

The arrow knows the way.

Munetaka drew back the bow in one perfect motion.

Father, guide my hand.

He let fly.

The entire crew held their breath as they watched the arrow streak through the blood rain.

The huge lid blinked open the instant before the arrow struck.

The arrow disappeared, sinking right through the clear jelly of the pupil.

It twitched.

The crew gasped.

There was an incredibly long pause. Then the creature's eye began to spasm wildly, like it was about to leap from its head. It leaned back, head jerking, tentacles thrashing. Webbed fingers clutched at its face. The horrific noise it let out threatened to split the world. The noise trailed off into a moan.

"Turn hard to port! Hard to port!" Munetaka ordered. "Now!"

The crew did as they were told. Seconds later their hull made a sickening sound as it ground against the rocks. Salt spray came up over the side from an impact, but they kept moving. To stop was to perish.

Lumbering forward, the Great Sea Beast continued to clutch madly at its misshapen head, but it was too late. The blessed arrow had worked its way deep into vulnerable tissue, and no living thing could survive for long, bleeding from inside its brain. It stumbled, then began to fall. It was like watching a great tree being felled by an ax, only they were beneath the tree.

Munetaka's crew knew what to do. They understood what would happen if they didn't get out of the way in time. There was no need to give instructions because they were already working hard. So Munetaka simply stood there, watching, as the Great Sea Beast fell. Live or die, it no longer mattered. His duty was complete.

The Great Sea Beast collapsed. The gradual impact of its bulk threw up a huge wall of water before it. They were lifted and pushed on the wave as sailors held on with all their might. The *Friendly Traveler* was hurled through the maze of rocks. They hit open water, violently spinning, and a few men were flung over the side. Yet, they were through the rocks. Normally that would have raised a cheer amongst the crew but the monster was still collapsing on top of them, and all they could do was watch and hope.

It struck. The world was consumed with thunder. For a moment, all of them were blinded by spray.

The Great Sea Beast's head smashed into the rocks right next to them, tons of flesh and bone compacting and rupturing against the unyielding earth. A spine came crashing down, shearing effortlessly through the *Friendly Traveler*'s mast and rigging. Captain Munetaka stepped calmly aside as the razor tip of the spine cleaved through the deck where he'd been standing.

And then they were away.

The Great Sea Beast lay still, ooze pouring from its head in such great quantities that the *Friendly Traveler* was floating on a sea of black.

It was silent except for the creaking of wood and rope.

"It is finished."

They were heroes.

The crew of the *Friendly Traveler* were welcomed in Kamakura and showered with gifts. Lord Minamoto Yoritomo granted every member of his crew lands and titles. Songs were sung about their long journey along the shores of foreign lands, and their battle against the Great Sea Beast grew larger with each telling of the story.

Captain Nasu Munetaka sat alone beneath the shade of a tree, watching the tide come in. It was good to escape the noise of the adoring crowds, but the silence made him realize a few things. His father was avenged. His family's honor restored. Yet, what good was a samurai without a purpose? He took out his flask and raised it to his lips. He was a great captain and probably the best archer in the world, but he did not know what came next . . .

Are there other monsters in the world?

Then perhaps I shall find them.

He poured the rest of his sake into the grass.

His hands did not tremble.

SOMETIMES STORY IDEAs come from the strangest places, especially when you are motivated by deadlines. I had agreed to provide a story to the *Kaiju Rising* anthology, but I kind of forgot about it until the last possible minute.

I needed a story *fast*. Luckily, I had run a Legend of the Five Rings RPG campaign, during which one of my players had an alcoholic samurai/pirate/archer who just so happened to have a blood vendetta against a giant sea monster which had ruined his life, and the resulting story had worked out really well. So I took that campaign, ground off the serial numbers for the IP, changed the names and settings to match real world history (only with more giant monsters), and wrote "The Great Sea Beast."

It turned out pretty good, and made the Distinguished Stories list for Best American Science Fiction and Fantasy 2015.

So, thanks, Tony Battaglino, for letting me steal your role playing game character.

FORCE MULTIPLIER

"Force Multiplier" originally appeared in V Wars: Blood and Wars, *edited by Jonathan Maberry, and published by IDW.*

THERE WERE FOUR GUARDS manning the Russian security checkpoint. Two were inside the guard shack, huddled next to an electric space heater. The other two were outside, next to the DhSK heavy machinegun mounted on a tripod.

He clicked his radio. "Execute," Kovac ordered.

The snipers fired simultaneously. The wet impact of the bullets was far louder than the suppressed rifles. The soldiers next to the machinegun emplacement collapsed, leaving behind a fine red mist floating in front of the spotlight. *Clean shots.*

A split second later a shadow moved inside the guard shack and was immediately followed by a large quantity of blood splattering against the interior of the window. Basco's genetic heritage was Indonesian, and his mutation made it so that he could move like a fucking magic ninja.

There was no alarm. *Quick and quiet,* just like they'd practiced.

The smell of torn-open bodies and fresh blood wafted over. It made him hungry. Kovac keyed his radio again. "Checkpoint is clear. Bring up the trucks." He lifted himself out of the snowbank he'd been lying in for hours. Cold didn't bother him anymore, and his body seemed immune to frostbite or hypothermia; that was one welcome change . . . among many.

Kovac used hand signals to order his squad to move out. Ten

figures rose from the snow. Their snipers would remain on the mountainside and cover their approach. Everyone knew their individual assignments, and responded quickly. A few of them were so fast that they seemed to simply vanish, while others were slower, but nearly invisible in the dark.

There was only one road in. The terrain here was unforgiving, consisting of iced-over rock, steep angles, and deadly cliffs. It was an excellent location for a secret research facility. Assaulting this place would have been suicide for humans.

In typical old Soviet military architectural style, the facility was a concrete cube. The main doors were designed to stop a tank. Breaching those would take too long, and the Russians would call for reinforcements. Instead, his squad moved down the mountain, toward the side that the Russians considered impossible to climb. The snow here was a thick, clinging slush, but most of the squad had no problem moving across it at in incredible rate of speed.

Their intel said the Russians ran constant patrols through this area, normally consisting of two men and a dog. Kovac sensed the approaching patrol before the guard dog smelled them. He flashed a signal at Meeker, who gave him a nod, then disappeared into the trees. Thirty seconds later, there was some commotion as the possessed German shepherd latched onto its surprised handler's throat. There was a thud as Meeker eliminated the other guard, and then a yelp as he dispatched the confused animal.

Meeker reappeared, covered in steaming blood, carrying an AK-74 in each hand, and wearing a new fur hat he'd taken as a trophy. He grinned, revealing a mouth filled with hundreds of needle-shaped teeth.

Gregor was the fastest, so he took point. Kovac ran after him, down a narrow rock shelf. The closer they got to the facility's wall, the more treacherous the footing became. One slip would mean a three-hundred-foot drop, but he wasn't worried. It was hard to imagine that he used to have to concern himself with things like balance. The mutations took on various forms, so he'd given out assignments to the team based on their different abilities. The slowest would bring up the rear and would need help scaling the wall, while the quick ones eliminated the opposition and secured their entrance.

Kovac was running out of mountain. He studied the rapidly

approaching edge of the cliff. There was a twenty-foot leap to the icy wall on the other side. Gregor's ancestors were from Ghana, where their legends told of vampires living in trees. He had already jumped across and was climbing so quickly and effortlessly that that bit of folklore seemed very plausible.

Kovac didn't hesitate. Hurling his body across the gap felt as natural as breathing. He hit the smooth concrete of the far side and began to slide, but he latched on and clung there like a spider. Wind and weather had created handholds that he never would have found when he'd been human.

He waited a moment to make sure his impact hadn't made too much noise. There was a flashlight moving high above, but the patrol wasn't lingering. There was no adrenaline in the guards' scent. They were unaware, dull from the aching cold. Kovac began climbing upwards. His bare skin stuck to the wall, and it burned each time he had to peel his hand away. It took him nearly twenty seconds to scurry up the side. The others who were physically capable had jumped across and were following him. They'd throw down ropes for those who were not so *athletically* gifted, but even the least of his men were more than human.

Kovac reached the top and hesitated, listening, smelling, and *feeling*. He could sense that the humans had their backs turned. He'd developed an instinct that told him where mortal eyes were lingering, and how to put himself in the places where people weren't looking. There were several soldiers up here. His senses were so sharp he could smell the grease on the bolt carriers of their AK-74s and what brand of cheap cigarettes they were smoking. The squeak of boots against the metal catwalk told him their position, their stance, even their weight.

Gregor was already over the railing and moving down the catwalk, stalking a guard. Kovac picked another guard and went the other direction. This soldier smelled old. His sweat had vodka in it. In the old days, he'd have used a knife for this kind of business, but he didn't need to do that anymore. Instead, he simply reached out, took hold of the back of the guard's neck, and dug his fingers in until he had a handful of spinal column, and twisted. Lowering the body to the catwalk, Kovac noted that Gregor was feeding on his victim and Bennett had secured the climbing rope for the others. Silent as a ghost,

Kovac had snapped two more necks before the next member of his squad arrived.

It took him a moment to find Lila, and that was only because of the leathery rustle of wings. He couldn't actually see her. In fact, when she was in her hunting form, she was nothing but a dark blur, until you caught her out of the corner of the eye. He turned his head until she appeared in his peripheral vision. She was crouched, naked, on top of a railing, her bare feet curled around the pipe like a raptor's claws. Security cameras didn't have peripheral vision. He'd tested her, and knew that her presence would be confusing every camera within a hundred yards. It was nothing too overt, more like a simple blur. The guards watching the monitors would probably think that snow had gathered on the lenses, nothing more.

Kovac wiped his bloody hand on his pants and unslung his AKS-74U. Stomach rumbling, he stepped over the last dead man, confident he'd feed later, preferably on someone that didn't taste like bad cabbage. Gregor finished and tossed the partially drained human over the side. The soldier was too weak to scream on the way down. Gregor went to the door, tilted his head to the side and listened. "There is no one on the other side," Gregor said as he tested the door. Of course it was locked.

The roof door was reinforced steel, but he'd brought flexo linear shaped charge in case they needed to breach, though he was hoping to be deep inside the facility before they went loud. As soon as Doroshanko came floating over the edge, Kovac signaled for him to move up. They kept him masked and hooded, because otherwise the weird pale glow his skin gave off would give them away. Though not worth a damn in combat, it turned out Moldovian DNA possessed some handy traits. Their vampires could go anywhere they felt like. Doroshanko took his glove off, revealing oddly translucent flesh that gave off a glow like a lava lamp, and placed his hand on the door handle. The handle began to vibrate, and that spread out through the whole door. He moved out of the way. "It is unlocked. There will be no alarm."

They stacked up, ready to enter. Some would fight with firearms, others with their natural gifts. Most of them would stick together, but a few were better suited ranging around on their own as solo killers.

Kovac keyed his radio. "Strike team is in position."

"Extraction team is in position."

"Overwatch is ready."

Those were the responses he'd been expecting. There was a heat in his chest, and this wasn't like the rush he'd used to feel before an op. This was different. This was *better*. He'd found them, brought them together, given them a mission and a purpose. Kovac had taken several individual apex predators and molded them into a lethal pack. Now they were going to fulfill their destiny.

"Execute."

Every country reacted differently to the I1V1 virus. When it was revealed that latent vampire DNA was activating among a small percentage of the population and causing strange predatory mutations, some governments saw this evolutionary offshoot as a threat and immediately cracked down. Others were more lenient, and tried to reconcile with their new vampire citizens.

Neither response worked.

The outcome had been inevitable from the minute patient zero was made known to the world.

There were two things Kovac had studied exhaustively during his mortal life: war and history. The topics were hopelessly intertwined and rather complex. History was rather clear about what happened whenever a superior group clashed with an inferior one. The inferior society was always eventually conquered, absorbed, subjugated, or eliminated.

The real question was, Which species was the inferior?

Evolution had made the vampire physically and mentally superior. Humans were their *food*. On the other hand, humanity had vastly greater numbers, established command and control, and infrastructure. It was now believed that vampires had existed before, hence the various cultural myths about them, as the folklore about their various subtypes was turning out to be far too accurate otherwise. If that was the case, despite the vampires' evident superiority, humans had wiped them out once before. He knew that many of his fellow vampires—those with enough sense to actually think about the future at least—assumed that it would happen again. It was just a matter of time.

Kovac had pondered on the implications of this prior loss. It suggested that humanity was better suited to win their competition and vampires would eventually be hunted to extinction once again. Of course, vampires had lost last time. Individuals, no matter their skill, would eventually be destroyed by the side with superior numbers and logistics. Direct action between the two would always end the same way.

History demonstrated that there was only one way for a smaller force to defeat a much larger one.

The last twenty-five years of his mortal life had been spent learning the ins and outs of asymmetrical warfare. He'd spent a decade fighting an army made up of illiterate Third World goat rapists. His side had been armed with drones, satellites, and cruise missiles, while the other side had been armed with the technological equivalent of a Radio Shack and whatever the Iranians could smuggle in, and they'd managed to remain a pain in the world's collective ass the whole time. Approximately twenty thousand jackoffs in a country the size of Texas had held out against the most advanced military coalition ever assembled. They were motivated. They had direction. They could disappear among the locals. And most importantly, their opponent's political leadership did not have the stomach to go far enough to exterminate them because of collateral damage.

Vampires were spread across the world. Most of them could blend in, and in fact, millions of them were living and feeding off of the humans around them now with no one being the wiser. On their own, they were nothing. Vampires were pests, vermin, just murderers and cannibals with super powers. They were lone wolves that would be hunted down and eliminated, just like last time.

But if all vampires had direction, motivation, and coordination, the only way man could stop them was if they had to guts to kill everyone they suspected might be a threat. The minute mankind faltered and lost their nerve, when they lacked the balls to get the job done, then the competition would be decided.

To fight this war, he would need an army.

It was a good thing the Russians had already done so much recruiting for him.

"Status?" Kovac asked as he walked into the secret prison's command center. Bodies were strewn everywhere. Very few of them were in one piece. Shell casings rolled underfoot. His own AK was still smoking from the heat. He'd just shot a *lot* of people. Basco and Gregor, who'd both had extensive military experience during their mortal lives, were waiting for him.

"We're secure," Basco reported. "Most of the humans are dead."

"Prisoners?"

"Ours or theirs?" Gregor shrugged. "We beat the shit out of the surviving humans and crammed them all in a few cells. We're freeing the vampire prisoners and loading them in the trucks now. Some of them are pretty fucked in the head. I'm talking psycho crazy, Boss, like they've gone feral."

His best intel had estimated that there were a hundred vampire prisoners being experimented on here. It turned out there was nearly twice that. They didn't have enough room on the trucks to get all of them out. "Anyone who doesn't cooperate, leave them. We don't have time to fuck around with drama queens . . ." Kovac checked his watch. Seven minutes had passed since the first shots had been fired at the checkpoint, and two minutes since the alarm had been sounded. They'd have a good head start. This place was so isolated that it would take time for reinforcements to arrive by helicopter, but if there were a bunch of savage vampires running loose in the facility, it would take time for the Russians to get the place secured enough to realize it had actually been a prison break. "Last thing we do before we leave is unlock all the cells. They're on their own."

"We should kill the rest of the humans," Gregor spat. "I cleared the medical wing. They were *dissecting* us. The vampires in there were still alive, but they were being peeled like fruit."

Basco nodded. "The cells aren't much better. They were penned in their own filth. It looks like most of them were being fed pig blood through hoses."

"On second thought, toss the surviving humans in with the vampires we leave behind. Maybe a good meal will cheer them up. Good work, men." They'd only taken one casualty, with Clark getting his brains blown out by an alert guard, and Meeker was missing, but it could be assumed that psychopath was off somewhere playing with his food. They'd killed at least a hundred Russian soldiers and an unknown number of support staff. He noticed that there was a human lying under a desk. He couldn't see her, but he knew she was trying to control her breathing so as to not make much noise. He could even smell that there were salty tears streaming down her cheeks. "Who is that?"

"One of their doctors, I believe," Basco answered.

She certainly didn't smell like cabbage. "Leave her to me."

There was a muffled squeak from beneath the desk.

"Tell Lily to take off. We need the cameras to work. Take video of the worst-looking captives, those shitty cells, and that medical wing. We'll stick it on the internet. That's propaganda gold. Get moving. We're out of here in five."

"Do you still want to leave your message, Boss?" Gregor asked as he removed a small video recorder from a pouch on his vest.

"Of course. The more scared they are, the harder they push, the better we recruit." Kovac went to the desk, grabbed the doctor by the hair, and pulled the now screaming woman from her hiding place. "That's half the fun."

Langley, Virginia

The man in charge of America's vampire response shook hands with a CIA operative whose job didn't officially exist.

"Thank you for coming on such short notice, General."

"You know my time is valuable, so this had better be good." General May glanced around the situation room. Considering the level of spooky mischief that was decided in this place, it was remarkably humble. It looked like a conference room you'd find in any corporate office building. There were three CIA men shifting nervously in their seats, clutching folders sealed with *literal* red tape. He only knew one of them by name and the others hadn't made an effort to introduce themselves. "I've got a global crisis to avert, so let's make this quick."

"I'm really sorry." The CIA pukes seemed more squirrelly than usual, and that was saying something. "How is the containment going?"

"Get to the point, Stuart. V-8 is on an op right now. A couple vamps kidnapped a school bus and took a bunch of kids hostage. Nasty business. We're going in soon, so I'd much rather be watching that live than listening to your bullshit."

That just made Stuart's minions even more jittery, but they didn't realize that Director Stuart and the General went way back. He had been at Special Operations Command before his current posting at Red Storm, so he'd been giving Stuart—head of the National Clandestine Services branch of the CIA—grief for years.

"I'm afraid we've got a complicated situation on our hands."

Terrorists, vampires—for General May, it didn't really matter who the bad guy was. Men like Stuart would feed him the intel, men above them both would give the order, and then it was his job to figure out how to get his boys in place to pull the trigger.

"The situation is only as complicated as you make it out to be, which knowing you fuckers are involved, means it's probably bad," the General snapped. Director Stuart had always reminded him of Mr. Rogers. He even wore a sweater at work. How the hell could a self-respecting spymaster wear a fuzzy sweater? But General May knew that looks could be deceiving, and Stuart was a fellow merciless badass who knew how to get the job done. "So what's the deal?"

It was one of the unnamed minions who asked him the question. "Are you familiar with a Lieutenant Colonel Marko Kovac, US Army Special Forces?"

"Yeah, from Seventh Group. We first met at SOCSouth in Panama, only it was Captain Kovac back then, but I'm sure you already knew that."

"What do you know about his record?" asked the other.

This was a rather suspicious line of questioning. "Enlisted man, 82nd if I remember right. Then Rangers. Went OCS, made it through Selection, got his long tab. Went to the War College. In between that, he volunteered for every deployment in every war we've had since Panama." The general pointed at the man's folder. "I've got a feeling that's all in there. Somalia, both Iraq wars, a couple trips through scenic Afghanistan, and every other shitty FID mission the Army could find, and that's just the official part . . . And I know that you know about Libya when he wasn't supposed to be there, and you probably know of some deployments that *I'm* not even cleared for. When he died in that helicopter crash, it was a sad day for the Army."

"How would you assess Kovac's leadership capabilities?"

"Superb."

"And his loyalty?" added the other.

That hung in the air like a poisonous cloud.

He slammed his hand on the table. "*Loyalty?* Are you fucking kidding me?" General May had a terrible poker face, and the minions unconsciously pulled back from the table as a result of his angry glare. "I'd say that he was one of the best soldiers I've ever had the privilege of knowing. Who is talking shit? Is that what the CIA brought me in here for? Somebody is accusing Marko Kovac of selling state secrets or something? Bullshit. There's no way."

"And you're certain of that?" Stuart asked.

"Let me put it this way, if he was still alive when all of this I1V1 vampire virus crisis started, Kovac would have been the very first man that I requested for Operation Red Storm. The man was a tactical genius. He was like a Green Beret poster child. You can always tell the real quality of an officer by his men's loyalty, and anyone who served under Kovac in combat would gladly follow him into hell. Whatever turncoat son of a bitch you rolled up selling classified intel is trying to cover his ass by implicating a dead officer who isn't around to defend his name. We've seen it before."

"You have no idea how much I wish that was all this was about . . ." Stuart took a deep breath and held it for a moment. He exhaled, then shoved one of the folders across the table toward May. "Okay. Here's the deal. Lieutenant Colonel Kovac wasn't killed in a helicopter crash three years ago. That cover story came out of my office. He was MIA on an op in Syria."

"I didn't know we'd lost anyone in that aborted clusterfuck of a mission." That was terrible news, but not unheard of in his old line of work.

"We had Kovac checking out possible allies, but some of the rebels turned on us."

"There was a meeting with the rebel leaders, but it was a trap. It turned into a firefight," said one of the minions. He was younger than the other two, and he was in extremely good shape, which suggested he was a field agent rather than an analyst. "I had to pull us out."

"We don't leave men behind."

The man looked him square in the eye. "We were outnumbered a hundred to one and hanging in the wind with no backup, deniable and expendable. I saw Marko get shot. I had six other guys who were still alive and half of them were injured. I made the call and we ran . . . I did what I had to do . . . I thought he was dead."

General May stared back at him. He sensed no lies, distortion, or bullshit. It was the simple truth, one warrior to another. The General nodded. *Explanation accepted.*

"Turns out I was wrong," the field agent muttered.

"Play it." Stuart gestured at the other minion, who promptly began pushing buttons on a remote control. A giant TV on the far wall came on. "This video was made a little while after the Syria incident, but only recently discovered."

When the CIA was that fuzzy on dates, it meant that they had something to hide, but General May held his tongue and watched.

The picture was a closeup of a man with his face wrapped in cloth, concealing all of his features, except for a fanatic's eyes. He was speaking in Arabic. The camera pulled back, revealing that two more masked thugs, and a third man down on his knees between them, shirtless, filthy with dried blood and scabs, wrists zip-tied together. They jerked his head back, and through the swelling, bruises, and lacerations of repeated beatings, General May could barely recognize the face of Marko Kovac. He struggled, but one of the rebels slugged him in the mouth.

The original speaker held up a rusty old butcher knife for the camera.

The office minion began to translate. "He will demonstrate to the Great Satan what happens when we meddle in their affairs—"

Stuart shushed him. They had all seen this sort of thing before.

The thugs shoved Kovac facedown on the floor. They'd laid down a tarp. He struggled. Kovac was an excellent fighter and extremely fit for his age, but he was severely injured, his hands were tied, and he was being held down by two giant slabs of meat. There wasn't much he could do. One of them pulled back on his jaw, exposing his neck, while the other knelt on his back. The speaker went to them, placed the edge of the knife against the side of Kovac's neck and began to *saw.*

"Jesus . . ." General May had to look away. This was a friend.

"You're going to want to keep watching," Stuart suggested.

There was blood all over the tarp. The knife was dull. Kovac was thrashing. The speaker was still shouting propaganda as he worked. There was blood up to his elbows.

It was hard to tell what happened next. Kovac's hands had gotten free somehow. He placed them on the tarp and lifted himself off the floor. The speaker stepped back, confused. The two thugs tried to push him back down. One started kicking him, putting the boot to Kovac's ribs. Blood was still pumping from his neck as he struggled upward. Kovac stood. One hand flashed out, hitting a terrorist so hard that the thug flew off the screen in a blur. More blood splattered the tarp, the walls, even the ceiling.

"What the hell . . ."

The camera jerked wildly as the cameraman stumbled backwards, revealing that they were in the living room of an apartment, with average furniture and decorations on the wall, then back to Kovac and the terrorists. The other big man had wrapped Kovac up and was lifting him off the floor while the speaker slammed the knife into his chest. Kovac moved and it was almost too fast for the camera to track. He broke free of the thug and sent the speaker crashing away. Kovac grabbed the thug by the arm and . . . *ripped it off.*

He'd just pulled it right off the man's body. "Holy shit!"

The cameraman must have been too startled to run, as his friend thrashed and screamed, blood spraying out of his torso, because he kept it focused on the action as Kovac walked toward the speaker and clubbed him with the severed arm. Kovac reached down, hoisted the speaker into the air, and dragged the screaming man next to his body. For the briefest instant, the camera picked up a flash of long white teeth, and then Kovac was biting down on the speaker's neck.

But he didn't just bite that son of a bitch; oh no, he shook him like a terrier with a rat. The speaker screamed and screamed as Kovac ripped him from side to side, flinging him about with impossible strength. Kovac drove one of his hands through the terrorist's flesh and into his guts. The cameraman came to his senses, dropped the camera, and probably ran for his life. They could hear him crying for help. The camera landed on the ground, but they could still see Kovac's legs, planted solid, and the lower half of the speaker's body thrashing about. Droplets of blood splattered against the lens as Kovac tore him apart.

There was one last, wet gurgle, and the speaker's mangled corpse was tossed aside to crash against the wall. Kovac's bloody bare feet came toward the camera. He got down on his hands and knees. The hilt of the butcher knife was still sticking out of his chest. Kovac's blood-soaked face filled the screen. The laceration in the side of his neck was still drizzling. His eyes had turned solid red, like the orbs had filled with blood. His canines were far too long. When he spoke, his voice was far too deep.

"You wanted to send a message to the Great Satan? Well . . . I'm listening."

Kovac looked up and let out an animal growl. There was a noise off screen. It was the clack of a Kalashnikov's safety. He launched himself upward and was gone. There was gunfire. Then crashing and a sound like the ripping of wet cloth, more gun shots, and so much screaming.

The minion hit stop. "The sounds go on like that for a long time."

General May put his hands on the table. They were shaking.

Marko Kovac was a vampire.

Stuart was studying him. "We tracked this video back to a village outside of Damascus. Thirty-seven men, women, and children were killed there in one night. The rebels blamed the regime and the regime blamed the rebels. Now we know what really happened. Lieutenant Colonel Kovac had been infected with the I1V1 virus, and was one of the unlucky ones. He underwent a mutation while being held prisoner by the rebels and we just saw the results."

"Please tell me they found Kovac's body in that village?"

"No."

It had been too much to hope that the terrorists would actually do them a favor for once. The General leaned back in his chair and rubbed his face in his hands. It was all a genetic crap shoot who ended up getting their junk DNA activated by I1V1. Talk about shitty luck. *If Kovac was still out there . . .* "Gentlemen, this is bad."

"We were hoping you could help us assess the situation. You're the expert on vampires."

"No, Stuart . . . There's no such thing as an expert with these things. It's all too new. We've documented almost a hundred types of vampire now, and they're all over the board, abilities and psychology. Some go bug nuts murder crazy. Others hide it. Some are supposedly playing nice and trying to be good, not that I buy that for a second, but they can at least be semirational. Some vampires have wild personality changes. Who knows? I'll need a copy of this for my tech guys. They at least might be able to guess what genetic type he is . . . Damn it all to hell, I can't think of a worse person to end up infected."

"Lieutenant Colonel Kovac was cleared on many of our top secret operations," the analyst minion said.

The General snorted. "Cleared? That's nothing. I don't think you realize the magnitude of the situation. The US Army has spent the better part of the last thirty years teaching that man how to overthrow countries and wage guerilla wars. He knows all our dirty tricks and came up with a bunch of new ones. He knows our responses, our defenses, our plans, and how we think, because he is *us*. At this point, I'm just hoping that Kovac *does* fall into the bat-shit crazy, blood-lust category, because I can deal with that. That's just another animal looking for its next meal. But if he retains all his knowledge and reason? Holy shit. There are smart vamps out there forming terror cells, but I can deal with amateurs. The last thing we want is somebody like Kovac on the other side capable of plotting and molding those cells into a real fighting force . . . That would be a nightmare."

The CIA men shared frightened glances.

May felt a sinking feeling deep in the pit of his stomach. "Oh no . . ."

"We got this video a few hours ago from our liaison at the FSB. There was an attack on a facility the Russians were using to hold vampires."

The Russians were far more direct in their vampire response than this administration had allowed Red Storm to be. "Facility, as in one of their secret prisons they're using to experiment on vampires . . . Come on, I'm not stupid. All professional courtesy to my Russian colleagues, those boys don't fuck around. When a Russian grows fangs and starts eating people, they don't stop to *open dialogs* about civil liberties."

"This recording is from a few days ago," said the minion with the TV remote.

"That's remarkably forthcoming by Ivan's standards."

"The FSB really thought we should see this," Stuart said.

The camera had been set on a desk or something of equivalent height. It showed a room filled with computers and monitors. There was blood spatter and bullet holes on the walls. The angle wasn't quite right to see for sure, but there were hints of bodies; a bit of red-stained clothing peeking around the back of a swivel chair, a shape in the corner that might be an outstretched hand, and peeking into the edge of the picture was a mass of blonde hair without any clue what it was attached to.

Blood began to pool under the hair.

There was movement in front of the camera, and a torso appeared, wearing Russian body armor and covered in mag pouches. The man pulled up a chair and sat directly in front of the camera. His face was momentarily covered, and the General realized that was because he was wiping blood from his mouth with a rag—No . . . a lab coat. Face cleaned, he tossed the lab coat aside.

"I am Marko Kovac. This is my declaration of war."

He appeared entirely human, though he looked much younger and stronger than the last time they'd met in person. Marko was in his fifties, but what was age to a vampire? They still weren't sure about that. But his eyes . . . They were different. They were frighteningly vacant of anything approaching humanity.

"This message is for the leaders of the efforts against vampires, and especially for my old friend, General May, of America's Operation Red Storm. I can't say that I was surprised to hear that you got the job. I have just finished liberating a vampire prison in Siberia. I'm sure most of you know of the place, even if you won't ever admit it. By the time you watch this, I'll be long gone, but don't worry. I took a few souvenirs. All those millions of vampires that are still sitting on the fence, thinking they can sneak by, or live in peace with you . . . Once they see that humans consider us nothing more than lab rats, they'll join the cause."

"The videos are already all over the internet," Stuart supplied. "NSA is trying to track the origins."

But that wasn't the part that had concerned the General.

When Kovac smiled, he didn't even have fangs. "You heard me correctly. Millions. Not thousands . . . *millions*. I've seen your estimates. You have no idea how wrong you are. Most of us are hiding in plain sight. There are more of us every day. The virus has swept the planet, but the awakening isn't instantaneous. For some, it is faster than others. So far, you've only seen the tip of the iceberg. The newly awakened have an advantage over the first of us . . . They know how the humans around them will react, so they'll continue playing at their mortal lives, pretending to be like you. They'll live with you by day and hunt you by night. The more they kill, the more you fear them, the more desperately you search. You've got no choice. The vampires among you have access to your food, your infrastructure, your money, even your secrets, so you can't afford *not* to eradicate us. So you have to push, and that means you'll make us push back. There are suckers on both sides who think we can work this out, but that's wishful thinking. You know it, and I know it, but the rest of the world hasn't caught on yet. I *will* convince the undecided."

General May knew exactly where this was going, and he didn't like it.

"One of the first things you taught me, General, was that if you're going to fight a war, you fight to win. Anything other than a total commitment gets your men killed. Your governments are weak. They want peace. They don't realize they should want *survival*. Your hands are tied. Mine won't be. Vampires are coming for you. I will train them. I will arm them. I will forge them into the scythe that will harvest you like wheat. There won't be any frontal assaults in this war. This is a war of attrition and time is on my side. This is a war of shadows and that is where we *live*. Every time a dam breaks or plane crashes, when vampires bomb your cities or poison your water, you'll wonder if that was me. Only you'll never know the answer for sure."

His voice had gotten deeper and deeper as he spoke. There was no trace of the good man General May had known before. Kovac got out of the chair and picked up the video camera. The view temporarily shifted to show that the hair belonged to a young woman missing half her neck, then it was back on Kovac's face

"From this point on, my existence is like a black hole. You will only know I am real by the absence of light."

The picture went black.

Fort Bragg, North Carolina

General May studied the latest reports. Killings were happening all over the country, and they were occurring at a steadily increasing pace, and beneath those average murders, he looked for a pattern. His search was interrupted by a knock on the frame of his open office door. It was one of his V-8 strike team leaders. "You wanted to see me, General?"

He returned the salute. "Yes, I do. Close the door and take a seat, Captain."

He was a handsome young man, and all indications were that he was one hell of a soldier. His strike team loved him. It was saying something when a twenty-six-year-old, newly promoted Captain could command that much respect from a group made up of hardened combat vets. The Captain waited, probably suspecting that he'd done something wrong, because why else would the General in charge of Red Storm call him in for anything other than an ass chewing.

"I read your report on Peoria. Moving that soon after hitting the ground was a gutsy call."

The Captain tried to think of a good response that might lessen the expected ass chewing. "I assessed the situation. The lead vampire seemed erratic. I recognized what type he was, and how he was behaving made me think the hostages were in imminent danger, so I made the call."

"You smoked four vampires, rescued twenty school kids, and your men didn't get so much as a scratch on them. Excellent work."

"I have an excellent team, sir. They train hard."

"Take the compliment, Captain. I don't give them very often."

That put him slightly more at ease. He even smiled a bit. "Thank you, sir."

This was more difficult that he'd expected it to be, but he had to plow forward. "I'm putting together a team for a special assignment. I'm thinking you might be an asset for it, but first I need to ask you a few difficult questions. I want your no-bullshit response. This isn't a PowerPoint to make the General happy. No political correctness. I need to know the God's honest truth of how you see some things, Captain."

It was obvious he hadn't expected General May to call him in to discuss philosophy. "Yes, sir."

"I think you know vampires better than anyone. You've worked with Luther Swann several times now and I know you've read all his stuff. He thinks we can coexist with vampires. Do you?"

"That's a tough one, sir. Personally, I like Dr. Swann. I think he's a smart guy and he means well. The President says that we can and we should try to—"

"This is off the record. Don't blow smoke up my ass. Can humans and vampires coexist peacefully?"

"Some of the types? Maybe. There are a few mutations where they can survive without feeding off of humans. Them, you can treat it like a genetic disorder."

"And for the rest."

"Most of them . . ." The Captain paused, probably deciding how bad he wanted to sabotage his career. "No. Not only no, but hell no. I'm sorry, sir, and I know we answer to a civilian authority, so I will follow my orders, but I don't think they realize what we're up against out there. The people talking about coexisting are living in ivory towers. This is an academic thought exercise for them. They've not crawled down in the corpse piles like I have, or looked some ghoul in the face while it's eating a baby it just sucked out of a pregnant woman."

"So you think that our direction is incorrect?"

The Captain swallowed hard. He was treading on dangerous ground and he knew it. "We're their food, sir. Sure, we can coexist, just like we do with cows."

"And what about their civil liberties?"

"I'm a very big fan of the Constitution, General, and I took a solemn oath to defend it. I had to think long and hard about that when I accepted this assignment. All the guys on the strike teams have to. These aren't foreign soldiers. They're not even terrorists. A little while ago they were regular folks who got a disease. I believe all men are created equal and should enjoy equal protection under the law, but these . . . *things* . . . the feeders, and the ghouls, and the suckers and freaks, the heart stealers, and the spear tongues, they are *not* men anymore. If somebody gets infected, turns, and they never harm a fly, I've got no problem with them, but the others . . . Give me a clean shot and I will put them in the ground."

The Captain was a tough one, but considering some of the weird, violent shit he'd seen over the last year, it wasn't a surprise. "And what about the *regular folks* that turn? They were good people before. Hypothetically speaking, do you think they're actually still the same person they were before? Do you think they've just been overpowered by the disease?"

"No, General, they aren't the same person they were before. The way I see it, once they've crossed that line, there's no coming back. They have to be destroyed. By their fruits, ye shall know them."

"Are you a religious man, Captain?"

"Does it matter?"

"For this assignment, yes."

He nodded. "I wasn't before I had this job, but when you've seen what I've seen, there comes a point when blaming a virus doesn't cut it . . . This may sound crazy, General, and I don't know what else to call it, but I believe in the soul . . . I know that in some of these vampires at least, when they turn, that human soul is gone. It's extinguished. *Replaced.* By what, I can't tell you, but it is evil. Pure, absolute, literal *evil.*"

"That'll do . . ." General May picked up a folder which had been sealed in red tape. He handed it across the desk. "We need to talk about what really happened to your father. I'm afraid I've got some bad news for you, Captain Kovac."

THIS IS THE ONE which I always refer to as my Green Beret Vampire story.

The V Wars series is an interesting shared world concept. The basic idea is that all of the world's vampire legends originate because of a virus which has been dormant for centuries. When the virus escapes into the world again, people with certain genetic markers begin turning into vampires. It gets pretty crazy.

At this point in the storyline, humanity and vampires have gone to war. Since humans have superior numbers and resources, I went to a friend of mine who has provided me with a lot of technical advice before. He was a Lieutenant Colonel in Army Special Forces before going to work for a federal law enforcement agency, and now his son is an Army officer. So I asked him what he would do if he turned into a vampire. Authors' friends get asked all sorts of weird questions like that. His answers were so chilling that I just stuck him in the story.

It turns out the last person you'd want turning into a vampire is somebody who studies how to overthrow governments for a living. I want to thank Marcus Custer for all the brilliant technical advice he's given me over the years.

THE ADVENTURES OF TOM STRANGER, INTERDIMENSIONAL INSURANCE AGENT

This story was originally only available in audiobook, produced by Audible Studios, and narrated by Adam Baldwin. This is the first time that it has appeared in print.

CHAPTER 1:
Tom's 9 AM Client Meeting
Washington D.C.
Earth #345-B-98081

PRESIDENT BALDWIN surveyed the White House underground war bunker. The greatest minds in the country were gathered there, appropriate for their greatest time of crisis. It had only been two days since a hole had been torn between worlds and the invasion had begun, but already all of Europe and half of Asia had been conquered and consumed by the slimy purple bastards.

The Secretary of Defense stood at the front of the room, giving the most important PowerPoint presentation in human history. SecDef had even worn his nicest eye patch. It was the black one with the embroidered USMC bulldog on it. The fate of all mankind rested on the decisions that would be made in this room in the next few minutes. So, of course, PowerPoint wasn't working. They'd wasted ten minutes trying to get it running.

"Piece of crap skuzz-knuckle pisspot!" the SecDef shouted as he kicked the projector. "What's the deal, Ed?"

"It says it suffered a *fatal error*," the Secretary of Education said as he poked ineffectually at the keys.

"Fatal error?" SecDef drew his .45. SecEd was smart enough to get the hell out of the way. "I'll show you a fatal error!" POTUS covered his ears just in time as the computer exploded in a very satisfactory manner. The Secret Service detail was used to these kinds of outbursts, and barely raised their collective eyebrows.

Tom Stranger was seated just behind POTUS. He leaned forward to whisper, "It doesn't really matter which dimension you're in, Mr. President. Windows still does that. There's even one Earth where Bill Gates' cyborg head is god-emperor, and they're still forced to use Vista."

POTUS shuddered at the thought.

"Syphilitic monkey bangers," SecDef grumbled. "I'll do this the old fashioned way!" He snapped his fingers and two generals and an admiral brought in a dry-erase board. "Dismissed, you wretched sphincter stains!" SecDef bellowed as he drew a dry-erase marker from his dry-erase marker holster. He popped the cap and started drawing stick figure versions of the alien invaders.

"They call themselves the Horde of Righteous Purification, but they don't talk much, because they're usually too busy eating babies!" SecDef deftly drew a frowny face on one of the blobs. Then he thought better of it and drew a bunch of sharp teeth as well. "They travel from planet to planet. They face-hump the ever-livin' snot outta that planet, eat everything, steal all the resources, and then stick a black hole in the core before they leave, just to be dicks about it!"

"Have we tried *negotiating* with them, Mr. President?" the Secretary of Health and Human Services asked.

POTUS groaned. He didn't really know what Health and Human Services did. "Duh. You think I'm stupid, Tina? Of course we did. But they ate the ambassador. And then they ate the Secretary of State. Then they ate his *dog*. We even tried playing the keyboard, like in that one movie with the mashed potato mountain, but they ate John Tesh, too. John Tesh and his keyboard! I've depopulated half the State Department. It was like an all-you-can-eat bureaucrat buffet."

"But what if we were nice to the—"

SecDef hurled his dry-erase marker at the SecHeHum. "Shut your pie hole, hippie!" Sadly, because he only had one eye, he lacked depth perception and struck the Press Secretary in the nose. But the Secretary of Health and Human Services hid under the table just in case. Victorious, SecDef drew another marker from his holster, purple this time, and continued his briefing.

"The Horde lives for war. They've been biologically augmented for the last million years to be perfect killing machines. They don't have tanks. They *are* tanks!" He colored the many tentacles and murder sparklers and eyeball cannons purple. "Their air power is made up of giant purple pterodactyls, with scramjets for buttholes. They fart themselves to Mach 4 and sexually assault F-22s!" He switched to red to draw flames as little stick figure human soldiers were crushed mercilessly beneath the tentacles. "Their vats grow a fully combat-effective Death-Mauler in ten minutes!" SecDef made explodey noises as he drew.

"And you don't even want to know about their Harvesters!" POTUS added.

"What do they harvest?" the Secretary of Agriculture asked suspiciously. He knew a thing or two about harvesting.

"*Scrotums!*" SecDef shouted.

Every man in the room cringed and crossed their legs protectively. "Nuke 'em!" screamed SecEd as he pounded the conference table. "Nuke the hell out of 'em!"

The room began to chant "*Nuke! Nuke! Nuke!*"

"That's the spirit!" SecDef answered. "Too bad we've been nuking them left and right since breakfast. France is now a glass parking lot with permanent nuclear winter so the Horde went ice skating on it! They are immune to radiation, bullets, electricity, disease, lava, and personal insults. We've tried everything. They sweat nitro and sneeze acid, and when they're not killing, they're practicing killing, or sharpening things so they can do some stab-killing! They exist only to blow things up . . ." he trailed off, a single tear forming in his good eye. "My God, they're beautiful."

The greatest minds available began to panic, which was understandable, since half the world's population had died in the last twenty-four hours. But POTUS knew he needed to get this situation under control, right the hell now, so he stood and flung his chair dramatically across the room. He went through a lot of chairs that way, but it got the point across. He'd risen to fame and popularity by playing a decisive man of action during the five seasons of the number one most successful Libertarian Space Cowboy show ever to air on television, so everyone knew not to screw with him. The room grew quiet.

"Ahem . . . That'll be all."

SecDef didn't hear. He was drawing a bunch of little stick figure army men and saying "No. Not my scrotum!" Sadly, the purple blob thing got them. "*Ahhhh! Noooooo!*" "This will look good on my trophy necklace." Then more exploding noises.

"Ladies and gentlemen," POTUS spoke calmly, "this situation is under control. All is not lost. What you are about to hear is classified way beyond super black ultra-top secret. It's like Bigfoot-riding-a-Unicorn level secret. Allow me to introduce Tom Stranger."

"Hello."

Tom Stranger stood up and waved.

"Your reality took out a policy with my company back when John Wayne was your president." Tom walked to the front of the room, handing out his business cards as he went. They read simply:

TOM STRANGER
INTERDIMENSIONAL INSURANCE AGENT

He was wearing a suit and a green polka-dot bow tie. Tom was about average height, average build, average looking; so average, in fact, that it was almost like he had been genetically manipulated to be totally unremarkable. It was like he *existed* simply to provide excellent customer service.

"Interdimensional insurance?" the Treasury Secretary asked. "What's that?"

"It's just like home owners' insurance, but for events relating to rifts between realities," Tom answered.

"Are you the insurance guys with the cute little gecko?" SecHeHum squeaked from beneath the table.

"No," Tom said.

"What about the duck?" a Secret Service agent asked.

"No."

"What about that weirdly attractive red-headed woman with all the makeup who lives in that somewhat Orwellian white room?" the other Secret Service agent asked.

"Flo?" POTUS asked. "Damn, yeah, she is hot."

"No," Tom answered as he adjusted his bow tie.

SecDef looked up from his dry-erase massacre. "Cartoon secret agent chick that fights robots?"

Tom shook his head sadly. "I am afraid my firm does not have any sort of attractive, ironic, or humorous mascots. What we do, however, offer is a full line of Interdimensional Insurance services. Since this Horde incident originated on Earth #789-Alpha-12567, it falls under your extended Space Marauder Protection. We'll just need to fill out some paperwork, and by paperwork, I mean blow up a bunch of aliens, but we'll get this all wrapped up in no time."

The room breathed a collective sigh of relief. This was why Tom Stranger had been voted Number One in customer service for three years running.

"So there are other Earths?" SecAg asked.

"Every time a Planck event warps the geosynergy matrix, a Thorne incident will cause an alteration in Hawking space," Tom said happily. When the Secretary of Agriculture looked at him blankly, Tom continued. "My apologies. I must simplify my explanation for this universe's Cow Lord. Yes, a whole bunch of Earths. A different one for every decision ever made."

POTUS whistled. That was a lot of Earths. There was an Earth where he'd had oatmeal for breakfast, and he didn't even *like* oatmeal. "So what happened to 789 whatever?"

"Sadly, that version of America hadn't kept current on their policy and they were harvested. It was a strange planet. You see, they spent all their budget on odd things like tarps, or buying perfectly good cars so they could destroy them so they could buy new cars, or acorns, or Canadian-style healthcare."

"What's a Canadian?" Secret Service Agent Number 1 whispered to Number 2. Number 2 shrugged. Whatever it was, it sounded silly.

"I wonder how that America could possibly have gotten in such bad shape?" POTUS asked. "We were doing awesome until this whole invasion thing."

"What I say may shock you, but in my extensive travels across the multiverse, I have seen some truly terrible things. In a few horrible realities, rather than five seasons and a trilogy of hit movies, *Firefly* was cancelled after just one season, your Excellency," Tom Stranger explained. Everyone present recoiled in horror. "There was never a Libertarian Space Cowboy revolution and you were never elected."

"Impossible!" SecDef shouted. "Lies!"

"In that alternate universe, you had a show on their History Channel where you shot watermelons with machine guns. Only you didn't have the eye patch."

SecDef put on his war face. "OooRah! Now that would be sweet!"

Tom Stranger nodded. "Now, if you'll excuse me, I have work to do. The claims have been filed. The Horde mother ship is in orbit and I will be meeting them for arbitration shortly. Thank you for picking Stranger & Stranger for all your Interdimensional Insurance needs." He clapped his hands twice and his giant battle robot crashed through the White House's bunker wall. The fifty-foot-tall monstrosity of bio-armor and plasma weapons had a single bumper sticker between its death ray and napalm sprayer. It read: *You're in Strange Hands with Tom Stranger.*

"Thank you, Tom Stranger!" President Baldwin shouted.

Tom leapt into the cockpit of his battle mech. It was time to kick ass and adjust claims.

CHAPTER 2:
Tom's 10:00 AM Arbitration

THE BATTLE seemed to be going well, which made Tom Stranger happy, since even the slightest error could destroy their mech and eject them into the hard vacuum of space. Tom, having been biologically and cybernetically augmented by the finest tech available from a thousand worlds, would easily survive, but atmospheric reentry was hell on the wardrobe, and he'd worn his favorite bow tie. The charcoal three-button suit from Men's Warehouse was easily replaceable—since it was a well-known fact that 92% of the cataloged alternative Earths in the Multiverse did, in fact, have Men's Warehouse—but the tie was irreplaceable. He had found it in a thrift store on Home Office World. It was green, with small black polka-dots, which his secretary said brought out the color of his eyes—the green of which was actually the color of the holographic targeting system implants—but regardless, it was Tom's favorite bow tie, and blazing through the atmosphere in a five-thousand-mile-an-hour fireball would surely destroy it. His new intern would probably not fare too well, either.

Curious, Tom Stranger turned to the new intern. "What's your rating on the Grylls Survivability Scale?" The GSS was the industry standard measurement of survivability in unforeseen circumstances. A 1.0 represented the amount of trauma necessary to kill a single Bear Grylls, which was a remarkably consistent measurement across many worlds. Being ejected into space was a solid 4 on the GSS, or enough to kill four Bear Gryllses, or a single Bear Grylls four times. Tom Stranger's GSS was a 142.9.

But Stranger & Stranger's newest intern was busy staring out a porthole, holding onto the overhead strap in white-knuckled terror. "There are space monsters shooting lasers at us!"

"Well, obviously," Tom replied as he steered them around an exploding starship. "That's what our evasive maneuvers and countermeasures are for."

The new intern had been rather emotional since he'd come out of cryo sleep. Tom checked his infolink. Apparently he was named Jimmy Duquesne, and rated a measly .07 on the GSS, which was a rating just above that of a standard Earth chicken.

"Purple eyeball monsters, man!" Jimmy the Intern shrieked. "They're coming right at us!"

"You know, Jimmy, back when I first got into Interdimensional Insurance, we had to be at least as tough as a space marine. Are you sure you're up for this internship?"

"Dude! Man! No way—" Jimmy turned away from the porthole and vomited, which was an especially bad move in zero G. Tom activated his personal energy shields to protect his suit from the incoming secondhand nachos. It took Jimmy a moment to compose himself. "I just needed the last couple credits to graduate. I signed up for Insurance Agent because it sounded easy. I didn't know about extra dimensions or outer space or nothing."

"And you didn't notice when we went through the Thorne Gate to get to this dimension?"

"I thought all the flashing lights were because my roommate made 'shroom brownies last night."

"And when we boarded the shuttle back on your Earth 169-J-00561?"

"Shuttle? It looked a lot like my older brother's Nissan Pulsar, man! How was I supposed to know?"

"There were solid rocket boosters mounted on it," Tom pointed out.

"I don't know, dude, I thought they were like . . . pontoons or something."

Jimmy seemed to be even dumber than most college interns. Curious, Tom checked his infolink again. Jimmy only had a 1.4 GPA and had majored in something called Gender Studies. He was from a relatively backwards Earth where the populace had very limited exposure to the Multiverse. Plus, Jimmy had attended that reality's Chico State, which explained the sorry condition of both Jimmy's brain cells and liver function.

He was beginning to suspect that this intern's placement had been a clerical error. The last time he'd gotten an intern this unprepared, one poor Earth had wound up dominated by a religion based on the *Fifty Shades of Grey* novels. Tom shuddered at the memory.

"Jimmy, since you're unfamiliar with Interdimensional Insurance, you should watch this brief infomercial to acquaint yourself with what we do here at Stranger & Stranger."

Tom activated the hologram. When the glowing images appeared, Jimmy screamed something incoherent about *tripping balls*. Tom did not understand whose balls he meant, or why anyone would trip over them, but then he had to concentrate on their epic space battle while the commercial played in the background.

EXTERIOR SHOT—DAYTIME IN A PARK: Children play on a jungle gym. Happy parents look on. There is giggling and birds singing. Suddenly a tear appears in the fabric of space and time and dinosaurs wearing Nazi uniforms spill out onto the playground. Parents scream as children are plucked from the slide and eaten.

VOICEOVER: "Has this ever happened to you?"

CLOSEUP: A doll lies on the ground and is squished beneath a dinosaur foot with a swastika on it.

CAMERA PANS BACK TO REVEAL TOM STRANGER: "Hello. I'm Tom Stranger, of Stranger & Stranger Interdimensional Insurance. Did you know that more than a million paradoxical Hawking rifts occur every day across the Multiverse?"

EXTERIOR SHOT—STATUE OF LIBERTY: A giant Cthuloid tentacle horror beast is humping the Statue of Liberty's leg like a deranged poodle.

TOM STRANGER: "Well, now you do."

MAN-ON-THE-STREET INTERVIEW: "It was horrible. One minute we were eating dinner, and the next, this buffed guy wearing a hockey mask and driving a dune buggy crashed through our dining room. He said his name was Lord Humungous. The next thing I knew I was hanging from a bungee cord, having a chain saw duel against some guy with a bucket on his head! Master Blaster! No!" (HE BEGINS TO SOB.)

Tom Stranger appears and pats the sobbing man on the back in a reassuring manner.

TOM STRANGER: "There, there."—TOM LOOKS AT THE CAMERA—"But because Mr. Lawson here had Stranger & Stranger Post-Apocalyptic Barbarian Insurance, he was fully covered."

CUT TO—INTERIOR SHOT—THUNDERDOME: Tom Stranger is arguing with Lord Humungous and somebody that looks like Genghis Khan. Hell, it probably is Genghis Khan. Lord Humungous throws his hands up in the air and stomps away, obviously frustrated.

TOM STRANGER VOICEOVER: "I was able to get Mr. Lawson's dimension fixed back the way it had been, and they even had to pay to vat-grow him some new legs."

MR. LAWSON: "These new legs are way cooler than my old ones!" — *MR. LAWSON TWIRLS*— "Wheee! Thanks, Tom Stranger!"

EXTERIOR SHOT—THE PLAYGROUND: Nazi dinosaurs are all trying to do that Heil *salute, but it is difficult with their stubby little arms. Tom Stranger falls out of the sky and lands, crouched, in the middle of the Nazi dinosaurs. They turn to look at him, surprised. Tom Stranger reaches both hands into his suit coat and comes out with an advanced CorreiaTech Combat Wombat pistol in each hand. A Tyrannosaurus with a little mustache roars, but then Hitlersaurus Rex explodes into a shower of blood and meat chunks as a 3mm hypervelocity round strikes it at more than 50,000 feet per second.*

VOICEOVER: "Rated Number One in customer service, three years running, Tom Stranger is here to help."

EXTERIOR SHOT—PARIS: Gritty shaky-cam style—The Eiffel Tower is on fire. It is chaos as an army of My Little Ponies runs through the streets with chainsaws. A mime silently pleads for his life but is brutally chainsawed by Sparkle-Butt. Blood splatters the screen as the camera falls with a clatter.

VOICEOVER: "No one thinks they need Interdimensional Insurance until it is too late. Don't let this happen to you . . ."

CUT TO—A hand wipes mime blood from the camera lens. The camera is picked up. In the background a Stranger & Stranger Battle Mech stomps the stuffing out of Sparkle-Butt, then turns to the camera and gives a robotic thumbs up.

TOM STRANGER SITS BEHIND A DESK, LOOKING CONCERNED: "Think of us as homeowner's insurance, but for your dimension. All three of my hearts swell with sadness every time I see a planet destroyed when it doesn't have to be. Because here at Stranger & Stranger, we care." TOM STRANGER ACTIVATES A HOLOGRAM ON HIS DESK. HE IMMEDIATELY CHEERS UP. "And we'll even provide a free rate quote from us and each of our competitors."

CLOSE UP OF HOLOGRAM: Stranger & Stranger is billions of dollars cheaper. The next quote is from Conundrum & Company.

TOM STRANGER: -mutters as he stares into the hologram- "I hate you Jeff Conundrum, so very much."—VOICE DROPS TO A DEADLY WHISPER—"You'll pay, Conundrum. I swear you'll pay."—TOM REMEMBERS HE IS ON TV. TURNS BACK TO CAMERA AND GIVES A FRIENDLY SMILE.

The hologram faded to black.

"Whoa. What the hell did I just watch?" Jimmy asked. However, as the hologram disappeared, his now-unobstructed view out the front window showed that they were about to crash into a giant Horde space squid. "Look out!"

But Tom simply rammed the monster. Purple guts sprayed across the glass. Tom turned on the wipers to clean off the goo. It left purple streaks, but at least he could see again. Judging by the number of explosions, it was clear that they were rapidly closing on the Horde mother ship.

"Excuse me for a moment, I need to call my office," Tom told Jimmy, not that it mattered, since Jimmy was too busy sobbing incoherently to hear him.

Home Office World picked up on the third ring. *"You're in strange hands with Stranger & Stranger."* Muffy the Secretary sounded bored. *"How may we best satisfy your insurance needs today?"*

"Good morning, Ms. Wappler."

She perked right up. Muffy "Sparkles" Wappler was a consummate insurance professional and a vital part of his team. *"Oh hey, Mr. Stranger. How's your ten o'clock arbitration with the purple people eaters going?"*

"Fine," he said as they narrowly dodged a death ray. "However, I think there's been a mistake with the new intern. Interdimensional Insurance is the most demanding and grueling profession in the Multiverse. But this one actually has something called a Gender Studies degree."

"Wow. Seriously? That's a thing? Some universes sure are super lame."

"Indeed."

"Hang on . . . Okay. There's been a mix-up in HR. The doofus you're stuck with was supposed to stay on his world. It says here his last job was occupying a street. That can't be right. It looks like your real intern was accidentally sent to a call center in their Nebraska to provide auto insurance quotes."

Well, that explained everything. "Thank you, Ms. Wappler. That'll be all."

"Good luck, Mr. Stranger. Try not to die!"

"I'm sorry, Jimmy, but according to my secretary there has been a mistake. Someone else is supposed to be my intern. I'm afraid that Stranger & Stranger only accepts the best."

"I'm totally cool with that!" Jimmy screamed as their battle mech bounced off the hull of the Horde mother ship. Missiles exploded against their energy shields, but they held long enough for them to rip through an airlock. They were inside.

"Very well, Jimmy," Tom said patiently as he used the mech's 20mm chain guns to mow down the mob of crazed, scrotum Harvesters charging at them. "Once we're done here, I'll take you back to your home dimension."

"How about we go now instead?" Jimmy squeaked.

"I'm afraid that I can't do that. You see, the most important duty of an Interdimensional Insurance Agent is to take care of our customer's needs, no matter the risk, no matter what the cost. I've made a sacred vow that good customer service is more important than my life. And this mission is the deadliest type of all. We'll be lucky to get out of here alive."

Jimmy's eyes widened. "What're we doing?" Then he flinched as a floating nacho struck him.

Tom lowered his voice to a dangerous hiss. "Expect the unexpected. Stay behind me. Stay low. Do not make any noise. Do not make eye contact. And for heaven's sakes, pull up your pants and turn your hat around the correct way. This is *Arbitration*."

"Well, howdy, *Stranger*!" Jeff Conundrum shouted in greeting as Tom Stranger and Jimmy the Intern entered the Horde mother ship's conference room.

"You . . ." Tom muttered. Instinctively his hand moved to the CorreiaTech Combat Wombat concealed beneath his suit, but Tom hesitated. Blasting Jeff Conundrum into a red mist would be satisfying, but wouldn't necessarily be providing his client with the finest customer service possible.

"Howdy, Stranger. Ha, ha, ha! Get it?" Conundrum was rotund and, as always, bore an expression of red-faced, forced joviality. Conundrum's neon-blue hair and glowing suspenders offended Tom's conservative senses. His rival Interdimensional Insurance Agent was always loud, always *on*, and always, always annoying. "That never gets old!"

"Yes. It does." Tom glared at his nemesis. "What are you doing here, Jeff?"

"I'm here for the arbitration." Conundrum jerked one fat thumb at the space alien sitting at the head of the conference table. "Conundrum & Company has been hired to represent Goreblog the Death-Slayer."

The space monsters seated around the table were all massive piles of steroid-enhanced muscle, armored plates, and tentacles, but Goreblog was by far the biggest. The Horde King was sitting, but still towered several feet over Tom's average height. Every inch of his purple torso had been tattooed with images of his dark god, Garfield the Cat, and various scenes of Garfield engaging in acts of violence and depravity. Goreblog the Death-Slayer stopped absently scratching his back with a running chainsaw, long enough to nod his spiked helmet toward Tom.

"'Sup?"

"Mr. Goreblog," Tom said politely. "Your fleet has invaded Earth 345-B-98081 and committed a series of atrocities, including trespassing, vandalism, genocide, and the indiscriminate playing of Insane Clown Posse music in public at extremely high volume. This dimension is covered by Stranger & Stranger. This is a violation of–"

"Hey, whoa there, Stranger in a Strange Land," Conundrum said, holding up one bloated hand. "Save it for the Arbiter."

Tom resisted the urge to blast Conundrum through the bulkhead. "Very well."

Conundrum laughed. "What did I tell you, Goreblog? Doctor Strangelove here is all business, all the time." He reached up and slapped the massive Horde King on the back. Goreblog growled and Conundrum stepped back. Jimmy the Intern huddled behind Tom's legs.

"Mr. Stranger?" Jimmy's voice was meek. "I don't feel so good."

"That's probably because of the sub-optimal gravity created by this ship's rotation, and the fact that my scans are showing you possess a blood alcohol level sufficient to incapacitate an adult water buffalo."

"I'd offer you some refreshment, but you don't take *candy from Strangers*! Har! Am I right? Get it?" Conundrum asked Goreblog, but the alien clearly didn't get it. "Never mind. Have a seat, Tom."

Tom Stranger sighed and pulled up a chair.

Conundrum tried to make small talk. "So, Tom, how is your home world?"

"Totaled."

"Oh . . . That's right. Forgot. Sorry about that."

The Arbiter arrived a few minutes later. Interdimensional Insurance Agents never knew which Galactic Arbiter would be assigned to their claim, only that they would always be fair, their judgment wise, and their justice swift. Tom had worked with this particular one before.

"All rise," grunted the alien serving as the bailiff. Everyone did so, including Goreblog, who had to duck to keep from impaling his helmet spikes into the ceiling. "The honorable Chuck Norris of Earth 872-Round-House-Kick presiding."

"Holy crap, it's Walker, Texas Ranger!" Jimmy cried. Tom kicked Jimmy where he'd been hiding under the table. You didn't want to upset a man so incredibly awesome that they'd renamed his home planet after one of his karate moves.

The Arbiter scowled, took off his cowboy hat, and took a seat at the head of the table. "Gentlemen, this is cutting into my Total Gym time, so let's make this quick. What seems to be the issue?"

Tom Stranger cleared his throat as he activated his holographic display. "The Horde has invaded this dimension without provocation. My client planet needs them to leave immediately and seeks damages for th—"

"Easy there, Strangers in the night, exchanging glances," Jeff Conundrum interrupted. "This dimension clearly provoked my client. They were just begging for Goreblog's unholy wrath."

"Is that true?" Chuck Norris asked. "And I warn you, Mr. Goreblog, I eat space mutants for breakfast. Literally. In fact, I had one on my waffles this morning, so do not test my patience."

Goreblog reached one purple tentacle inside his armored carapace and removed a single Polaroid photo. Chuck Norris took the picture, studied it for a moment, then passed it to Tom Stranger without comment. The picture showed a white fence with the words *Space Monsters r teh suck and lame* spray-painted on it.

"As you can clearly see, teenagers from this dimension defaced Mr. Goreblog's fence. He had no choice but to destroy their entire planet in reprisal." Jeff Conundrum stuck his thumbs through his neon glowing suspenders. "Ergo, all the damages from this invasion are not Mr. Goreblog's fault. In addition, his mental anguish and suffering from this vandalism requires compensation."

"The Horde already ate Europe," Tom said.

"I'm still feeling peckish," Goreblog grumbled.

Chuck Norris stroked his manly beard thoughtfully. "I'm afraid Conundrum's got a point, Mr. Stranger. Sounds like your client started it, and as galactic law clearly states, don't start shit if you can't finish it." Much of the galactic code of laws had been based upon the Planet of Texas.

But Tom Stranger hadn't been given the award for best customer service for three years in a row for nothing. He flipped the photo over to hide it from view. "So, Mr. Goreblog. This fence of yours that was defaced, what kind was it?"

The Horde leader swiveled his multitude of eyes over and looked to Jeff Conundrum in confusion. Conundrum seemed surprised at this development. "What's that got to do with it?"

"Answer the question," Chuck Norris ordered.

Goreblog looked back at Tom Stranger. "Uhhh . . . pokey with stabby spikes?" Tom shook his head. "Uhm, does it have skulls on it?" Tom shook his head again. "Metal with razors and land mines?"

"Three strikes," Tom made a *tsk-tsk* noise as he passed the photo over to Chuck Norris. "And no touchdown."

"That not how sports work, man," Jimmy whispered from under the table.

The Arbiter took one look at the photo and frowned. "That is clearly a vinyl fence, Mr. Goreblog. This photo is staged. Did you just try to fabricate evidence during my arbitration?"

"I didn't know anything about this, your Awesomeness!" Conundrum begged.

Chuck Norris slammed his fist into the table, because only a wuss needed a gavel. "I haven't been this offended since Jade Helm. I find in favor of Stranger & Stranger's claim. The Horde of Righteous Purification needs to pay for all the damages, pain and suffering compensation, and return to their own dimension immediately. Arbitration is adjourned."

"ENOUGH!" Goreblog rose, grabbed the conference table and flipped it across the room, revealing Jimmy the Intern, who screamed and crawled under Chuck Norris' chair. "Foolish humans, Goreblog has no fence! I swear on the soulless void of Arbuckle that you will feel the wrath of Goreblog! ATTACK!"

Tom's targeting eye scanned the forty enraged Horde monsters and then the structure of the spacecraft itself. "I'd suggest keeping small arms fire and energy weapons usage to a minimum," he said to Chuck Norris. "Or this whole place will come apart."

"Fine." Chuck Norris stood and cracked his knuckles. "I haven't face-punched anything to death yet today anyway, and it's almost *lunch*." Chuck and Tom stood back to back as the slavering mutants surrounded them. "What about your friend?"

Tom looked to where Jimmy the Intern had assumed the fetal position on the floor and had begun sucking his thumb and rocking back and forth. "Please, try not to trip over him, Mr. Norris. He's new."

The Horde attacked in a screaming wave of tentacles, meat cleavers, and 'roid rage. Tom pulled one of his cufflinks off and threw it to the deck, where it exploded into a cloud of nanobots. The microscopic robots immediately began to devour the first rank of enemies. Tom leapt through the purple cloud of dissolving tissue and melting bones, and landed in their midst, where he really got down to business. Tom Stranger moved faster than their many eyes could follow, striking with surgical accuracy and superhuman strength, each blow of his hardened fists sending an opponent flying.

Meanwhile, Chuck Norris had responded with sheer badassitude. Tom looked up from decapitating an alien with a length of monomolecular wire to see Chuck Norris round-house kick Goreblog's head entirely through his own torso and out his rectum, literally turning the Horde King inside out. Tom's encyclopedic knowledge of biology had not considered that possible. He automatically updated the Chuck Norris Wiki on his infolink.

They had been outnumbered twenty to one—13.333 to one if you counted Jimmy, which Tom did not, since Jimmy had spent the entirety of the battle being kicked back and forth like a fleshy soccer ball—but it was over in seconds. Tom dispatched his final opponent by chopping its head off with the reinforced edge of his hand.

The mother ship shuddered as a drop ship launched from the dock. Tom watched out the window as Jeff Conundrum escaped. "We'll meet again, Conundrum," he promised.

Chuck Norris dusted off his jeans. "I got alien on my boots. I think they're ruined," he stated flatly, then spotted Goreblog's corpse and cheered up. "I think I'll skin that big purple fella there, make me a new pair. Thanks for the assist, Stranger."

"Always a pleasure, Mr. Norris," Tom said happily, moving aside as a purple torso fell from the ceiling and splattered on the floor. "Will that be all, then?"

"Don't forget him," Chuck Norris said, pointing at Jimmy. "I think he wet himself. Sheesh. These kids today. Back when I got into Interdimensional Insurance you had to have guts."

"It is truly sad, Mr. Norris. Good day." Tom Stranger grabbed Jimmy by one foot and dragged the incoherent intern down the passageway.

Jimmy's crazed babblings struck a chord and Tom had a sudden thought. Since he'd been given this intern by accident that meant Stranger & Stranger's proper intern had been accidently sent to work in a call center. A proper Interdimensional Insurance Agent Intern had to be a scholar and a warrior. The thought of somebody with so much potential being chained to the soul-crushing abyss of a call center filled Tom with dread. He dragged Jimmy faster.

"Ow, hey! Dude!" Jimmy shouted as Tom tossed him through the airlock. "What's the dealio?"

Tom Stranger did not know what a "dealio" was. "Quickly, Jimmy, we must return to your world."

"Yay!"

"To Nebraska."

"Huh?"

CHAPTER 3:
Tom Works through His Lunch Hour

THEY WERE SPEEDING toward the nearest rift when Tom Stranger placed a call to his secretary, Muffy "Sparkles" Wappler, back on Home Office World.

"Ms. Wappler, I've had something come up. Could you let my twelve o'clock know I will be running late?"

"Jimmy Hendrix and Kurt Cobain will be disappointed if you have to miss lunch again, Mr. Stranger."

"My friends know I have to put insurance first, but see if they'll order some mammoth for me. Scratch that. Applebee's has the best dodo fingers. If I'm late, just put it in the fridge. I'll microwave it later." He hated missing out on his regular Thursday client lunch appointment, but this was far too important. Interdimensional insurance was not just a job. It was a calling. "Could you be a dear and send the paperwork and a check over to President Baldwin? The Arbiter found the invaders at fault."

"That's great news, Mr. Stranger."

"And don't forget to remind him that if they fill out our customer satisfaction survey, they'll receive a five percent discount on their next month's premium."

"You did just save their whole planet from total annihilation, sir."

Tom figured that was worth at least a seven or an eight on the satisfaction survey, but he strove for tens. "There's always room to improve our customer service, Ms. Wappler." Tom ended the call.

Jimmy the Temporary Intern was strapped into the seat next to him. "Your secretary sounds smoking hot."

"Muffy Sparkles is an insurance professional. The love of providing good customer service shines through. Of course she is attractive."

"Can't wait to meet her!"

Tom thought about opening the airlock so Jimmy would be sucked out into the cold vacuum of space, but it would have been rude to deprive the Nebraska call center of its rightful intern. Tom would never steal from another insurance company in such a disrespectful manner.

Jimmy continued trying to make awkward conversation. "So, dude, like all that krav kickboxing tai-bo back there, you look all normal, like mild-mannered and stuff, but then you're all like pow, boom, ninja flip, and I think you decapitated a dude with your bow tie and I'm like, whoa, are you a Terminator or something?"

Tom found that grammatically incorrect question to be racist. "No, I am not. However, I will have you know that some of my best friends are cybernetic organisms, and they would find your language offensive. Terminators may be living tissue over a metal endoskeleton, but they still have feelings, Jimmy. Not to mention Skynet is a valued customer."

"Whoa, chill out, man. I didn't mean nothing by it."

Tom shook his head sadly. In addition to being as survivable as a standard Earth chicken, Jimmy seemed terribly unsuited to provide quality customer service.

"So like with all this Multiverse stuff, pretty much everything we can imagine gets its own universe?"

The answer to that profound philosophical question was incredibly complex, requiring advanced mathematical equations to even begin to comprehend the never-ending cosmic dance that stretched the boundaries of human imagination, but since Jimmy wasn't very bright, Tom abbreviated his answer to, "Sure. Why not?"

"Mind *blown*." It turned out Jimmy was full of questions. "So, like, if I imagine that dolphins took over, there's an earth ruled by dolphins?"

"Fourteen to be exact." Though Tom did not enjoy doing business with aquatic mammals. They tended to be rather flippant about doing their paperwork correctly. Well, except for manatees. The noble manatee was meticulous and always paid their premiums on time.

"So there's even like a universe where the Cubs win the World Series?"

"Don't be absurd." There were *some* limits to probability.

"What about that fat guy with the neon-blue hair on the spaceship? Was he like you?"

If they'd not been hurtling through space, Tom would have pulled the giant robot over and given Jimmy a stern talking to. "Jeff Conundrum is nothing like me."

"Sounds like you guys got a beef."

Tom was not sure why he would share a cow with his sworn nemesis.

"I meant this Conundrum dude is like an Interdimensional Insurance Agent too, right?"

"I am afraid so, Jimmy. Only you need to know that the insurance business has a dark side."

"Dark side? Whoa . . . You are a friggin' Jedi! I knew it, man! I knew it!"

"Their customer service is poor."

"Just like the Sith!"

In Tom Stranger's belief system, poor customer service was the ultimate sin. Sure, Jeff Conundrum was also personally responsible for the totaling of Tom's home universe, but bad customer service was simply unforgivable.

"Aw, man, Conundrum can't be that bad. They've got really funny commercials!" Jimmy began to sing the Conundrum & Company jingle. "*Wreck your car, sink your boat, flood your house, leave a sponge inside a patient's brain. Conundrum is there! Look, an ironic caveman! How do we save you so much money? It's a conundrum!*"

Tom looked wistfully over at the airlock button. It was big, red, and just tempting him to push it. But Tom sighed and continued trying to explain his complex industry to a moron.

"They avoid payouts. They do not vigorously pursue their clients' best interests. They hide their terrible service with clever marketing to prey upon the gullible. Not only have they brought dishonor onto all Interdimensional Insurance Agents, but Conundrum & Company has grown wealthy across the entire Multiverse by doing everything they can to stall or deny their clients' righteous claims."

"What's a claim?"

Before Tom could push the airlock button, a hologram appeared over the dash. The warning klaxon told him this was an emergency call from one of his biggest clients. "I must take this. It's CorreiaTech."

"What's a Korea Tech?"

"Only the most powerful megacorporation in the Multiverse."

"Like Korea the country?"

"No. It is merely pronounced the same way, which is why the CEO purchased the North and South Korea on his home planet and had the countries renamed to avoid confusion." The countries now known as Commie Jerk Face Land and Gangnam Style had not been pleased, but CorreiaTech was just that powerful.

Luckily, it wasn't the terrifying and merciless Interdimensional Lord of Hate himself calling, but rather one of his chief minions. The image of an enormous fish tank formed in the holographic field. Floating peacefully inside was CorreiaTech's Chief Financial Officer, Wendell the Manatee. Judging by the lettuce floating in his tank, the CFO had interrupted his lunch to make this call. That meant it was serious.

"Hello, Wendell."

"Meeeeeeerrrrp," Wendell said by way of greeting, but then he got right down to business. "Flooooooo?"

Tom was fluent in Manatee as well as six hundred and eighty four other languages. "Why yes. What a fortuitous coincidence, I happen to be on my way to Earth 169-J-00561 as we speak."

"Dude! It's a magic narwhal!"

"HOOOOOOOOOON!" Wendell bellowed.

Those were fighting words. "Forgive Jimmy. He's new." Tom leaned in closer to the hologram and whispered. "He has a *Gender Studies* degree."

The manatee gave Tom an understanding nod. Luckily Wendell knew how difficult it was to find good help nowadays.

"How can I provide quality customer service to you today, sir?"

"Mehwwhoooooooooooo," stated Wendell as he chewed his lettuce ominously.

"The very gates of hell have opened?"

"Meewooo hooooooon." As usual Wendell was a courageous voice for fiscal responsibility. "Mooooo-*gurgle gurgle*."

"Of course such events are fully covered in CorreiaTech's

comprehensive platinum policy. In fact, I believe this is your tenth paradoxical Hawking event, so your next one is free."

Wendell held up the punch card in his flipper, indicating that Tom was correct.

"Don't worry. I'll take care of everything." Since Wendell's boss was the most important man in the Multiverse, he added, "Please give my regards to the Interdimensional Lord of Hate."

As Tom ended the call, he redlined the mech's engines and accelerated to maximum speed. The sudden extra gravities violently squished Jimmy into his seat. "Urg! Fuuurk?" Jimmy managed to gasp through his gritted teeth.

That was not from any of the six hundred and eighty five languages Tom was familiar with, but he got the gist of it. "You heard the manatee, Jimmy. We must hurry. Your home reality is in terrible danger."

CHAPTER 4:
Hell Comes to Nebraska
Earth 169-J-00561
Nebraska
KhanQuanCon XIV

VIOLENCE nearly erupted when a fat man wearing elf ears cut in line in front of an even fatter man dressed as a Klingon. Insults were exchanged in Klingon and Elvish. Shoving ensued. Larry Correia, the novelist—not the CEO of the ultra-powerful megacorporation— looked up from the authors' signing table, surely hoping for some good old-fashioned, nerd-on-nerd face punching. Sadly, the shoving match didn't last long, as both men quickly became too winded to continue. Grumbling and out of breath, they got back in line, hoping to get an autograph from the lady that played Bystander #14 in *Superman 2*, and the authors went back to autographing books.

"Crap, I was hoping to see somebody get stabbed with that goofy Klingon sword," Jimmy the Temporary Intern said to the other convention attendees standing around them.

"It's called a *Bat'leth*," corrected one of the fans waiting in a different line. The sci-fi fan—or so Tom Stranger assumed judging by his Star Fleet pajamas—regarded Jimmy with barely concealed disdain. "It is a weapon of honor. You would know that if you weren't such a *Ha'DibaH*."

"Huh?"

"I believe he is communicating his dislike for you," Tom clarified. "Be silent and do not provoke the locals, Jimmy." Satisfied that his Temporary Intern would not further violate the local customs, Tom went back to patiently waiting his turn to speak to his client.

KhanQuanCon XIV was crowded with people in colorful costumes, and smelled faintly of an odor known as *con funk.* There were several authors signing books at the booth just ahead of them. His client was among them. Tom was eager to get this over with so he could get back on schedule, but Interdimensional Insurance Agents were unfailingly polite, and terrible impending destruction was no excuse for cutting in line. Luckily, they were next.

Larry Correia passed over a freshly signed novel to the waiting fan. "I'm glad you liked it."

"Not really. I thought it was boring and derivative. I'm just going to sell it on eBay." The "fan" scowled as he looked at the title page. "You call that a signature? It looks like a lightning bolt. You suck." He waddled off, swishing his triple extra-large cape of invisibility for dramatic effect.

"Hey, let me personalize that for you!" the author shouted after him. "I can make it out *To my dear friend, Ass Bag!*"

Now it was Tom's turn. "Hello. Are you the prestigious La Mancha-award-winning fantasy author, Larry Correia?"

"That's what the sign says."

"No," he looked down at the cardboard placard, then turned it around so Larry the Writer could see. "It actually says James Gandolfini."

"Well, shoot. Con organizers get us confused all the time."

"Yes. The resemblance is eerie." Tom handed him a paperback.

"Who should I make this out to?" Larry the Writer readied his signing pen.

"Tom Stranger."

"To Tom." He made a quick squiggle, drew a happy face with horns, and passed the book back over.

"Thank you, Mr. Correia." Tom Stranger stuck the book into his suit pocket and it disappeared so cleanly, it was almost as if the pocket was somehow bigger inside than it appeared. His manner turned deadly serious. "Now come with me if you want to live."

The large, bald author stared at him stupidly. "Huh?"

Tom had to remind himself that Jimmy's home reality was backwards and not overly familiar with the greater Multiverse. He handed over a business card, and his client seemed rather impressed. Probably because unlike most business cards received at cons, this one was not printed at home, nor did it have any unicorns on it. It looked *professional*.

"Interdimensional Insurance?"

"That is correct. I am afraid that a rift has occurred here at this KhanQuanCon XIV science-fiction and fantasy convention event. You are covered by Stranger & Stranger, so I must protect you."

"That's great." It was apparent that Larry the Writer was just humoring him. Tom did not take offense. Lame dimensions were not familiar with his career field. "It was nice to meet you, but I'm super busy. Next!"

"I am the only person left in line."

"Ouch." Larry the Writer looked past Tom and confirmed that was true. He sighed. "Still not a *real writer* . . . Look—Tom, is it? You've got the wrong guy. I've never bought Interdimensional Insurance."

"No. But the Larry Correia on Earth 686-Gamma-13006 has purchased our *comprehensive* plan. Thereby indemnifying all Larry Corrieas in existence across the known Multiverse."

"Sounds expensive."

"Indeed," Tom Stranger explained. "It is exceedingly expensive. In fact, the annual premium is greater than the GDP of most planets. The Larry Correia of that reality is extremely wealthy."

Larry nodded appreciatively. "He must've had a few more *New York Times* bestsellers than I have. Damn it. I knew I should have branched out into Scottish time-travel romance."

Tom Stranger shook his head. "No. He does not write books; though he does have a popular web comic about an anthropomorphic moose that solves mysteries, that is not the source of his wealth. It is more of a hobby as I understand it. Rather, that Larry Correia is the founder of CorreiaTech, which has revolutionized warfare across the entire Multiverse. He is commonly considered the greatest genius of all time, having invented the inertial dampener, the cold-fusion miniaturized power cell, and true no-wrinkle slacks."

"That's kind of surprising. I'm not really that technically minded."

Tom checked his Wiki. That was an understatement. This reality's version of his client was so mechanically inept that he had once accidentally set his Chevy Caprice on fire inside his own garage while trying to change the water pump.

"The primary difference that my infolink can discern between you and that particular Larry Correia is that he attended a college physics lecture that you missed. Inspired, that version immediately invented the world's first energy shield using only a box of Wheat Thins and a medium-sized Holstein cow. You, on the other hand, missed that class, because you had somehow gotten your head stuck in a mailbox. "

"Yeah, I remember that. Good times. Wait a second . . . How do you know about that? The Great Mailbox Incident of '97 was so embarrassing that I've never posted about it on the Internet. And you weren't one of the responding paramedics. You must be from the *future!*"

"Not the future, but rather another dimension. Now, quickly, Mr. Correia, we must get you out of here. The demonic invasion has already begun. Luckily for you I was already on my way to this Nebraska to pick up my correct intern. Allow me to introduce my Temporary Intern, Jimmy Duquesne." Tom turned around, but there was no one behind him. "I seem to have misplaced my intern. Darn it, Jimmy, where have you wandered off to now?"

Suddenly, there was a scream from one of the game rooms. A man stumbled out into the hallway, covered in blood. His clothing was in tatters, his hands were twisted into razor sharp talons, and his glowing red eyes bulged out of his skull as he gnashed the air with his fangs. He lurched into the crowd, howling as he began to claw madly at the other attendees.

"Damn LARPers," muttered the writer, "thinking they own the place."

"Nice costume!" somebody dressed as Sailor Moon told the demonic Live Action Role Player. The LARPer's head rotated all the way around in a complete circle like in *The Exorcist*. "Cool effect!" but then it was too late, as Sailor Moon was dragged to the ground in a spray of entrails and giant yellow hair extensions.

Larry the Writer seemed rather shocked. "I don't think that's a costume!" When a lung flew over and knocked over a cardboard cutout of R2-D2, that pretty much confirmed it. "What the hell?"

Tom Stranger reached into his suit and withdrew his sidearm. The small, but extremely awesome CorreiaTech Combat Wombat was the finest combat implement ever designed. He aimed, and the demon exploded into a cloud of meat. Blood splattered the walls and attendees.

Unfortunately, the other con-goers who'd been scratched were already mutating.

"It's like a bad '80s Italian horror movie!"

"It appears that I arrived too late." Tom Stranger stated as the blood cloud rained down. He put one hand to his ear. "Hello, Ms. Wappler. Could you please postpone my one o'clock?"

The surviving con attendees were trapped and terrified. The main hall and game rooms had already fallen before the fearsome onslaught. The demons had swept through the convention, spreading death and mutant cooties. The remaining geeks, authors, gamers, and fan boys of KhanQuanCon XIV were making their final stand, and had barricaded the green room door with a pallet of self-published comic books, temporarily stopping the demons' advance, but they could hear the mad scratching of their instantly infectious claws on the other side.

"Those comic books won't hold forever," Larry the Writer stated with grim finality.

"They're *graphic* novels," corrected the comic book author with a sniff. He adjusted his beret. "They're about man's inhumanity to man and our existential struggle for—"

"Crap, dude, whatever. Fine, those *graphic novels* won't hold forever." He looked over at the last folks who'd made it in before they'd sealed the door. "What's it like out there?"

The girl in storm trooper armor was really shaken up. "The monsters attacked the room holding the panel on writing space-alien-on-human love scenes. It devolved into how to write Kirk-on-Spock slash fic. It was *horrible*."

"The panel discussion or the demons?"

"The demons . . . mostly." She began to sob. "Oh, John Ringo, *no!*"

"Keep it together, Trooper. We need to think of a plan. Has anybody seen Tom Stranger?" The other refugees exchanged confused glances. "Average guy, average height, average looking, has a bow tie? Awesome laser pistol?"

"Oh, that guy." A Jawa pointed at the barricade. Or maybe it was a short dude wearing a robe made out of brown carpet, but the LED-light eyeballs were a cool touch. "He stayed out there. Said something about having to find his intern."

"Crap. I barely find out I've even got an Interdimensional Insurance Agent, and I've already lost him. He seemed so polite and eager to provide good customer service, too . . . We're on our own." Luckily, Larry the Writer had been preparing his entire life for the zombie apocalypse so this wasn't a complete bummer. He'd been to worse cons. *Way* worse. "Okay, we're going to need weapons."

One of the Society for Creative Anachronism people stepped forward and lifted his sword. "Thou dost knoweth of our exquisite blades and skills, me Lord. The foul denizens of Hades shall taste our steel! Huzzah!" Everybody else wearing a tunic or chainmail also yelled huzzah. He estimated at least a dozen huzzahs, which was certainly an above-average number of huzzahs. "We may slay these beasts, if we can but liberate our stores in the marketplace, and thus arm the entire vanguard with halberds and falchions!"

"What are sandwiches and birds supposed to do?"

The SCA guy switched back to normal English. His name tag read Sir Galen. "I said there are a bunch of axes and swords over in the sales room. If we grab those, we can kill the snot out of these douche-nozzles."

Now, *that* Larry could understand. "Okay, you guys can do that while the rest of us do something useful. I meant who's got *real* weapons?" It turned out most of his fans had concealed weapons permits, as did everyone in a Jayne Cobb hat. One of them had even smuggled in an AK-47. "Damn, how'd you get that in here?"

"I stuck some gears on it and told security it was part of a Steampunk costume."

"Excellent. We're going to have to kill every last one of these things if we're—"

"Hey. Who put you in charge?" asked an exceedingly large woman wearing a Team Jacob T-shirt.

"That's Tony Soprano! Don't piss him off!" hissed her friend in the Team Edward shirt.

"Listen, lady, if we're going to live, we've got to fight."

"Violence never solved anything," the Jacobite answered with the grim finality of a hippy who'd never once read a history book, ever. "I say we hide here until help comes. We've got food." She pointed at the green room table that had a bowl of M&M's and a plate of Ritz crackers reserved for the guests. Little did people realize how many secret perks there were to being a writer.

Suddenly there was a rumble from the ceiling. The tiles broke apart and dust rained down. Immediately the fans began to engage the hole with small arms fire. Tom Stranger popped out of the hole and dropped to the floor, dragging another person with him. The bullets sparked harmlessly off his CorreiaTech personal energy shield, which made Larry the Writer realize that he really should have paid more attention in college.

"Cease fire! Cease fire! That's my insurance agent!" The wild gunfire tapered off.

Tom Stranger brushed the plaster dust from his suit coat. "Please excuse my rude interruption. I had to rescue my intern. " He frowned at the pathetic slob of a young man in his stained Chico State T-shirt lying on the floor. "I told you not to wander off."

"But, but Mr. Stranger. We're at a con!" Jimmy pleaded. "There are girls. In costume . . . Girls in costume!" Tom Stranger didn't respond. "Chainmail bikinis, leather corsets, and Princess Leia! Princess Leia, man! And some of them have really low self-esteem! I had to work my magic, know what I'm saying?"

"Is he drunk?"

"Usually. Jimmy, this is the client. Mr. Correia, this is Jimmy Duquesne."

"Dude, you were awesome as that gay hit man in *The Mexican*."

There was a sudden crash against the door, hard enough to shake all the graphic novels, followed by a sanity-rending scream of hate and sheer crankiness.

"What's that?" someone dressed as Dr. Horrible cried.

"They've summoned a Balrog," Tom Stranger stated with grim finality. "It is a nearly unstoppable force of evil. I would estimate it is at least a two hundred on the Grylls Survivability Scale."

Larry whistled. That was a lot of Bear Gryllses. "Why don't you just shoot it with your fancy laser pistol?"

Tom Stranger shook his head. "I lost it trying to save Jimmy from a demon."

Jimmy got upset. "Demon? But she seemed so into me. Are you sure she was a demon?"

"I thought perhaps her tail or bat wings would have been a clear indicator, but you are a remarkably unobservant little man." Tom Stranger turned back to his client. "I have many CorreiaTech devices on my person, but only my Combat Wombat is powerful enough to pierce the nether hide of a greater demon. I will have to retrieve it. It was by the swag table."

The Balrog crashed into the door again. They wouldn't have a chance in the enclosed space of the green room. Larry the Writer looked out across the sea of con-goers and saw grim determination on their pasty faces. It was time to go on the offensive.

"Are you guys ready? Let's do this! Nebraska is counting on us!"

"Can I get a huzzah?" Sir Galen shouted.

"Huzzah!" they shouted in return.

"I can't hear you!"

"HUZZAH!"

Even Larry the Writer was getting really psyched up, and this universe's Larry really didn't like to do cardio. "Let's go kick some demon ass!"

But by the time the angry mob turned around, they saw that the pallet of comics—sorry, graphic novels—had been shoved out of the way and the green room door was open. While they'd been trying to build enthusiasm for a suicidally futile noble gesture, Tom Stranger had simply walked out and started beating the ever-living hell out of a bunch of demonic mutants. And apparently you had to be a serious bad ass to be an Interdimensional Insurance Agent, because Tom Stranger was absolutely massacring them.

The fans and authors watched in amazement as Tom fought his way through two dozen zombified Deadpools. "Man, that is some Wu-Tang crouching tiger shaolin temple stuff right there."

"I know, right?" Jimmy the Intern said. "You should have seen him with Walker, Texas Ranger this morning." But Tom Stranger couldn't beat up an entire convention center full of monsters by himself, and Jimmy had apparently caught the Interdimensional Insurance Agent spirit. "Friggin' huzzah, bitches! Charge!"

Jimmy made it all of ten feet before he was clotheslined by a zombie furry in a panda costume. But the rest of the fans followed his valiant lead.

It was hard to see what happened next, because the con descended into a hyperviolent, blood-soaked melee. It turns out all those LARPers were just waiting for an excuse to wreck face with real swords, because *shit got real.* It seemed the con-goers were doing pretty good, maybe even winning, up until the part where the Balrog moseyed up and started popping nerds into its mouth like they were gummy bears.

As they retreated, Sir Galen bravely placed himself in front of the flaming super monster, planted his sword into the floor, and shouted, "YOU SHALL NOT PASS!" Then he turned around and looked back at the others. "I always wanted to say that!" It was so *metal* that Larry the Writer had to throw the horns. But then the Balrog kicked Sir Galen through the convention center wall.

The Balrog was thirty feet tall, on fire and, frankly, kind of a dick.

But right before it could squish the rest of the attendees, Tom Stranger appeared. He'd gotten his fancy laser pistol back, and used it to knee-cap the Balrog. The monster roared as lava blood splattered out of the hole, setting the carpet and the panda furry that Jimmy was still wrestling with on fire. *FOOOM!* And there went the other knee.

The Balrog toppled, hitting the floor so hard the whole convention center shook.

Tom Stranger walked around in front of the crippled monster. It glared at him with flaming eyeballs.

"Holy crap, insurance agents are awesome! So what now? Are you going to exorcise it, or cast it back into hell or something?" Larry the Writer was taking notes. This was fiction-writing gold.

But instead, Tom Stranger holstered his pistol, approached the beast, and pulled out a pen and some paperwork. "We need to exchange insurance provider information."

The Balrog tried to act offended. "Hey! I'm not at fault here. Someone fired up my hell gate, and their dimension just came out of nowhere right in front of it! I couldn't stop my Legions of the Damned in time."

"This dimension clearly had right of way . . . Let me guess. You're uninsured?"

The gigantic demon looked away sheepishly. "Well, this is embarrassing. Yeah."

That confession seemed to sadden Tom Stranger. "You can't just go blundering around the Multiverse uninsured."

"I had liability, but Conundrum & Company dropped me. I was only late on one payment!"

"Conundrum?" Tom snorted. "There's your problem right there. A greater demon obviously requires full coverage for his hellish armies. This collision is really going to cost you."

"Darn it," the mighty beast rumbled. "I can't afford any more points on my realm."

The flames started by the Balrog's lava blood were spreading up the convention center's walls. "Excuse me, Tom?" Larry the Writer called out. "The place is burning down."

"Of course, Mr. Correia. One moment." He turned back to the Balrog. "Listen, get your hellspawn back to your dimension, free the damned souls from their eternal torment, and then call my office." Tom handed over one of his cards. It immediately caught on fire when the demon pinched it between its massive claws. "Once you've paid for this mess, let's set up a consultation. Stranger & Stranger offers a Nether Realms Protection Package that's not only a great value but also covers inadvertent possession."

"What about locust plagues?" the demon asked as Tom Stranger walked away. "Or ravens made of congealed blood plucking the eyes from infants?"

Tom Stranger put his thumb to his ear. "Call me." The insurance agent paused long enough to pick up Jimmy the Intern by his belt so that he could carry him like a suitcase. They began to flee through the flaming wreckage. Once they were far enough away that the Balrog couldn't overhear, Tom looked over at his client and scoffed. "Liability only? That is so irresponsible."

"Yeah, demons are cheesy." Larry the Writer coughed as he was overcome by smoke. He managed to croak, "Cheap bastards," before passing out.

Tom sighed as he was forced to carry his temporary intern and his client. A giant flaming beam almost fell on them as they escaped. It was all very dramatic as Tom carried them both from the ruins of KhanQuanCon XIV.

Tom left Larry the Writer in the parking lot with the other stunned survivors, gave him some forms to fill out, and then disappeared as mysteriously as he arrived. The Interdimensional Insurance Agent had just saved their lives, and probably the whole planet. Which was why, later, Larry the Writer gave Tom all tens on his Customer Satisfaction Survey.

CHAPTER 5:
Tom and Jimmy's Big Call Center Adventure

IT HAD BEEN an extremely busy day. Tom had already been able to provide quality customer service twice, but he'd also been forced to postpone his other appointments. He needed to get this intern mix-up taken care of so he could get back on schedule. According to his directions, they would be landing at their destination soon. Tom could get his proper intern, and Jimmy could get on with . . . well, whatever it was that Jimmy did.

"We will reach your correct employer shortly, Jimmy. Do not worry. I will explain the mistake to them so that you do not get off on the wrong foot with your new insurance masters. Some firms can be rather harsh. It was not uncommon for rookies to commit ritual seppuku back when I was but a lowly intern at Mifune & Eastwood."

"Wow. Really, Mr. Stranger? You were an intern? That's hard to imagine with you being such a bad ass and all."

Tom had to check his infolink to see why Jimmy was comparing him to a disobedient donkey. It turned out it was meant as a compliment. "Thank you, Jimmy, but all insurance agents must start somewhere. It takes decades of rigorous training in order to become proficient at Interdimensional Insurance. It is a solemn calling, meant only for the most stalwart of souls."

"How did you get into this?"

Tom's home reality had been underinsured, and had paid a terrible price. "For some, there comes a time when the Multiverse needs help, and then you must peer deep into your soul and discover your inner Insurance Agent."

"Do you think I could ever be an Interdimensional Insurance Agent?"

"*No!*" Tom had turned around and said that so fervently that he nearly crashed their battle mech.

"Aw, come on! You just said everybody has to start somewhere. I'm somewhere!"

Tom blinked a few times.

"You saw the way I was kicking that panda's ass. I had him right where I wanted him. I was all like *boom*, bitch! And it was like *aaaaaaarghh!*" Jimmy pantomimed what was probably supposed to have represented fighting moves. "It was wicked cool."

"In truth, it looked like you were having a grand mal seizure."

"Dude. Harsh."

Jimmy was correct in his assessment of harshness. Insurance agents should always be truthful, but never impolite. "I apologize, Jimmy. I am very sorry and did not intend to hurt your feelings. What I meant to say is that Interdimensional Insurance is an extremely difficult job, and that because of your general lack of intelligence, courage, commitment, integrity, physical fitness, character, communication skills, work ethic, and hygiene, you might not be the best fit for such a position."

His Temporary Intern sulked. Tom was not very good at apologies.

"I could totally do anything if I put my mind to it, Mr. Stranger. Even be an insurance agent!"

That was doubtful. There was a common misconception among people with pampered origins that they could coast through life carefree, but then when they actually faced a real challenge, they would somehow be able to rise to the occasion if they simply *believed in themselves* hard enough. It was known as Kung Fu Panda Syndrome. But in most realities, regardless of how much self-esteem someone had, the fatty still got trounced by the warrior who had spent his whole life beating up ninjas and punching boulders under a waterfall.

Most Interdimensional Insurance Agents hailed from worlds where children had to work hard just to not be devoured by cave bears. Jimmy came from a culture that gave out trophies for *participation*. An insurance agent had to start out quick-witted and then further hone his mind to razor sharpness. Jimmy had a hundred thousand dollars of student loan debt and had occupied a street for weeks hoping somebody else would pay for it. When Tom was only ten years old, a horrible paper route accident had left him stranded alone on Mars, where he'd been forced to perform his own emergency appendectomy with nothing but a melon baller. Under the headline *Skills,* Jimmy's resume included "Twitter."

Tom's Multiverse-spanning career had left him with a keen understanding of probability. Truly, anything was possible, but some things remained extremely unlikely. In other words, he wasn't going to place any bets on Jimmy Duquesne making the cut to be an Interdimensional Insurance Agent.

"Perhaps you should try this call center position first, and see how that works out for you. It will be like dipping your toe into the giant pond that is insurance."

"Sure, whatever," Jimmy muttered.

Thankfully, they had reached their destination. To avoid causing any further chaos in this ignorant and backwards reality, Tom landed the Stranger & Stranger battle mech in the trees behind the call center. They would walk the rest of the way. It was a beautiful sunny afternoon. Birds chirped. The air smelled of corn. Jimmy grumbled under his breath and kicked at rocks the whole way.

The call center was a large, unadorned, windowless concrete building. There were no signs advertising what the place was. Tom found that odd. Insurance professionals were normally extremely proud of what they did. Most insurance offices had holograms or giant inflatable gorillas. Something was off here. Tom himself was not the flashy type, but even his office at least had a sign with his name on it. His sign was white with block print. Because Tom did not like to put on airs.

Tom checked his infolink. According to the internship records, this call center belonged to a company called Fail State. They were a relatively unknown player in the great galactic game of insurance. He activated an AI sprite and turned it loose in the universal datasphere to dredge up more information on Fail State as they went inside.

The lobby was almost as plain as the exterior. There were a few potted plants and a security guard who was nearly as interesting as the potted plants.

"This place is lame."

For once Tom was in total agreement with young Jimmy. He approached the slovenly security guard at the desk.

"Hello, good sir. I am Tom Stranger." The nano fabricator in his pocket instantly printed a business card, and Tom handed it over. "This is Jimmy the Intern, who I am delivering to you for educational purposes. May we speak to a member of your management?"

The security guard read the business card, and then looked Tom over with dull pig eyes. He grunted and pointed at a clipboard. "They've been expecting you. Sign in here."

Tom signed his name and the in time. It was the only signature on the visitors' sheet. Insurance facilities should be bustling, exciting places. This call center seemed suspiciously dead.

"Go on in." The security guard pushed a button, and the door behind him emitted a buzzing noise. It was dark on the other side.

"I'm scared, Mr. Stranger."

"Don't worry, Jimmy. I'm sure everything will be fine."

Tom and Jimmy entered the call center. The heavy door slammed shut behind them.

The fluorescent lights on the other side slowly flickered to life. The scene before them was one of abject, soul-crushing misery. Tiny cubicles seemed to stretch on for eternity. Squished between the carpeted walls of each cube was an employee, wearing a headset and staring at a monitor.

"What're they doing?" Jimmy whispered fearfully.

Tom walked to the nearest cubicle. Once he got closer he could overhear the employee crammed into the cubicle speaking. "Hello, Mr. Smith? I'm calling about an exciting new offer. Yes, I know I am interrupting your dinner but it is a super exciting new offer."

They were making *cold calls*. They were harassing innocent people in their homes. Telemarketing was the greatest evil in all of insurance, and had been banned on all sane worlds. "Abomination!" Tom hissed.

He went to the next cube.

"This is Lisa with Fail State . . . Oh, you're on the Do Not Call List? Well, I'll be super happy to update our records." But Lisa pushed no buttons on her computer.

"Lies!" Tom Stranger exclaimed. Fail State would continue to call that poor person over and over and over and over. *For eternity.*

"Oh, you're unsatisfied and would like to speak to my supervisor? No problem," said one of the employees. Only he didn't pass the call to someone else. Instead he just changed his voice, made it sound deeper, and started talking again. "This is the supervisor."

A real supervisor—you could tell by the bullwhip in his hand—stopped at an adjoining cube. "Way to hassle those innocents, Tim, but your English is way too good. If they can clearly understand everything you say, you're doing it wrong. On this next one, I want you to make up a terrible accent."

"Okay, sir," Tim said. His computer screen read Faulkner. He pushed the button to take another call. "Ez Meester Fooook Nur home?" The accent was horrid and incomprehensible.

"Excellent," the supervisor crowed.

The idea of his real intern being trapped here shook Tom to the very core of his insurance-loving soul.

"What is this place?" Jimmy asked, terrified.

"I think we may be in Hell."

Tom's infolink chirped. The data had been heavily encrypted, but the AI sprite had found some information on the call center. Tom gasped. "No. It can't be."

"What's wrong, Mr. Stranger?"

"Fail State is a wholly owned subsidiary of *Conundrum & Company*."

Suddenly, a voice boomed over the intercom. "That's right, Perfect Strangers! And I've been expecting you!"

Hidden autocannons fired. Tom activated his personal energy shield, but he was too late, and several darts pierced his suit. Powerful neurotoxins flooded his system. To add insult to injury, they dropped a giant net on him. Tom was barely able to shove Jimmy out of the way before becoming hopelessly entangled.

"Curse you, Jeff!" Tom shouted, shaking his fist at the ceiling. "Where is my real intern?"

Conundrum did his best supervillain laugh. "There never was a real intern, Tom! The whole thing was my clever plot to get you out of the picture. I'm tired of you always making me look bad."

"You make yourself look bad, Jeff."

"There you go, with that holier-than-thou attitude again. Nobody likes a smart ass, Tom!"

The nanites in his blood were fighting off the poison, but Tom was rapidly losing consciousness. This potent mix must have been genetically engineered specifically for him. It had to be strong enough to drop at least a hundred Bear Gryllses. Terribly disoriented, Tom fell to his knees.

"Mr. Stranger!" Jimmy yelled as he futilely plucked at the net. He grabbed Tom's suit and tried to pull him free, but Jimmy just wasn't coordinated enough to accomplish much.

"Didn't your mother tell you never talk to Strangers? Guards, seize him!" Conundrum bellowed over the intercom. Several guards appeared, clubbed Jimmy hard enough to knock off his trucker hat, and dragged him away. "I made sure you got an intern so idiotic that you'd have no choice but to rush here. You walked right into my cunning trap."

"You'll never get away with this, Jeff."

"Oh, I will. And with you out of the way this year, I'm finally going to be ranked number one in customer satisfaction!"

"NOOOOOOO!"

Jimmy the Intern woke up sitting in a crappy office chair inside a tiny carpeted cubicle. He was groggy, had a splitting headache, and couldn't remember how he'd gotten there, but for Jimmy that was pretty normal. When he tried to get up, he realized that he was chained to the office chair. The first thing Jimmy did was make sure he still had both kidneys.

"Whew . . ." That was a relief.

"Hey, rookie," said a voice. Jimmy turned around and saw a supervisor with a bullwhip.

And then it all came rushing back to him. He was trapped in an evil insurance call center, and Tom Stranger had been captured. This day had really sucked.

"Okay, Jimmy. Let me catch you up. You're property of Conundrum & Company now. Beatings will continue until morale improves."

Jimmy laughed. The supervisor didn't. "Oh . . . I thought that was like a meme."

"Nope." The supervisor pointed at the equipment. "You'll wear the headset at all times. If you get caught taking the headset off, that's what Betsy here is for." The supervisor patted a big stainless steel staple gun on his belt.

"That sounds like it would hurt."

"Getting wood staples put in your skull would hurt . . . Ya think?" the supervisor shouted. "But it won't hurt as much as when I have to super glue your eyelids open. You can blink on your own time. The rest of the time, eyes on the screen."

Jimmy hurried and swiveled his chair back toward the monitor. It was covered in names, private personal information, and what would be the absolutely most inconvenient times to call and bug them. So, of course, that was when the calls were scheduled for.

"What about bathroom breaks?"

"There's a bucket under the desk."

Jimmy shrugged. He'd Occupied Wall Street. He was good at improvised pooping. "What is that fat blue-haired guy going to do to Mr. Stranger?"

"The boss is going to kill that goody-two-shoes. Serves him right. All day long we're calling people, and they're all like mew mew mew, we're happy with Stranger & Stranger and don't want to switch. Screw those guys! We have better commercials! Right?"

"Right." But Jimmy wasn't feeling very enthusiastic.

"Just so you know, calls may be monitored for training purposes. Ha! Just messing with you. There is no training! We just turn you maladjusted rage monkeys loose to terrorize the populace. Shake enough trees and some suckers are bound to fall out! We just record the calls so we can find little things to yell at you talentless dorks for."

"I'm not talentless. I have a Gender Studies degree," Jimmy squeaked.

"You think that makes you special? Look around you!" He gestured at the thousands of cubicles. "So do lots of these mooks! Where to you think all the people with useless expensive degrees end up after college, Jimmy?" He lowered his voice to a dangerous whisper. "*Call centers.*"

Jimmy began to cry. His parents had tried to talk him into honest work, like accounting or decorative beadwork. He should have listened to them. "I only got into that major because it was supposed to be super easy and I wanted to impress chicks by being all sensitive and stuff! Only the girls were all bossy. All they ever did was complain about manspreading and the patriarchy! Man, I don't even know what a patriarchy is!"

"The patriarchy can't save you now, Jimmy. Because you're here *forever*!" The supervisor cracked the whip. "Now, start calling some fools. Every day you meet your quota, you get a fresh bucket!"

Tom Stranger found himself chained to a wall in a dungeon. He had been in a lot of dungeons over the years, and this one was actually rather nice, with hand-cut stone walls, vintage wall torches, a rather extensive collection of exotic torture devices, and . . . could it be? "Are those real giant plague-carrying rats?"

"I had them flown in special just for you," Jeff Conundrum replied. "They set a certain ambiance."

That was just like Conundrum. Go cheap on paying claims, and then blow all the profits on a top-of-the-line torture dungeon.

"So here's the dealio, Strangers on a Train. We're going to kill you eventually, and it is going to be really painful, but we're going to torture the names of your client list out of you first."

"That is proprietary information. An Interdimensional Insurance Agent would never share such things and violate their clients' privacy."

Jeff snorted. "I opened a portal to the nether world at a science fiction convention already today. Do I look like I give a crap about not sharing clients' private information? As soon as one of my goons gathers somebody's info for a rate quote, I sell their secrets to the most ludicrously evil organizations I can find, like the KGB, or Google."

"The attack on KhanQuanCon, that was you?"

"Well, yeah. I wasn't covering those demons anymore, so I didn't have to worry about liability. I figured best-case scenario I could zombify most of Nebraska, and use them as call center employees. Just imagine the savings!"

"That is evil, even for you, Jeff."

Conundrum was obviously proud of himself. "You've not seen anything yet, Tom. Without you meddling, I'm going to revolutionize the insurance business. Heck, in this reality's America, I got them to make health insurance *mandatory*, which made it *more* expensive, and then you can get fined for not having it!"

"But . . . but that doesn't even make any sense."

He grinned. "I know, right! It's a conundrum!"

Tom tugged on his chains, but they were too strong, and he was too injured to escape.

"Well, it's been fun, but I've got work to do." Jeff gestured at the waiting goon squad of professional torturers. "These guys are going to mess you up now. They're the best torturers in the business. The guy in the black hood? He's even a consultant on Eli Roth movies."

"Impressive."

Conundrum snapped his fingers as he walked away. "Get to work, boys."

"I'll never talk, Conundrum."

"Oh, you'll talk, believe me . . . Start with his bow tie."

Jeff Conundrum was *super* evil.

A couple hours of soul-crushing cold calling later, Jimmy Duquesne was about to break. He just couldn't take it anymore. This internship sucked balls.

Now, Stranger & Stranger, *that* had been a sweet internship. Sure, he'd been super confused or thought he was going to die for most of it, but it had never been boring. Mr. Stranger was a cool boss. Plus a giant flying gundam robot was a dope ride. Jimmy figured that Interdimensional Insurance Agents got all the chicks. He didn't know what it paid, but Mr. Stranger always had that pimp Men's Warehouse look going on, so he had to be rolling in the benjamins.

He also felt kind of bad that Mr. Stranger was going to get murdered, and figured he should do something about that. But he also didn't want to get his headset stapled on permanently, so he'd not dared move from his cubicle.

Jimmy risked looking over his shoulder. There was no sign of the call center supervisor. He'd wandered off to yell at someone else. Now was his chance to save the day.

It was time to look inside himself and find his inner insurance agent.

What would Tom Stranger do?

Probably some bad ass karate shootery but, his earlier claims to the contrary, Jimmy knew he was lacking in that department. He had once lost a fight to a troop of Girl Scouts. In his defense, he'd thought those Thin Mints were free samples, and he'd tried to explain that through a mouthful of delicious cookies, but that hadn't stopped the hail of tiny, unforgiving fists, and they'd chased him from the minimall.

So he wasn't much of a fighter . . . But Jimmy had snagged Mr. Stranger's bitchin' laser pistol when he'd tried to get him out of that net. So there was that.

Jimmy pulled the CorreiaTech Combat Wombat out of his pants. Sadly, everything Jimmy knew about guns he'd learned from Call of Duty, and this thing had all sorts of buttons, switches, and levers on it.

Since it could blow up dinosaurs, Jimmy was smart enough to not point it at any of his body parts. He thought about checking online to see if there was an instruction manual, but he knew Conundrum & Company monitored their call center employees' Internet use. Some dude in the next cubicle over had been caught playing Candy Crush Saga, and when he'd gotten caught, it had been staple and bullwhip city!

Luckily, Jimmy noticed a tiny button on the back of the pistol that had HELP on it. When he pushed it, a cool heavy metal riff played, then a holographic logo formed shimmering in the air.

"Welcome to the CorreiaTech Combat Wombat plasma, laser, particle beam, missile, and explosive projectile system 4.0! Now with 70% more wombat! Please check out our other exciting CorreiaTech products, like Power Glove, Robo-Bear, A Sound That Kills, Atomic Pen, Tentacle-Proof Underwear, or Space Axe! Click here to learn more!"

Jimmy was still getting used to all this groovy sci-fi stuff. A little hologram of a big dude materialized. He was cut, like super-ripped— he probably did CrossFit—and had a long flowing glorious mane of hair worthy of a White Snake video. He was smoking a cigar and had a voice like thunder.

"Hi. I'm Larry Correia. You may know me as the ultra-powerful Interdimensional Lord of Hate, or from my hit web comic, The Yard Moose Chronicles. Welcome to this CorreiaTech instructional video. Warning. CorreiaTech products are not intended for use by sissies, liberals, or crybabies. Now, a word from our manatee. Take it away, Wendell."

The super handsome buffed guy disappeared, and a tiny holographic manatee appeared floating in Jimmy's cubicle.

"HOOOOOOOOON!" It bellowed.

"Shhhh!" Jimmy looked around in a panic. Hopefully the supervisor hadn't heard. "Keep it down, dude!"

But it was just a recording. The imaginary laser manatee couldn't actually hear him. It proceeded to give instructions on how to use the Combat Wombat. *"MEEEEWHOOOO—"* Luckily Jimmy found the volume controls and got it turned way down. That had been close.

Only a bunch of other employees had heard the manatee's instructions, and their heads automatically popped up over the tops of their cubicles like a bunch of prairie dogs who had sensed danger. He was made.

The holographic manatee was holding a Combat Wombat in its flippers. It pushed a button and launched some missiles. *"Flooooorp."* Another button and it was throwing lightning bolts. *"Hoon."* Jimmy was trying to keep up, because he knew he was running out of time, but sadly, he didn't speak manatee.

There was an option for subtitles and other languages. Jimmy selected that and began scrolling through the available languages. "Darn it! No. I don't speak Gangnam Style!" This was all very frustrating.

"Wait! There's English." He tried to select his native language, but he fat-fingered the button, and the manatee started yelling at him in German.

"Nein!" the manatee wagged one flipper disapprovingly over the *Kill Everything* button. *"NEIN!"*

Of course, he'd had to go and pick the shoutiest language ever. The other employees were loudly muttering about how somebody else got to watch YouTube and how come they couldn't. A bullwhip cracked. The supervisor was coming back down the aisle. Jimmy hadn't actually read the employee handbook, but dinking around with weapons of mass destruction at work had to be *way* worse than Candy Crush.

Jimmy had to get out of here, fast. He tried to stand up, only to forget that he was still chained to the chair. *Clank.* Then he realized that the chair had *wheels!* So Jimmy began to kick his feet against the carpet. He rolled himself out into the aisle. It wasn't exactly a high-speed getaway, but it was a start. As Jimmy shuffle-kicked furiously backwards down the hall, the helpful manatee continued to educate him on how to use the ultra-deadly Combat Wombat.

"Okay, let's do this!"

The holographic Wendell covered his eyes with his flippers.

Jimmy flipped a lever and yanked the trigger. A brilliant blue beam instantly burned a flaming hole through a hundred cubicles, lanced up the ceiling, and blasted a hole through the roof. Sparks and flaming debris rained down. He hadn't meant to do that. The manatee made it look so easy!

The supervisor saw him and gave chase. "Where do you think you're going, dumbass?"

"Oh crap!" The office chair was hurtling along at a staggering one, maybe even two, miles an hour.

"*Schnell! Schnell!*" urged the manatee.

Jimmy was so distracted by the bullwhip and Betsy the staple gun that he didn't see he was rolling directly for the stairs.

Tom Stranger had been extremely fond of that bow tie. He shed a single manly tear as it disappeared into the flames of the torturer's blowtorch.

"That was simply uncalled for," he told the torturers.

"Give us your client list, and this can all stop."

Tom Stranger never thought of himself as a hero. Hero was a title reserved for real men of courage, like George Washington or Harry Dresden. Tom was a simple insurance agent, but he would rather die than betray the solemn trust of his clients.

"Never."

The head torturer nodded. "I expected as much. Your reputation precedes you, Mr. Stranger." He turned to one of his underlings. "Fetch my sack of rabid raccoons and my complete DVD collection of *The View.*"

"Joy Behar is banned by the Geneva Convention."

"Not in this dimension."

Tom cringed. This was truly one of the worst dimensions ever.

"You expect me to talk?"

"No, Mr. Stranger, I expect you to die." The torturers high-fived each other. It didn't matter what reality you were in, torturers loved to use that line.

Just then, Jimmy the Intern rolled down the stairs in an office chair in a most violent and haphazard manner. He collided with one of the torturers, who dropped the sack of rabid raccoons. It burst open. Vicious foaming mammals sprang forth and the torturers screamed as they were attacked.

Tom had to admit he was rather surprised to see Jimmy attempting to rescue him. Perhaps he had underestimated him . . . But, of course, Jimmy was immediately set upon by raccoons.

But that was okay, because Tom had only needed a distraction. While they had been tormenting his poor bow tie, he had been working on the lock's mechanism with the picks subcutaneously implanted in his thumbs. The shackles fell away and Tom stepped free.

The head torturer saw Tom heading his way and his eyes widened fearfully. "You're free? Uh . . . I'm really super sorry, Mr. Stranger. It wasn't anything personal." He held up the DVD of *The View* defensively. "Conundrum ordered us to inflict these awful harpies on you, I swear. I had no choice."

"No one deserves Joy Behar." Tom slugged the torturer in the face and left him to the raccoons.

Jimmy was thrashing about with a raccoon gnawing on his arm. Tom removed the thrashing animal and placed it gently aside. "Thank you for rescuing me, Jimmy."

"I found my inner insurance agent, Mr. Stranger!"

"Yes, it appears you have. I am sorry you were bitten by a rabid raccoon in the process."

"Yeah, man! That wicked hurt! Wait. Rabid? Dude, does that mean I'm going to gain its powers?"

"No. You are thinking of Spiderman. Sadly, that is not how rabies or radioactivity works. Luckily, these do not appear to be werecoons, so there should be no lasting side effects . . . other than the prolonged series of extremely painful injections directly into your stomach, of course. Now, we must hurry before Conundrum escapes." He helped Jimmy up. "Do you still have my Combat Wombat?"

"I must have dropped it falling down the stairs, but don't worry, Mr. Stranger. I did just like the imaginary glowing space manatee said and pushed the Kill Everything button nine times!"

Over the screams of the torturers and chittering of the raccoons, Tom heard a dangerous beeping noise. He spotted his Combat Wombat lying on the floor. The warning light was blinking red.

"We need to run away now, Jimmy." When his intern didn't react fast enough, Tom tossed him over one shoulder, and ran up the stairs.

"Why are you carrying me?"

"You set my Combat Wombat to self-destruct."

"That sounds bad. Is that bad?"

"The explosion is approximately one Kilo-Grylls."

Tom ran as fast as his cybernetically-enhanced legs could carry them. Once clear of the stairs, he squished the supervisor, plowed through several cubicles, and didn't even bother to see if the door was locked. Instead he just lowered one shoulder and made a Tom Stranger-shaped hole through it. In the lobby, either the security guard or the potted plants engaged them with small arms fire, but he didn't slow down enough to check. Tom smashed through the front door and sprinted across the parking lot.

"I'm not super good at math, but I watched *Miami Vice*. A kilo is a lot, right?"

"Yes, Jimmy," Tom panted as he ran across a field. Several cows were watching them curiously. He shouted at them in Angusian. "Flee, my bovine friends. The call center is about to explode."

"Moooo," replied one of the cows—which roughly translated to *thanks for the heads-up, insurance professional*—as she took cover.

Tom unceremoniously chucked Jimmy into a drainage ditch, and then he ducked down next to him. Jimmy peeked his head up over the edge. There was a small flash, a *whump*, and the call center shook just a bit as some smoke shot out the doors.

"That didn't seem so bad."

Jimmy didn't realize that was just a single round of the Combat Wombat's explosive ammo cooking off. There were another two hundred rounds in the magazine, and that wasn't even getting into the missiles, area denial system, or spider mines. Tom placed one hand on Jimmy's head and shoved him back down.

Then it sounded like popcorn popping, but only if each individual kernel was filled with enough high explosives to level a house. Then the good stuff went off. And each of those micro warheads was sufficient to flatten a city block. Then the power cell went critical, and the flash could be seen from space. In fact, just then there was an astronaut aboard the International Space Station who was all like, "Holy crap, somebody just nuked Nebraska!"

They slowly raised their heads over the edge of the ditch. Jimmy gawked at the expanding mushroom cloud. There was nothing but a giant crater where the Fail State call center had been.

"That was ten Michael Bay movies' worth of explosions, Mr. Stranger, but what about all those call center employees?"

"They were telemarketers, Jimmy. No one will miss them." Tom stood up and dusted off his suit. He hoped Jeff Conundrum had still been inside. If that were the case, then this was a fine day for insurance agents everywhere. "I am impressed. Despite your complete ineptitude, you believed in yourself enough to overcome all the odds and rescue me. That was very *Kung Fu Panda* of you."

"I sure did!" Jimmy said with pride. "Do you think I could maybe make it as an insurance agent now?"

Tom thought it over. Perhaps Jimmy was not totally hopeless. "Let's put it this way. If you gave me a customer satisfaction survey right now, I would have to give you at least a five. I am not mildly dissatisfied."

"Wow. Thanks, Mr. Stranger." Jimmy grinned. Then his expression changed as he looked over Tom's shoulder. "Look out!"

Tom turned to see that Jeff Conundrum had survived the explosion and freed himself from the wreckage. He was aiming a pistol right at Tom's head. Conundrum fired!

Only Jimmy had stepped in the way and was struck instead. "Oooof!" He spun around and fell in the grass.

Conundrum would have finished them off, except his cheap Commie Jerk Face knock-off of a Combat Wombat had jammed. He snarled, struck at the gun a few times in frustration, before dropping it and running away. "We'll meet again, Stranger Than Fiction!"

Tom knelt at Jimmy's side. "I can't believe you took a bullet for me."

"Yeah, I totally meant to do that. That wasn't just me tripping and getting in the way, I swear. But damn, dude, getting shot really freaking hurts!"

That was kind of the point. He patted Jimmy on the head. "There, there."

Jimmy coughed. "How about my customer service survey now?"

"I would have to give you at least a six. I am now *mildly satisfied.*" That was one of the highest compliments Tom had ever given anyone.

"I'm scared, Mr. Stranger. Dude, man, freak, I don't want to die. I can see a light. I can totally see a light, Mr. Stranger!"

"That's because you are staring up at the sun, Jimmy." Tom had already produced an emergency med kit, squirted healing nano jell into the bullet hole, and given Jimmy a shot full of painkillers. "It's just a flesh wound. You'll be perfectly fine."

Jimmy sat up. "Oh." He looked down at the bloody hole in his Chico State t-shirt. "I've always heard chicks dig scars."

"That is true in every universe."

"Sweet. But, hey, if I'm not going to bleed to death or anything, you should totally go whoop that blue-haired fat guy's ass."

Tom saw Conundrum running across an open field. He would

avenge his intern and his favorite bow tie. "That is an excellent idea, Jimmy."

Only the painkillers had kicked in, and Jimmy was too busy staring at his hands to hear him. He wiggled his fingers. "Whoa. Hey there, little space manatees. How ya' doing?"

So Tom left Jimmy to his hallucinations and went in pursuit of Jeff Conundrum.

CHAPTER 6:
Tom's 3:00 PM Epic Dimension-Hopping Boss Fight

CONUNDRUM was far faster than his rotund form suggested. Like most Interdimensional Insurance Agents, he was also genetically and cybernetically augmented, but Tom was still gaining on him, because while Jeff had grown soft and cynical, Tom had trained constantly in pursuit of superior customer service. Conundrum looked back, saw Tom catching up, and pulled a complicated device from beneath his suspenders. It was a portable riftmaker. Such black market devices were incredibly dangerous, but Conundrum was desperate. He mashed the button. "So long, Tom!"

A glowing hole appeared in the air in front of Conundrum and he stepped through. Tom didn't know to where in space or time the gate would lead, but he had to hurry and leap through before it closed on him.

Jeff had paused on the other side to catch his breath. He stared in disbelief as Tom popped out after him. "Don't you ever give up?"

"Give up? That's a two-or-three-on-a-satisfaction-survey talk."

Though he didn't know which reality they were in, Tom recognized the building. They were in the White House. Jeff Conundrum ran toward the Oval Office, shouting for Secret Service agents to tackle Tom. He easily avoided the unaugmented humans, and chased Jeff into the President's inner sanctum.

Only what appeared to be an alcoholic circus clown was sitting behind the desk. Tom did not recognize the man.

"Vice President Joe Biden, I need your help," Jeff shouted. "Where's the President?"

"Huh?" He looked up from his stupor. "I'm only filling in for the big guy while he's golfing. What's my insurance agent doing here? Where are the strippers I ordered?"

"So he left you in charge? Then I command you to use your superpowers to destroy Tom Stranger!"

Confused, Joe Biden lifted one arm, revealing that he had a suitcase handcuffed to his wrist. "What? Oh, you mean this?" Tom recognized it as the dreaded *nuclear football* that held the country's top secret launch codes. Only when Joe Biden opened it, confetti and festive balloons popped out. "Oh, so that's what the guys left in there for me! Ain't that something?"

"Dang it, I should have known!" Conundrum went to activate his portable rift generator, but Tom Stranger swept the Karl Marx bobblehead from the President's desk and hurled it at him. The bobblehead struck the device, but rather than knock it from Jeff's hands, it stuck the selector to *random*.

There was a flash of light.

Then Jeff, Tom, and Vice President Joe Biden were free-falling through the air. The rainbow-colored ground rushed up to meet them. Luckily, it was a giant, world-spanning ball pit that broke their fall. He'd been here before. Tom hated this dimension. It was very silly.

As he swam and struggled through the balls toward the floundering Conundrum, Joe Biden could be heard shouting, "A ball pit! This is the best birthday ever!"

Curse these infernal balls. Tom reached Conundrum, and punched him in his ample gut. "Surrender, Jeff."

"Never!" Jeff shouted as he struck the button again. There was a flash as Jeff and Tom were torn from that universe, leaving Vice President Joe Biden to have a wonderful time throwing rainbow-colored balls in the air . . . until the ball sharks arrived.

The two of them appeared in a very dark reality. Tom and Jeff looked around, saw all the strange leather accoutrements and odd devices surrounding them, and simultaneously realized they'd entered the universe dominated—literally—by *Fifty Shades of Grey* novels.

"Awkward," Conundrum said, as he realized they were being watched by pervy weirdoes and bored housewives.

"Push the button again, Jeff." Tom suggested. "We can fight to the death somewhere tasteful."

"Yeah. Good call, Tom. Pushing the button."

There was a flash, and the two of them were standing at the top of a giant volcano that was actively spewing smoke and lava, under a blood-red sky filled with lightning and swirling-fire tornados. It was a proper showdown location.

"Now this is more like it!" Conundrum said as he sucker-punched Tom in the face.

The two of them fought across the narrow ledge at the top of the volcano. Lava gurgled, bubbled, and spat below them. It was more than four hundred degrees on the ledge, so Tom broke into a sweat. Both of them had dozens of fighting styles downloaded directly into their brains, their bones were hardened with armored molecular weave, and they were capable of moving at speeds that made Jackie Chan look like a tree sloth. When two Interdimensional Insurance Agents throw down, it gets pretty crazy.

Only Tom was still recovering from being poisoned and tortured—not to mention he'd skipped lunch—so Conundrum got the upper hand. With a spinning back kick, he knocked Tom down and sent him rolling to the edge. He clung there, precariously balanced. One slip and it meant falling to certain lava-filled doom.

"You know why I always win, Tom? It's because I cheat. You know why your reality got totaled? Because it was a loser reality for losers who lose! I know that's why you have it in for me. Sure, you were only a boy and had to watch your whole planet explode. That's a bummer. I get that! But it's no excuse to make me look bad in front of Chuck Norris! Your stupid dimension brought it on themselves for being underinsured."

"That was pretty irresponsible of my Earth," Tom agreed. "Maybe if their insurance agent had done his job, they would have bought the correct coverage. But this isn't personal, Jeff. This is professional. You've committed crimes against insurance. Surrender yourself to the Licensing Board for peer review."

"And pay a fine? I don't think so!" Conundrum laughed as he kicked Tom over the side. The intrepid Interdimensional Insurance Agent barely hung on by his fingertips. Conundrum stepped on Tom's fingers and ground them into the rock beneath his Kenneth Cole oxfords.

Tom winced. "Last chance, Jeff. Give up."

Conundrum snorted. "You're about to fall to your death, People are Strange. You're hardly in any position to threaten me. What's to keep me from just murdering you once and for all?"

"You're forgetting one thing, Jeff."

"What's that, Tom?"

"We're from different dimensions."

"So?"

"I'm insured with Stranger & Stranger."

Someone tapped Jeff Conundrum on the shoulder. He reflexively turned around only to discover that he was facing another Tom Stranger, who promptly shoved him. Off balance, Jeff's arms windmilled wildly—it would have been comical if not for the whole burning lava death thing—before he tumbled over the ledge.

"Straaaaaaaaanger—" Conundrum disappeared into the sulfur clouds below.

"Hello, Tom."

"Tom," the other Tom Stranger said in greeting as he extended a hand to help Tom up. "It appears that you've had a difficult day."

"Indeed. Thank you."

Once safely back on the ledge, Tom dusted off the tattered remains of his suit. The other Tom's attire was in pristine condition. Tom Prime was a little jealous that the other Tom still had his green bow tie. That Tom had a goatee, which meant he was Evil Tom, but regardless of his alignment, right or wrong, good or evil, just or unjust, that all paled before the importance of providing quality customer service.

Evil Tom made a *tsk-tsk* noise as he looked over the sorry state of Tom Prime's suit. "It looks like we've got that business sorted out. I'll have my Muffy send your Muffy the paperwork."

"Excellent. Are we still on for golf this Saturday at Dick Cheney's secret moon base?"

"Of course. I will bring the chips."

The two Tom Strangers shook hands before they parted ways.

Tom limped back to the edge and looked over the side. As he peered down into the sulfur clouds, he spotted Jeff Conundrum far below. His nemesis hadn't perished. Instead, one of his neon suspenders had caught on a cliff, leaving him dangling helplessly a few feet over the lava flow.

"It seems you are in a predicament, Jeff."

"It's a bit of a conundrum . . . Damn . . . You're right. That *is* annoying. Now can I get a hand here, Tom?"

"Sorry. You're not covered by Stranger & Stranger."

Just then something stirred in the lava beneath Jeff. A gigantic, terrifying figure rose from the molten rock. Tom recognized it as the Balrog he'd fought in Nebraska earlier. So *that* was whose horrible hellish dimension they'd wound up in.

"Hello." Tom waved.

"Greetings, Tom Stranger. You are early. I set up a consultation with your secretary, but I didn't think our meeting was until tomorrow . . . Who is this other flabby blue-haired mortal dangling over my pain cave? Wait. It's you!" The horrific demon got right in Conundrum's face. "You jerk! You cancelled my liability policy and tricked my legions into invading Nebraska!"

"Oh, hey, yeah, about that, I can totally explain—"

"Screw that. You're on my turf now, Conundrum. You will pay for your sins. Your stupid call center put me on hold for what seemed like eternity, but now I get to show you what eternity really means! Get it? Because eternal torment is sort of our thing around here. I'm going to stick you down in the seventh level with the murderers and the Fox executives who cancelled *Firefly*. We call it the Pineapple Room."

"That sounds awful!"

"Oh, whatever it is you're imagining we make you do with the pineapples, it's *way worse*."

Panicked, Jeff looked at Tom. "Hey, Tom, can I buy a Stranger & Stranger policy real fast?"

He thought about it for a moment. Maybe if Jeff hadn't shot his intern and burned his favorite bow tie . . . But every once in a while, it turned out that goodness and justice did still matter.

"Denied." Tom Stranger turned his back and began to walk away.

"Wait! Why?"

"Preexisting conditions."

EPILOGUE:
Tom Pencils in a 3:45 Team Meeting

BACK ABOARD the Stranger & Stranger giant battle mech, Tom changed into his spare suit and red bow tie. It was a clearly inferior bow tie, but sometimes there were casualties in this business. Sacrifices had to be made.

Jimmy Duquesne was sitting in one of the seats in the cockpit, repeatedly poking his finger into the gunshot wound on his chest. "Ouch!" Then a few seconds would pass, and he would inevitably do it again. "Ouch!"

Tom interrupted him. "Well, Jimmy, we are running late, but if we hurry and take a shortcut through a few other realities, we could still make our four o'clock. It seems that on Earth 123-S-4567, our client Cookie Monster has inadvertently fallen in with Somali pirates and has overthrown the democratically elected governments of several African nations. It appears he has gotten into the shortbread again. The damages are staggering."

"Wait . . . Our client?"

"Yes. Do not let the adorable children's programming of your universe fool you. He is the most feared and deadly mercenary in the Multiverse. Big Blue, as he is called in the mercenary community, is paid in cookies, and wherever he treads, there is blood and bodies. When he is spun up, he leaves a path of devastation and crumbs across worlds. To look into his googly eyes is to know madness."

Or, as Muffy Wappler's message had warned him, this latest revolution had been brought to them by the letters C, M, and the numbers seven point six two.

"No, no, man. I'm cool with all that. Murderous puppets, whatever, it's all good. I mean the part where you called him *our* client."

"Why yes, Jimmy. As long as his premiums are paid, then he is our client, and it is our solemn duty to provide him with the best customer service possible. When universes collide, Stranger & Stranger will be there."

"But does that mean that you're making me your real intern, Mr. Stranger?"

"You still have much to learn, young intern, but you have demonstrated your commitment to quality customer service. Sure, according to every simulation I have run, your odds of success are minimal, and your odds of survival are even worse, but I sent the paperwork over to Chico State earlier. You are now officially my real intern."

"Kickass!" Jimmy pumped one fist in the air. "Wait . . . My survival is what now?"

"Unlikely. But don't worry. There are other perks."

"You mean I'm going to be rolling in the dough, G."

Tom wasn't sure why Jimmy would want to cavort in raw bread. Tom checked his infolink. "Oh, you mean money. Were you not aware this is an unpaid internship?"

"But you said there were perks!"

"Yes. For example, you get to see our new commercial before it airs. Muffy just finished editing it and sent it over." Tom turned on the hologram projector while he prepared to launch them toward the nearest rift. The new commercial began to play and Jimmy's protests about unfair pay and unsafe working conditions were drowned out by the audio.

VOICEOVER GUY: *"Everyone knows that Stranger & Stranger has been rated number one in customer service for three years running, but why? Let's hear testimonials from some satisfied customers."*

A SATISFIED CUSTOMER APPEARS: *"I'm Secretary of Defense on Earth 345 whatever Tom called it. We got invaded, but my dimension had Stranger & Stranger extended space marauder coverage. After being screwed over by a horde of purple egg sucking puke rags, Tom kicked their asses back to space! It was a Mach 4 pterodactyl rodeo! OooohRah! Tom Stranger's customer service is outstanding!"*

CUT TO ANOTHER SATISFIED CUSTOMER: *"I'm Adam Baldwin, President of the United States of America on Earth 345-Bravo-98081. Tom Stranger saved our entire planet with his—"*

GOES TO SPLIT SCREEN—ANOTHER CUSTOMER APPEARS: *"And I'm Barack Obama, the American president on Earth 169-J-00561. After our old insurance agent blew up Nebraska and left my vice president stranded on another planet being menaced by ball sharks, Tom Stranger was kind enough to return Joe to our universe—"*

"Hey, I was talking, jerk."

"Well, I got bored. And that hat makes you look stupid."

"I think it makes me look cunning. You take that back."

BARACK OBAMA STICKS HIS NOSE IN THE AIR AND LOOKS SMUG: *"Let me be clear, I'm very important on my planet."*

"And I swear on Charlton Heston's magic laser sword that I truly do not give a flying crap. Apologize to my hat."

"I only apologize to dictators and terrorists. And occasionally I bow to a small town mayor, but only if I'm caught up in the moment. It'll be a cold day in hell before I apologize to a libertarian space cowboy!"

THE SECRETARY OF DEFENSE SHOVES HIS WAY BACK ONTO CAMERA: *"Let me through, Prez. Nobody talks trash to my dimension! Hey, I know you! You're that guy who can't even pronounce corpsman correctly! Nobody disrespects my beloved Corps or my President's hat! I'll plant my Space Marine size 12 combat boot in your cornhole! Hey! Yeah, I'm talking to you! Eyes over here, maggot. Your teleprompter can't save you now!"*

BARACK OBAMA APPEARS CONFUSED: *"You kiss your mama with that mouth?"*

"No, but I kiss yours with it!"

"What? This means war!"

CUT TO—TOM STRANGER AT HIS DESK, PERPLEXED: *"Well, that just goes to demonstrate that when multiple alternate realities collide, things can get a little . . ."*

VOICEOVER GUY: *Strange?*

TOM: *"I suppose so."* TOM SIGHS AS THERE IS A HUGE EXPLOSION IN THE BACKGROUND. *"It looks like I've got more work to do. Until next time, you are in strange hands with Stranger & Stranger."*

The commercial faded away.

"Okay, Mr. Stranger, about this unpaid intern thing—"

But Tom activated the rocket boosters, crushing Jimmy into his seat, and launching them toward their next claim.

"Welcome to Stranger & Stranger, Jimmy. Buckle up."

THE ADVENTURES OF TOM STRANGER started out as a silly blog post way back in 2010. The idea came from my Dead Six coauthor, Mike Kupari. One day we were driving down the street and saw a sign for Tom Stanger Insurance. As we went past, I misread the sign as *Stranger* instead of Stanger, and said so out loud. Mike immediately said, "Stranger Insurance, huh? I bet he sells multidimensional insurance." I kid you not. That's pretty much how it happened. (On that note, I would like to apologize to the real-life Tom for any confusion or really odd customer requests which he may have received as a result.)

So I wrote a really silly little story about an interdimensional insurance agent and stuck it on my blog. The fans thought it was funny, so I ended up writing a few of them.

Since one of my favorite actors had recently written some very articulate political think pieces of a libertarian persuasion, and this alternate universe required a president, it seemed reasonable to give Adam Baldwin the job. Years later I met Adam and had to explain that I did actually once use him as a fictional character. Which I suppose is kind of weird when you think about it, but Adam was cool.

Then in 2015 I was at Book Expo America in New York, and ate lunch with Steve Feldberg of Audible. They are always looking for voice talent, so I introduced Steve to Adam. Then Steve approached me about an Audible exclusive novella for Adam to narrate, so I gave him the big list of everything I'd ever written . . . Only instead he asked for the weirdest, goofiest, silliest piece of fiction I'd ever stuck on my blog—Tom Stranger.

So I cleaned it up, made it more of a coherent story (well, as coherent as a story guest starring an eloquent manatee can be), Adam turned in one heck of a performance, and that's how Tom Stranger came to be. It's been really successful and most people found it hilarious (excluding the easily offended and dolphins, obviously).